STUDIES IN MAJOR
LITERARY AUTHORS

T0304175

Edited by

William E. Cain
Professor of English
Wellesley College

A ROUTLEDGE SERIES

STUDIES IN MAJOR LITERARY AUTHORS

WILLIAM E. CAIN, *General Editor*

READY TO TRAMPLE ON ALL HUMAN LAW
Financial Capitalism in the Fiction
of Charles Dickens

Paul A. Jarvie

Routledge
Taylor & Francis Group

NEW YORK AND LONDON

Published in 2005 by
Routledge
711 Third Avenue,
New York, NY 10017

Published in Great Britain by
Routledge
2 Park Square,
Milton Park, Abingdon,
Oxfordshire OX14 4RN

First issued in paperback 2015

Routledge is an imprint of the Taylor and Francis Group, an informa business

© 2005 by Taylor & Francis Group, LLC

International Standard Book Number-13: 978-0-415-86946-1 (pbk)
International Standard Book Number-13: 978-0-415-97524-7 (Hardcover)

Library of Congress Cataloging-In-Publication Data

Catalog record is available from the Library of Congress

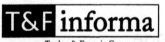

Taylor & Francis Group
is the Academic Division of T&F Informa plc.

Visit the Taylor & Francis Web site at
http://www.taylorandfrancis.com

and the Routledge Web site at
http://www.routledge-ny.com

For Sharon

Contents

Contents

Acknowledgments

This book began as my doctoral dissertation. It could never have been written without the creative insight and thoughtful guidance of my advisor, Dr. Joseph Litvak, of Tufts University. I am grateful also for the constructive criticism and kind encouragement of my committee, Drs. Sheila Emerson and Carol Flynn of Tufts, and Dr. Julia Prewitt Brown of Boston University.

In addition, I am indebted to Peter Noble of Performance Systems, Inc., for his generosity and warm friendship, without which this project would have been impossible; to Dr. Michael Maginn for his unwavering support; and to Dr. Larry Wallace for his enthusiastic encouragement.

Finally, I would like to thank Dr. William E. Cain, editor of this series, for the interest he showed in this manuscript and for his valuable suggestions for its revision; and Max Novick, the Routledge editor, for guiding me through the process of preparing this book for publication.

Introduction

Dickens's Evolving Critique of Financial Capitalism

Dickens's writings form part of what Mary Poovey has called "a discursive system in which Britons constructed ideas about finance and money alongside the system of finance itself." [1] This system, Poovey notes, was both incomplete and evolving, and thus texts on finance were actual "participants in the financial system itself" (Poovey, *Financial System*, 6):

> [T]he lack of readily available information means that every piece of writing about finance in this period was an attempt to understand and interpret something that was only partially visible and constantly in a state of change. [. . .] Even [apparently straightforward publications like] like McCullough's *Dictionary of Commerce and Commercial Navigation,* need to be read as *interpretive descriptions,* which are informed both by their authors' relative proximity to existing sources of information and by their own theoretical and political positions on issues that were often highly controversial and imperfectly understood. [. . .] Because the operations of the financial system are extremely sensitive to the circulation of information (or rumors), efforts to understand the system—to represent and dramatize its parts—could actually affect the system itself. (Poovey, *Financial System*, 4–5; Poovey's emphasis)

As Poovey notes, such influences could be readily seen in the impact of newspaper reports during financial panics, for example. [2] But this "discursive system" also contained other kinds of texts, "from McCullough's *Dictionary* to Trollope's novels" (Poovey, *Financial System*, 7).

In this book I will examine some of Dickens's major contributions to this discursive system, and explore the relationship of these texts with the financial system itself, both as reflections of the evolution of that system, and as attempts to shape and influence, if not the system itself, at least public opinion about the system and the actions of those who participated in finance. Specifically, this book will examine elements of Dickens's work that form a critique of financial capitalism. This critique grows out of the nature of nineteenth-century commercial society, a world in which the commodity had become a central factor in the economic relations between people. Dickens's critique is rooted in the difference between use-value and exchange-value, and in the difference between productive circulations and mere accumulation. The critique details how, in a money-based society, exchange-value and accumulation become dominant to the point where they infect even the most important and sacred relationships between parts of society and individuals. The core concepts of this critique parallel Marx's views of nineteenth-century financial capitalism, and reflect an uneasiness with accumulation of money for its own sake that relates back through medieval concepts of usury to Aristotle's distinction between "economics" and "chrematistics."[3]

These core concepts and their fundamental relationships are constant in the novels, in my view, but the critique itself broadens and becomes more pessimistic over time. The ill effects of living in a money-based society are presented more as the consequences of individual evil in earlier novels, while in the later books they are seen as far more systemic and pervasive. In *Nicholas Nickleby* (1839), such evils cluster around Ralph, and fighting Ralph, as Nicholas does, can lessen but not contain them. In *A Christmas Carol* (1843), individual benevolence is presented as a corrective—though more an act of imaginative faith than a prescription—to capitalism's evils. In *Little Dorrit* (1857), the evils cluster around Merdle, but insinuate their way into every corner of society—including the use-value stronghold of Doyce and Clennam; Merdle embodies these evils, but his death will have little or nothing to do with ending them. Finally, in *Our Mutual Friend* (1865), the evils of capitalism are reflected in the very fabric of the world itself, as the infection of the exchange-value ethic permeates everything, including the biology of our own human bodies.

In addition, Dickens's critique alters over time in the choices and outcomes it offers for those who would oppose the way of life inherent in a world of financial capitalism. This evolution is not one of progression from "hope" to "hopelessness." Rather, it is a movement from apparently successful opposition to capitalism, undercut by the very forces being criticized, to a definition of "success" that becomes increasingly narrow and personal. Thus in *Nickleby*, while the creation of a protected, non-capitalist enclave supported by the Cheerybles' benevolence is presented as a potential "solution," this solution itself is undercut in multiple ways by the forces to which it is intended to be opposed. The scope of such solutions continues to narrow as Dickens's career progresses. *A Christmas Carol's* attempt to convert individuals to benevolence gives way to an embattled isolation at the conclusion of *Little Dorrit*. And in *Our Mutual Friend*, the only credible "solution" is not social but individual—the attempt to isolate and preserve the true value in oneself outside of a pervasive capitalist system that implicates even the biology of the human body.

NICHOLAS NICKLEBY

To begin, I will look at *Nicholas Nickleby* to examine where Dickens's critique of financial capitalism began, and how it evolved into the comprehensive view we see in the later novels. In *Nickleby*, the distinction between use-value and exchange-value drives much of the moral action of the story. For example, Ralph's relations to others exist primarily in terms of money and the power money brings him over others, paralleling Marx's comments about the danger of the modern commodity, represented by money, "as tending to destroy the economic and moral order."[4] Ralph is a usurer, echoing the outcast Jew, and a type of small-time City operator who was traditionally a loner. Solitary and paranoid, he trusts no one, and is at war with everyone. His attitude toward the world, in fact, mirrors one part of the injunctions about usury in Deuteronomy, where the Jews were allowed to "lend upon usury" to "strangers" but not to "brothers."[5] The implication of this portrayal of Ralph is that the ill effects of financial capitalism stem from individuals' outlooks—an individual's failure to find "brothers" in his fellow humanity.

At the same time, the Cheerybles' view of money as a means to a variety of charitable ends represents, however unconvincingly to modern critics, the ethic of use-value. They mirror the opposite injunction of Deuteronomy, where one is forbidden to lend at interest to one's "brother." To the Cheerybles, of course, humankind (or at least "deserving" humankind) is their brother, and through them the novel asserts that one may choose to oppose the tide of financial capitalism and, with the help of such exemplars of middle-class individual benevolence, manage to carve out a living more or less uninfected by the evils of the system. As in *Pickwick*, such an existence involves retirement from business to a protected enclave insulated from the capitalistic system which enabled it— but it is possible to survive, even thrive, the novel asserts, in a kind of opposition to the system.

Although *Nickleby*'s "solution" is a heartfelt call for individual benevolence, it is undercut in several ways. For one, the solution of individual
benevolent action, while real enough in terms of the Grant Brothers on
whom Dickens modeled the Cheerybles, is highly circumstantial and random, and as such hardly seems a match for the pervasive evils of capitalism
on which the novel dwells. Secondly, this model is, in fact, coercive in its en-
forcement of the Cheerybles' paternalistic and, indeed, obsessive control of
the world around them, and demonstrates a kind of accumulative desire (for
power and control) too close in spirit to the chrematistic accumulation of
wealth Ralph practices. Finally, though the novel tries to "market" individual
benevolence to its readers, its best efforts are spent in the highly effective
marketing (in terms of meeting our "needs" as consumers of entertainment,
and purchasers of Dickens's commodity text) of Ralph himself—a character
of pungency and presence who dominates the novel even in death.

A CHRISTMAS CAROL

This story extends and deepens the themes raised in *Nickleby*. The *Carol*
presents the same opposition between use and exchange-value, and it also attempts to foster individual benevolence as a solution to the evils created by
financial capitalism. The story's power derives from its identification of the
values and point of view of childhood with the ethic of use-value, in opposition to the obsessive, self-referential ethic of exchange-value. In the *Carol*,
Scrooge is converted through a series of spectacles which force him to return
to his childhood values of imagination, openness to non-financial relations
with others, charity, etc. Thus the *Carol*, like *Nickleby*, proposes a change of
heart as the solution to the problems of living under financial capitalism.
The *Carol* goes further by illustrating Scrooge's change of heart, and further
still, through its construction as a series of spectacles and a form of figural
prophecy, to the point where its project is to covert us, the readers, as we
watch Scrooge's conversion.

Contemporary reactions to the *Carol* support the view that in this project it had some success. But the story's project, at length, is undermined by
its powerful representations of the pervasive nature of commodification and
the "infective" ethic of exchange-value. For example, the spectacle of the
fruiterers' shops in Stave III draws Scrooge in and makes him feel the lack, in
his own case, of middle-class familial and heterosexual values. At the same
time, running underneath this spectacle is a riot of imagery suggesting unbri-
dled and uncontrollable sexuality—the "polymorphous perverse" associated
with childhood sexuality. These insistent images describe a non-generative

"circulation" (an accumulation of pleasure for its own sake) very much akin to Marx's description of the self-referential, essentially entropic circulation that creates capital.[6] These images undermine the story's project because they suggest that a tendency toward entropy, chaos and disorder is inherent even in childhood itself; they thus link childhood with capital, whose teleology is also disorder and death.

The pervasive teleology of capital as death—underscored heavily in the rag and bone shop scene in Stave IV, where all commodities, even the human body itself, seem to end as offal and rubbish—seems too powerful, in the end, for Scrooge's conversion to individual benevolence to overcome. For one thing, money, the presence of which leads inevitably, according to Marx, to the kinds of social problems the story is trying to mitigate, is also absolutely necessary for survival; even Tiny Tim, the Christ-like avatar of childhood imagination and sensibility, cannot survive without an infusion of Scrooge's money.

Another example of this undermining is the obvious linkage of Scrooge (an old-fashioned money-lender, rather than a stock operator, merchant or banker) and the type of the Jewish usurer, whose conversion was never complete and always suspect. Scrooge, in the face of the suspicion traditionally attached to Jewish conversion, essentially has to buy his way into the society he is made to want to join, thus reinforcing the seeming impossibility of a "pure" (moneyless) solution to the problems of living in society under financial capitalism.

In the end, these doubts form a sort of "anti-*Carol*" running under the conversion story, and force Scrooge's conversion to become more of an "act of hope" (bolstered by Dickens's formidable artistic powers) rather than a prescription for programmatic change. Finally, this "anti-*Carol*" seems to me solidly rooted in Dickens's own equivocal position in 1843 as a famous and successful artist chronically short of money—the intention and the powerful act of hope represented by Scrooge's story is pervasively undermined by a reality in which money is absolutely necessary for survival.

In my view, this undermining and discrediting of potential solutions to the problems described above points the way to the "infection" metaphor of *Little Dorrit*, and to the acceptance there of a more limited, individual solution to the problem of living in a financial-capitalistic society. At the same time, the "act of hope" inherent in Scrooge's story demonstrates that, underneath it all, Dickens was unprepared to give up on finding a solution to the problems he was posing—a determination that leads, I think, to the insistence in *Little Dorrit* on the assertion of a powerful use-value ethic to balance the pervasive, infective exchange-value ethic.

LITTLE DORRIT

Little Dorrit represents a very clear and comprehensive statement of the elements of financial capitalism, the interplay between these elements, their effects on society and individuals, and the limited, but real, possibilities for living in opposition to these forces. In my view, *Little Dorrit* is Dickens's most fully-worked out "statement" of the problem of financial capitalism, and it both reflects the development of his views through the earlier novels, and foreshadows the extension of those views in his later work.

Little Dorrit presents the fundamental conflict between use-value and exchange-value in the clearest possible way. The novel represents the exchange-value ethic in its purest, most dangerous form—as a widespread nervous "dis-ease" and ultimately an infectious disease capable of penetrating into every corner of society. This disease brings madness and death with it; Merdle dies of it, of course, but it carries with it a deeper kind of death in which society and people are emptied of all meaning, and made to reflect simply the essentially meaningless numbers of exchange-value. The novel underscores the point that the teleology of capital is death by presenting Merdle, dead in his bath, as an "anti-commodity" interpellating us, ultimately, to desire and partake in Merdle's fate.

Opposed to this disease, and again presented clearly and starkly, is a use-value ethic represented by Doyce and his productive activities and by Little Dorrit and hers. This ethic is presented as rugged, substantial enough—in the persons of Doyce and Little Dorrit—to survive years of frustration and hardship. At the same time, however, even this ethic is highly vulnerable to infection, as we see when Arthur succumbs and almost destroys both himself and Doyce. In Arthur's case, the exchange-value ethic is linked explicitly to a kind of out-of-control sexuality—Arthur is "seduced" to invest in Merdle's schemes—that makes the "disease" almost impossible to resist. In the end, the working out of a narrow, limited victory for the forces of use-value stresses the importance of individual choice and individual rectitude, and downplays any hope of a systemic solution to the problems inherent in a society based on financial capitalism.

OUR MUTUAL FRIEND

Our Mutual Friend (1864–65) plunges beneath the obvious outward representations of the capitalist system to grapple with the process (and the figure) at its heart: metonymy—an opportunistic trope that itself mirrors capitalism's processes within the text. The novel seeks to understand and arrest the process by which "value" moves from commodity to commodity, a process which seems, in capitalist society, to operate more or less autonomously. This process involves not only the exchange-value inherent in objects and money, but that inherent in the elements of the body itself, thus implicating human biological processes with those of capitalism. Then, given this understanding, the novel attempts to discover alternatives, ways for humans to choose their destinies in such a society, rather than simply succumbing to capitalism's powerful shape-shifting process.

Our *Mutual Friend's* "solutions" involve the attainment of a state disengaged from the metonymic world of the commodity—a state of which Jenny Wren's call to "come up and be dead" is emblematic.[7] For Bella, attaining such a state involves, first, being made to see the entropic tendencies of an exchange-value ethic, and, second, sequestration in Rokesmith's "doll's house," an island alleged to be free from the forces of the marketplace, as those in *Pickwick* and *Nicholas Nickleby* were imagined to be. But like that of the "walled garden" in *Nickleby,* the viability of Bella's solution to the problems of living in a capitalist society is more than suspect. Rokesmith's and Boffin's attempt to "convert" Bella is, first of all, a form of coercive violence, a pseudo-benevolent commodification, perhaps, but still a reduction of Bella to an object to be manipulated, and not far removed from the chrematistic mindset which it is supposed to oppose. In addition, the insistent portrayal of every aspect of the world of the novel, from the Stock Exchange to the dust mounds to human biology itself, as shot through with the autonomous, shape-shifting processes of capitalism renders the inviolability of the "doll's house" suspect, as does the fact that, in the end, the viability of this anticapitalist enclave depends on capital itself—the Harmon fortune.

The solution involving Eugene requires attaining some distance on the capitalist world by "dying" and returning to life—a change in mindset augmented by real changes to Eugene's face and body as a result of Headstone's brutal beating. Again, this solution is presented as a form of forced "conversion," where Eugene is brought to see the falsity and deathliness of an exchange-value ethic, and made to embrace an ethic involving marriage and home—an "economic" ethic to correspond with the "chrematistic" ethic embodied in the Veneerings. Eugene clearly pays a price for his change of heart, and his payment renders this solution, perhaps, more credible than Bella's change. But this solution, too, is undercut by the forces it is meant to oppose. Again, the "conversion" is coercive—Eugene, at one level, is beaten and disfigured to drive him to embrace marriage, home and "economic" values. In addition, Eugene's desire to marry Lizzie is explicitly represented as an act of bargain and sale, a "reparation" for his sins (*OMF,* 722, bk. IV, ch. X).

Thus the forces of capitalism creep in, even during the process supposed to destroy them.

In the end, *Our Mutual Friend* does not provide a global "solution" to the problems inherent in a society dominated by capitalism, but its author never stops trying to do so. In addition, the end of the novel may point the way to a more personal solution for its author of the problem of being both an artist and a capitalist—one who lived by his "products." In Dickens's postscript he links *Our Mutual Friend* with the disaster and death of the 1865 Staplehurst railway accident, and with his own death. As Catherine Gallagher notes, *Our Mutual Friend* is a text into which Dickens "dies," or imagines dying.[8] As such a text, the novel ceases to be about Dickens's authorial agenda or about his capitalist agenda and becomes something larger and separate from these, the repository of his "value" in the form of his struggles, insights, vision. In creating such a repository, the author gives up his own purposes and is forced to rely on the future reader to find and exploit the value being left behind. In so doing, the author-capitalist is finally free (in a way Bella and even Eugene are not) from the ubiquitous processes of capitalism, which depend, after all, on desire—for control, for commodities, for *something* other than what one has at any given moment.

OTHER VIEWS

To complete the book, I will briefly examine the critiques of capitalism offered by two other Victorian authors, Trollope and Eliot. In considering the treatment of financial capitalism in *The Way We Live Now* (1875) and *Daniel Deronda* (1876), I will focus on two broad themes which are also strongly present in Dickens's critique: the role of the "financial Jew" in the system of finance capitalism; and the attempt to develop "economic" alternatives to chrematistic capitalism, and to the potentially chrematistic role of the author.

In my examination of these works, I hope to show that, while the projects and even the values of these authors are very different, they share two important similarities. First, neither is able to decouple "Jewishness" and finance. Trollope's Melmotte may be a caricature of the stateless Jewish financier, but even Breghert, clearly a decent man, is presented as inescapably (and undesirably) Jewish. In *Daniel Deronda*, the "spiritual" Jew is represented heroically, but the Cohens stink of commerce, despite, again, their obvious decency. This inability to see finance capitalism as something independent of "Jewishness" has implications for both authors. In Trollope's case it blunts the satirical attack of *The Way We Live Now* ("Christians—the English—are as greedy as stereotypical Jews") by providing an "out" ("Yes, but the system is essentially and inescapably Jewish") which allows Christians to shift moral responsibility for their actions to the Jews. In Eliot's case, the inevitable taint of finance attaching to the "Cohen-like" Jew undercuts the eventual valorizing of the "spiritual" Jew by rendering the latter a special (and apparently rare) case—the "non-Jewish" Jew who is not driven by the chrematistic desires governing the "Jewish" Jews and who, therefore, is worthy of being represented heroically.

Second, both authors share with Dickens the difficulty in developing credible and robust "solutions" to the problems of living in a society increasingly dominated by finance capitalism. Trollope's "economic" solution revolves around the "English" values of Roger Carbury, whose project is the preservation and transmission of the value of Carbury Hall to future generations; but even Roger does not escape untainted by essentially chrematistic needs to control this property and those who will inherit it. In *Daniel Deronda*, Eliot proposes a kind of "spiritual" economy—principally through the creation of a Jewish state based in part on "economic" values. But this project is undercut, in the end, because we see that such an effort is no more than another Nicklebian walled garden: to be successful, it must take place outside of capitalistic England, but supported by Daniel's (English) fortune. Thus the struggles of Trollope and Eliot, in their own ways, echo that of Dickens. Artist in his ability to see the evils around him and to create texts which participate forcefully in the discursive system Poovey describes, he was also an "author," in Catherine Gallagher's terms[9], in his participation in the system he was critiquing, and a subject interpellated by the ubiquitous and inescapable spectacle of nineteenth-century capitalism. In my view, Dickens's inability to find a "solution" free from the taint of financial capitalism is far outweighed by his ability to see, understand and represent in powerful and convincing detail the evils of the system in which he himself was inescapably implicated—the fish trying to describe water, so to speak. This ability, a vision and awareness of complexity and its implications, and an unwillingness to gloss over those implications in the service of ideological coherence, is the hallmark of his art.

Chapter One

"I hold myself released from such hard bargains as these": *Nicholas Nickleby* and "Brotherly" Capitalism

Nicholas Nickleby's form and content mirror the difficulties Dickens faced in 1838–39 in formulating and delivering a critique of capitalism and a proposal to mitigate some of its evils. The form of the novel has long provoked critical discussion,[1] and while its critique of capitalism is clearly a harsh one, its "solution" for the ills of capitalism, embodied in the Cheerybles, has more often than not been dismissed as little more than a device to close off Nicholas's "adventures" if not his "life."[2] But *Nickleby*'s structure and content illustrate both the complexity and the contradictions inherent in the novel's project of critiquing capitalism and presenting a proposal for its mitigation, and are more interesting than many of these criticisms admit. Two short texts—one from the novel and one from an 1839 letter—will help to clarify both the novel's intent and the contradictions with which it is beset.

The first text occurs in chapter sixteen of *Nicholas Nickleby*, when Nicholas, having thrown up his job at Dotheboys Hall and returned to London with Smike, finds himself restless and unable to sleep:

> The unhappy state of his own affairs was the one idea which occupied the brain of Nicholas, walk as fast as he would; and when he tried to dislodge it by speculating on the situation and prospects of the people who surrounded him, he caught himself in a few seconds contrasting their condition with his own, and gliding almost imperceptibly back into his old train of thought again.[3]

This short episode is emblematic of the overall structure of the novel and its approach to its subject matter. Dickens labels Nicholas's activity in the above passage "speculating," a loaded term in this novel; in her essay "The Game of Speculation: Economics and Representation," Tatiana Holway notes several meanings of the word "speculation" which are relevant to an examination of *Nicholas Nickleby:*

> First denoting spiritual revelation and later economic prognostication, the word "speculation," deriving from *specere*, to look, and associated with *speculum*, or mirror, has always been related to vision and knowledge, imagination and representation. Indeed, as speculative practices and perspectives shifted from the sixteenth- and seventeenth-century search for insight into the divine to the eighteenth- and nineteenth-century attempts at foresight into the market, alterations in perception seem to have been as closely bound up in the creation of new and variable socioeconomic conditions as those conditions themselves were influential in changing modes of vision. These dialectical processes focus the relationship of economics and representation, one that begins as a transparency in the sixteenth century and becomes increasingly obscure in the nineteenth, when, posing a problem for demystification in the English novel, it also profoundly affects the novel's modes of representation.[4]

Nicholas's activity during his rapid walk can be seen as "speculating" in several senses. First, it involves the kind of imaginative looking Holway terms "*specere*"; Nicholas is observing and inferring or "completing" the economic histories of those he encounters. This speculation is also related to the sense offered by the word "*speculum*," as Nicholas is measuring ("contrasting") others' inferred prospects against his own economic situation. Finally, Nicholas as the "maker" of stories plainly doubles the author, whose own night-walks legendarily helped him in his own "making," and whose "making" of the novel, indeed a financial "speculation" in itself, was constantly troubled by intrusive economic issues.

These connections suggest a metaphor for *Nicholas Nickleby*'s structure: we might think of it as a kind of frantic forced march, where what is observed will be examined imaginatively, and will be constantly contrasted in economic terms with other things observed.[5] Moreover, this economic evaluation is obsessive, not something chosen by the observer, but something forced upon him, as it is upon Nicholas in the passage above, thus reflecting both the obsessive nature of capitalism itself, and the fact that it is an inescapable force in the society *Nicholas Nickleby* analyses. In the novel, this "speculative" process or structure, rapidly taking in and evaluating everything, is the basis for the "case" the novel builds against financial capitalism, which, taken by itself, is both clear and very harsh.

The second text I want to consider helps bring out the contradictions with which *Nickleby* must grapple in carrying out its project. On 21 January 1839, Dickens was writing to Forster about his deteriorating relationship with his publisher Bentley:

> The immense profits which *Oliver* has realised to its publisher, and is still realising; the paltry, wretched, miserable sum it brought me (not equal to what is every day paid for a novel that sells fifteen hundred copies at most); the recollection of all this, and the consciousness that I still have the slavery and drudgery of another work on the same journeyman-terms; the consciousness that my books are enriching everybody connected with them but myself, and that I, with such a popularity as I have acquired, am struggling in old toils, and wasting my energies in the very height and freshness of my fame, and the best part of my life, to fill the pockets of others, while for those who are nearest and dearest to me I can realise little more than a genteel subsistence: all this puts me out of heart and spirits: [. . .] I do most solemnly declare that morally, before God and man, I hold myself released from such hard bargains as these, after I have done so much for those who drive them[.][6]

This letter seems to me both to provide support for *Nickleby*'s project as I have described it, and to undercut that project at the same time. Certainly, the economic contrasts here ("immense profits" and "paltry, miserable sum") suggest the world of haves and have-nots ("starvation and repletion lay them down together") depicted in the novel (*NN*, 489; ch. 32). And Dickens's view of himself as "struggling in old toils" on behalf of "those who drive" "such hard bargains" suggests, too, the essential mechanism of capitalism, where the value of one person's labor is appropriated by another, an investor or capitalist who reaps rich rewards for creating nothing. To this extent, the letter helps identify some of the painful personal issues fuelling *Nickleby*'s harsh critique of financial capitalism.

But the letter goes further. In it, Dickens is envisioning a different sort of "bargain," one which we may infer would be more equitable, at some level, to him as author; and he seems determined to create such a bargain, though doing so would involve the re-creation of the business of publishing and of the customary relations between publishers (capitalists) and authors.[7] Such re-creation suggests the other main element of *Nicholas Nickleby*'s project: the need to create and present an alternative, "brotherly" or "familial" capitalism which, as I will discuss below, is calculated to mitigate the excesses of capitalism in a "safer" way than, for example, revolution or Chartism.

However, despite the support the letter offers, it also contains an implication that illustrates the contradictions inherent in *Nickleby's* project. The letter implies strongly that the new kind of "bargain" Dickens is seeking would
balance, or perhaps even reverse, the terms of the old: make immense profits
for *him*, and fill *his* pockets. Significantly, the letter does not say whether
Dickens is to be enriched along with his publisher or instead of him, although
the tone of the comments implies redress for grievances rather than partnership. These grievances are grounded in Dickens's sense of being treated un-
fairly, certainly, but also in his need to provide for "those who are nearest and
dearest to me"—that is, his family. Thus Dickens hints at a new kind of bargain that would be in some sense fairer, but does so in a way that is saturated
with the kind of self-interest and competitive hustling for scarce resources (the
profits) that such a bargain should, presumably, rise above. Moreover, the letter invokes "family" as one reason for its author's aggressive and competitive
attitude, even though, as we shall see, "family" is a key component in the ethic
of the "tamer" capitalism the novel is arguing for. The letter suggests the kinds
of contradictions we will find working against *Nickleby's* project, and suggests
that these contradictions arise from Dickens's own inability to extricate himself from his role as a "player" within the capitalistic system.

From here, this chapter will examine, first, the "case" *Nicholas Nickleby*
builds against financial capitalism, specifically capitalism's damaging psychological effects, its impact on childhood and childhood's redemptive powers,
and its ultimate tendency toward entropy and the destruction of the society
upon which it lives. Then I will discuss the alternative, "brotherly" capitalism
embodied in the Cheerybles, and will consider ways in which this familial or
"brotherly" model is meant to mitigate the ill effects of capitalism upon
which the novel dwells. Finally, I will consider how the portrayal of Ralph, as
well as other aspects of the novel's rhetoric and imagery, undercuts the
"brotherly" model of capitalism even as it is presented, leaving us, in the end,
with an ambiguous message: on the one hand the embodied wish that a
kinder, more humane capitalism can exist—must exist, perhaps; and on the
other hand the placement of the society created by this kinder capitalism
within a walled Eden, safely isolated from the destructive forces the novel so
clearly describes.

NICKLEBY'S CASE AGAINST CAPITALISM:
"DIS-EASE" AND DISEASE

In *Nicholas Nickleby*, the psychological damage created in people by living in
a society dominated by financial capitalism is postulated early and explored

throughout the novel. The groundwork for this theme is laid in chapter one: Nicholas senior is afflicted with what we might call clinical depression after his financial losses, while Ralph, under the mantra, "There is nothing like money," becomes an obsessive accumulator (*NN*, 61; ch. 1). But the psychological impact of the financial system on people in the book is more expansive than this. In fact, the effects of the system produce a general effect of "dis-ease"—an agitation or angst created by economic pressures—in the population of the book as a whole. This financial anxiety seems compounded of two factors. First, a good deal of the "dis-ease" in the novel springs from the fear of financial failure, strong in Dickens himself and in the Victorians, as C. R. B. Dunlop points out:

> Walter Houghton has noted the high value that Victorians placed on financial success. A corollary was the fear of debt and financial failure that appears throughout the literature of the period. John Vernon describes the common situation in nineteenth-century fiction of a character trying to find money to pay a debt. The situation is urgent, even desperate, and it carries a sense of guilt and retribution. Financial failure becomes the nightmare of a society which worships financial success.[8]

Second, financial anxiety was driven and exacerbated by the sense that financial markets were both irrational and crooked. Supporting the conventional wisdom of commercial and financial progress to a fairer, more rational financial system, theorists like Bentham and his political economist followers espoused the self-regulating orderliness and rationality of markets. As Benjamin Nelson points out, in his *Defence of Usury*, Bentham finds it strange "that the liberty of making one's own terms in money-bargains" should be restricted in free England. "In a word," Bentham declares,

> the proposition I have been accustomed to lay down to myself on this subject is the following one, viz. that *no man of ripe years and of sound mind, acting freely and with his eyes open, ought to be hindered, with a view to his advantage, from making such bargain, in the way of obtaining money, as he thinks fit:* nor, [sic] (what is a necessary consequence) anybody hindered from supplying him upon any terms he thinks proper to accede to.[9]

Bentham is talking about usury, but his assertions are relevant here as well because they imply that participants in financial transactions are normally rational and fully informed *homines economici*—a line of thinking *Nicholas Nickleby* seems to go out of its way to discredit. For example, the rigged nature of the game is made clear as early as chapter two, when Bonney and Ralph gloat over anticipated gains from the Muffin Company floatation:

> "'United Metropolitan Improved Hot Muffin and Crumpet Baking and Punctual Delivery Company. Capital, five millions, in five hundred thousand shares of ten pounds each." Why, the very name will get the shares up to a premium in ten days.'
>
> 'And when they *are* at a premium,' said Mr Ralph Nickleby, smiling.
>
> 'When they are, you know what to do with them as well as any man alive, and how to back quietly out at the right time,' said Mr Bonney, slapping the capitalist familiarly on the shoulder. (*NN*, 69; ch. 2)

Irrationality appears most obviously in the Muffin Company Meeting in chapter two, which packs all the frenzy of the bubble and panic of 1825 into one short episode. As Ralph and Bonney approach the meeting, they see

> half a dozen men [. . .] tacking across the road under a press of paper, bearing gigantic announcements that a Public Meeting would be holden at one o'clock precisely, to take into consideration the propriety of petitioning Parliament in favour of the United Metropolitan Improved Hot Muffin and Punctual Delivery Company, capital five millions, in five hundred thousand shares of ten pounds each; which sums were set forth in fat black figures of considerable size. (*NN*, 70; ch. 2)

The men are "tacking" because it is a "windy day," and we see immediately that finance is as much a business focused on the creation, proliferation and management of signs—both banners and "signs" like numbers and letters—as it is a business dedicated to management of money. We see also that such signs, when signifiers are not firmly linked to their supposed "signifieds," seem, like the wind-driven banner, to have a life of their own. This sense of signs out of control in the financial world is suggested by the "fat black figures" on the banner. We already know these are meaningless, since we know from Ralph and Bonney that the business is based on nothing, and that the amount of capital indicated has simply been made up, yet the numbers are used in Bonney's speech, along with the promise that the Company would "confer undying brightness and splendour upon England," to entice and entrap the crowd of potential investors in the meeting (*NN*, 73; ch. 2).

A little later, the "grievous gentleman of a semi-clerical appearance" demonstrates that signs detached from meaning, really metonyms opportunistically substituted for one another, can pass for currency in the financial world. This speaker weaves a tissue of nonsense stories about the supposed suffering of muffin-boys, particularly one who, "having been exposed to this inhuman and barbarous system for no less than five years, at length fell a victim to a cold in the head, beneath which he gradually sunk until he fell into a perspiration and recovered" (*NN*, 74; ch.2). Here, the rhetoric's content is absurdly unrelated to the financial flotation under consideration, and absurd in and of itself, given that a "cold" is hardly the logical consequence of "an inhuman and barbarous system"; and the form of this message, too, is irrational—a debased version of the language of reform, twisted to produce capitalist gains. But such signs have power in the financial world, as we learn immediately; after this speech, "the excitement was tremendous, and Mr. Nickleby whispered to his friend that the shares were henceforth at a premium of five-and-twenty percent" (74). Thus "signs" are immediately transmuted into money, yet in a way that had nothing to do with the rationality of Bentham's "man of ripe years and of sound mind, acting freely and with his eyes open."

What are the psychological effects of being at the mercy of such a system? First, generalized anxiety is present almost everywhere in the novel, even in the more secure sphere of the Cheerybles, where it is transmuted into the nervous "tics" (constant hand-rubbing, for instance) which help characterize the brothers, and into Tim Linkinwater's agoraphobic attachment to "the Square." This anxiety is very often tied to the need for money, as with the Nicklebys' money worries after Nicholas senior's death, or the Kenwigses' near-obsession about securing Lillyvick's legacies for the children. But the psychological impact of financial capitalism is also presented as true madness, as we can see in the case of the "Gentleman in smallclothes" who falls in love with Mrs. Nickleby after the family is settled in the cottage at Bow. The Gentleman, as Sylvia Manning notes, provides with his courting of Mrs. Nickleby a parody of some of the other courtships in the novel (from Gride's at one extreme to those of Nicholas and Madeline and Kate and Frank at the other) that reflects some of the novel's problematizing of marriage in a money-driven society.[10] But the Gentleman and his madness are also firmly linked to financial capitalism itself, of which madness is seen to be one potential consequence. Significantly, this character's mad love-making is couched in the language of the City: "[T]he statue at Charing Cross [has] been seen lately on the Stock Exchange at midnight, walking arm-in-arm with the Pump from Aldgate, in a riding habit" (*NN*, 621; ch. 41).[11] Such utterances are startling, imaginative and amusing, but they also parody the slippery, "opportunistic" system of signs we have observed as characteristic of the financial world; in fact, one gets the feeling in reading them that they might well fit into the speeches of the Muffin Company promoters without much difficulty. In addition, the marrows and cucumbers thrown over the wall as love-offerings (620) combine a grotesque sexuality with the metonymic proliferation of debased signs we have already noticed as inseparable from financial capitalism. Thus the Gentleman reminds us that finance unhinges language and meaning, and that a potential consequence of this is complete destabilization of human understanding.

Even more seriously, the Gentleman's true character, when it is revealed, links real personal insanity and money. The "coarse squat man" who is the Gentleman's keeper, explains:

> 'He was the cruelest, wickedest, out-and outerest old flint that ever drawed breath. [. . .] Broke his poor wife's heart, turned his daughters out of doors, drove his sons into the streets—it was a blessing he went mad at last, through evil tempers, and covetousness, and selfishness, and guzzling, and drinking, or he'd have drove many others so.' (*NN*, 628; ch. 41)

The Gentleman's life is an illustration of the impact of his love of money—his obsession with accumulation—on his own sanity and on his children and wife; this is how capitalism ends, the Gentleman seems to say. And the example is all the more striking when we recall that, in Marx's view, the capitalist and the miser are brothers under the skin—both driven by an obsession with "the unceasing movement of profit-making

> [. . . ;] while the miser is merely a capitalist gone mad, the capitalist is a rational miser" (*Capital*, vol. I, 254–55).

Thus the introduction of the Gentleman in Small-Clothes adds an episode of humor to the novel, but also insists on circling back to the novel's project of portraying the pain of the impact of the system of finance capitalism on the middle-class. The Gentleman is both a crazy individual and an embodiment of capitalistic accumulation: from a Marxist point of view, such pathologies are inescapable (even the text itself cannot escape them—it obsessively circles back to these themes), since they spring from financial capitalism itself.

NICKLEBY'S CASE AGAINST CAPITALISM:
THE DESTRUCTION OF THE CHILD

The second of the novel's examinations of the destructive effects of finance capitalism first assesses the power and limits of childhood as a redemptive force, then explores the danger that the system of finance capitalism poses for childhood itself, and for the society childhood is supposed to redeem. Malcolm Andrews notes that the redemptive nature of childhood, an outgrowth of the replacement of the "noble savage" ideal with something more innocent and manageable, is in Dickens a repudiation of "a certain model of adulthood developing in the Victorian period and represented in the major fictional characters of the middle years of his career: Scrooge, Dombey, Murdstone, Gradgrind":

> These are the formidable exponents of that habit of being 'too wise,' 'too stately,' 'too rough with innocent fancies.' They have no residual childlikeness in them and need to retrieve it from somewhere. Scrooge's change of heart is triggered by his enforced reintroduction to his own childhood, long abandoned in memory, and by his succumbing once again to the romantic charms of *Robinson Crusoe* and *Ali Baba*. These books, recalled in loving detail in the essay ["Where We Stopped Growing," *Household Words*, 1/1/53], have a redemptive power because they are, literally, rejuvenating. Dombey's change of heart is confirmed in our last glimpses of him, as an old man on the sea-shore, hand in hand with his small grandson and enjoying the sight of him at play. It is an image of the restored continuity of generations and of the redemptive liberation within Dombey of the spirit of childhood.[12]

This dynamic of childhood as a redemptive force in opposition to certain adult traits, while examined and explored in *Nickleby*, is realized only partially, as we can see in the case of Smike. When Nicholas is at Dotheboys, he tries to teach Smike to read. As we see in much of Dickens's later writing, the trope of the neglected child reading is a powerful symbol of the development of a childhood imagination which can later serve as a redemptive force (e.g., for Scrooge, for David Copperfield, and for Dickens himself in the "Autobiographical Fragment"). Yet for Smike, developing this capacity is impossible: he pores "hard over the tattered book [. . .] vainly endeavouring to master some task which a child of nine years old, possessed of ordinary powers, could have conquered with ease, but which to the addled brain of the crushed boy of nineteen was sealed and hopeless mystery" (*NN*, 210–11; ch. 12). When Smike despairs of success Nicholas says, "Do not try. [. . .] Do not for God's sake [. . .] I cannot bear to see you" (211). This is perhaps Smike's true death-warrant, as even in his benefactor's eyes he is seen as too damaged to survive, cut off from what would be for him a redemptive "mystery."

Yet childhood is not wholly ineffectual as a redemptive force even in Smike's case. His story demonstrates a measure of "redemption," though in a different sense from the conversions of Scrooge or Dombey, through a return to childhood via the power of memory. Nicholas's first thought is to take Smike to Devonshire when "the last chance and hope of his life depended on his being instantly removed from London" (*NN*, 830; ch. 55). Immediately, the narrator adds, "[t]hat part of Devonshire in which Nicholas had been himself bred when a boy, was named as the most favourable spot." Thus the childhood scene and the "wilderness" of London, the seat of finance capitalism, are set in opposition. This idyll cannot save Smike, but it does point up the redemptive value he receives from, in effect, possessing by proxy the childhood memories that mean so much to Nicholas. We learn that

> there was not a lane, nor a brook, or copse, or cottage near, with which some childish event was not intertwined, and back it came upon the mind as events of childhood do—nothing in itself: perhaps a word, a laugh, a look, some slight distress, a passing thought or fear—and yet more strongly and distinctly marked, and better far remembered than the hardest trials or severest sorrows of but a year ago. (*NN*, 858; ch. 58)

Thus Smike, whose "redemption" in this case involves not a change of heart but a completion through finally obtaining an actual childhood of his own, is partially healed, even as he dies. This redemptive process culminates when Nicholas describes a formative childhood moment:

> One of these expeditions led them through the churchyard where was his father's grave. 'Even here,' said Nicholas softly, 'we used to loiter before we knew what death was, and when we little thought whose ashes would rest beneath, and wondering at the silence, sit down to rest and speak below our breath. Once Kate was lost, and after an hour of fruitless search, they found her fast asleep under that tree which shades my father's grave. He was very fond of her, and said when he took her up in his arms, still sleeping, that whenever he died he would wish to be buried where his dear little child had laid her head. You see his wish was not forgotten.' (*NN*, 858–59; ch.58)

A few lines later, Smike completes his assumption of Nicholas's childhood by asking to be "buried near—as near as they can make my grave—to the tree we saw today." The promise is given, and shortly, Smike dies. Both the promise itself and Smike are therefore "redeemed," but not without the ambiguity with which resolutions in this novel are wrapped. Nicholas's promise to Smike doubles the (constantly unredeemed) finance-related promises (signs, speeches, figures) with which the book is filled; at one level, the redemption of the promise (and of Smike) thus shows us an alternative, another moral choice concerning promises. But this "redemption" is imperfect in two ways. First, the novel is crammed with meaningless "promises" (signs and banners, numbers and speeches—the basis, in fact for the whole monetary system) which debase the entire process of exchange within the novel, and undercut, or at least cast doubt on, the "currency" of *any* promise in the world of the novel. Second, the shattered Smike brings with him too much of the destructiveness of the system to which he has been exposed; his living presence allows the system that has destroyed him to enter the "Eden" Nicholas builds at the novel's conclusion. So Smike himself can only be "redeemed" after he is safely dead, and the doubt we feel about the extent to which promises can or will be kept in a world dominated by finance capitalism is reinforced.

If Smike is too damaged by the system to be fully redeemed, Ralph seems to have been born with an inability to partake in potentially softening memories of childhood that might have led him to a Scrooge-like conversion. In chapter one, Ralph is given the motto "There is nothing like money" and begins usury while a schoolboy—capitalism seems innate in him. Later in life, the power of memory is effectively blocked by a "haze" of gold: this effectively quashes any "recollection[s] of his old playfellow," and when any of these recollections manages to break through, Ralph dismisses them with the thought that "if [he and his brother] were intimate he would want to borrow money of him" (*NN*, 62; ch. 1). More significantly, Ralph is offered a second opportunity to go down memory's redemptive path in chapter nineteen, when he is putting Kate into a coach after the dinner party with Hawk and Verisopht. Seemingly softened by Kate and what she has gone through, Ralph sees a sudden vision of her face in the lamplight:

> The lock of hair that had escaped and curled loosely over her brow, the traces of tears yet scarcely dry, the flushed cheek, the look of sorrow, all fired some dormant train of recollection in the old man's breast; and the face of the dead brother seemed present before him, with the very look it wore on some occasion of boyish grief, of which every circumstance flashed upon his mind, with the distinctness of a scene of yesterday. (*NN*, 316; ch. 19)

Here, in a scene that prefigures Scrooge's encounters with visions of his own past, Kate brings Ralph's childhood into the present briefly. Ralph "staggers" and "reels" "as a man who had seen a spirit from some world beyond the grave," but he does not change. This scene is a "dress-rehearsal" for the conversion mechanism in the *Carol,* and shows Dickens experimenting with the redemptive power of childhood memories, assessing the power of this "weapon" against the capitalist's habitual ways of thinking. That Ralph is not allowed to redeem himself is, I think, consistent with the novel's attempt to present two "competing" forms of capitalism for the reader to choose from:[13] given the ideological load he carries (which I will examine in detail later in this chapter), Ralph must remain "the capitalist" until the novel works itself out, and we have had the opportunity to compare the system Ralph embodies with the better alternative embodied by the Cheerybles.

If the redemptive power of childhood is a force that is being explored and tested in *Nicholas Nickleby*, the destructive power of finance capitalism on childhood and children is already a given. *Nickleby* presents a highly commodified world where everything, including children, is assigned an exchange-value and is subject to circulation as an object. Squeers, for example, sees that boys are commodities to be traded in and profited from, and he is constantly valuing his pupils in money terms:

> "I took down ten boys; ten twentys—two hundred pound." (*NN*, 91; ch. 4)

> "I think you'd better get up behind. I'm afraid of one of them boys falling off, and then there's twenty pound a year gone." (*NN*, 108; ch. 5)

> "There's youth to the amount of eight hundred pound a-year at Dotheboys Hall at this present time. I'd take sixteen hundred pound worth if I could get 'em, and be as fond of every individual twenty pound among 'em as nothing should equal it!" (*NN*, 520; ch. 34)

The valuation of children as money (and their consequent appearance as objects for sale) occurs again and again in the novel. Sometimes this equation is comic. For example, when Nicholas announces Lillyvick's marriage to Mr. Kenwigs in chapter thirty-six, the latter's response is as hilariously melodramatic as Mrs. Crummles's "let the mutton and onion sauce appear" (*NN*, 372; ch. 23): "My children, my defrauded, swindled infants!" he begins, reminding us of the constant association of speculation and swindling in the novel. After the nurse admonishes him to be silent out of "regard for your baby":

> 'Let him [the new baby] die,' cried Mr Kenwigs in the torrent of his wrath. 'Let him die. He has no expectations, no property to come into. We want no babies here,' said Mr Kenwigs recklessly. (*NN*, 550; ch. 36)

Earlier, the Kenwigses have been presented as a fruitful, generative couple, their children as "olive branches" (*NN*, 229; ch. 14) in whom the parents are willing to invest by paying Nicholas to give them French lessons. Yet even here, where generativity and productive middle-class parenthood have been carefully, if comically, foregrounded, we see the invasive power of financial capitalism. When the family party sits down to play "Speculation" in chapter fourteen, we are immediately reminded of the links between card-playing, marriage and speculation in chapter one; this juxtaposition suggests that the Kenwigses, like the Nicklebys, are vulnerable to the need for money, and to the market forces and contingencies (the "Fortunes, Misfortunes, Uprisings [and] Downfallings," as the novel's full title puts it) money brings with it. The Kenwigses' "speculation" is in the cultivation and preparation of Mr. Lillyvick (a parodic, lower-middle class representation of the coercive power of capital in this episode of the novel)—an "investment" which is intended to provide a "return" of "a matter of a hundred pound a-piece, perhaps" as a legacy (*NN*, 545; ch. 36).

Mr. Kenwigs's response to Nicholas's news underlines the real vulnerability of the middle-class family to market forces. As Jeff Nunokawa notes, in the nineteenth-century novel, the "celebration of domesticity as a sanctuary from the vicissitudes of the cash nexus is everywhere spoiled; everywhere the shades of the countinghouse fall upon the home."[14] The implication of this invasion is shadowed forth by another symbolic element associated with the Kenwigs household. As the narrator tells us, the stairs of the house give the "curious visitor" indications of the "progressive poverty of the inmates." While the Kenwigses live on the first floor, their relative prosperity symbolized by the "real mahogany" table they keep on the landing, Newman Noggs and Crowl live in the garret, and their real poverty is symbolized by what is on their landing: "two crippled pitchers and some broken blacking bottles" (*NN*, 228; ch. 14). Recalling this symbol, and the enormous power it had for Dickens in later years, we come to the crux of Mr. Kenwigs's dilemma: in order to avoid the plunge into poverty suffered by Newman (doubling the fall of the child Dickens in this instance), the Kenwigses as prudent parents must "speculate," and, in so doing, must value even their beloved children in monetary terms, and must "market" them to Lillyvick ("Morleena Kenwigs [. . .] Go down upon your knees to your dear uncle" [*NN*, 247; ch. 15]) in a way that, perhaps, is different only in degree from Bray's "marketing" of Madeline to Gride.

The Kenwigs episode, in fact, functions as a parody of the more serious examples of the degradation of childhood by the financial system. Kate, Nicholas and Madeline are the major examples of this degradation, which involves both use and abuse—commodification and pain. Kate is commodified throughout the novel. She is quite baldly offered for sale (with an attendant "spectacle" during which Hawk examines her minutely) to Verisopht at the dinner in chapter nineteen. Verisopht puts a price on Kate immediately, calling her an addition to the group "that would almost warrant the addition of an extra two and a half per cent" (*NN*, 307; ch. 19). The sexual component of Kate's situation darkens the novel's picture of the potential fate of the commodified child—actual traffic in children for parental or adult advantage. The passage quoted above, where Mrs. Kenwigs orders Morleena "Down upon your knees to your dear uncle," can be read as a dark, if fleeting, parody of the real sexual danger children face in a commodified world. Madeline Bray's situation explores this danger and its meanings more fully. Madeline's vulnerability arises in part from her father's callous selfishness, and in part from her own pure, childlike love for Bray, which makes her, as Gride tells Ralph, "a slave to every wish, of her only parent, who had no other friend on earth." Typically, Ralph devalues Madeline's love for Bray (which indeed is strong enough to make her willing to sacrifice herself to Gride) by noting that "if she were a little more of the world, she wouldn't have been such a fool" (*NN*, 709; ch. 47).

We might, after reading Bray's first encounter with Nicholas in chapter forty-six, agree with Ralph on this point. In the context of the somewhat melodramatic story line, Madeline's motivation for self-immolation is not overtly explored. She prefigures Amy Dorrit in her love for her father and her exploitation by him, but she is more hastily drawn, more a stock victim or prop the novel can use in depicting a terrible evil. However, we see very clearly, when Nicholas visits Madeline to try to dissuade her, that the prospect of marrying Gride is slowly killing her:

> It was nearly three weeks since he had seen her last, but there was a change in the lovely girl before him which told Nicholas, in startling terms, what mental suffering had been compressed into that short time. There are no words which can express, nothing with which can be compared, the perfect pallor, the clear transparent cold ghastly whiteness, of the beautiful face which turned towards him when he entered. [. . .] Most beautiful—more beautiful perhaps in appearance than ever— there was something in her face which quite unmanned him, and appeared far more touching than the wildest agony of grief. It was not merely calm and composed, but fixed and rigid. (*NN*, 792; ch. 53)

In this description, the damage to the child—madness or death, and she is already presented as a beautiful corpse—is apparent; and along with Madeline will go the purity of her love for Bray, misused as it has been. But Madeline's situation is fraught with additional danger for children and for society itself. As implied in Kate's story, the commodification both young women suffer seems to have affected the order of social and familial relationships in the world of the novel. Kate's uncle is willing to sell her; Madeline's father actually makes the deal, but dies before the "closing."

This loosening of societal structures, the opportunistic elision of one relationship (father, or adult) into another (seller, or user) calls to mind Marx's warnings from chapter three of *Capital* on the effects of money on the social order. Marx calls money "a radical leveller" which "extinguishes all distinctions"; he contends that money itself is "a commodity [. . .] capable of becoming the private property of private persons" (*Capital,* vol. I, 229–30). These passages suggest that the leveling power of money and money's status as an ownable commodity both eliminate the distinctions between commodities (as between "daughter" and "sexual object") which make for an ordered society, and transfer tremendous power into the hands of individuals who happen to possess money—power that is ultimately destabilizing to society and to social relationships. While this destabilization plays out in *Little Dorrit,* for example, in an exploitative role reversal between Amy and her father, in *Nickleby* it plays out through an exploration of sexual disorder focused on Gride's desire for Madeline. While Gride is equivocal about this desire, allowing Ralph to conclude it is the "little property" he is really after, Gride's descriptions of Madeline as "a tit-bit—a dainty chick" and a "delicate morsel" center his lust not on money but on Madeline. His comments present her as food—something Gride intends to consume at his own pleasure— "any time I chose to name" (*NN,* 710; ch. 47).

Gride's lust grows more complicated in his discussion with Peg Sliderskew in chapter fifty-one. There, he explains to Peg that "we must be very careful" when Madeline joins the household, "more saving than ever with another mouth to feed. Only we—we mustn't let her lose her good looks, Peg, because I like to see 'em." In addition, Gride opines that Madeline "will be very cheap to dress and keep," and jokes that he will give her a "sparkling necklace" on their wedding day "and take it away again the next day" (*NN,* 766–67; ch. 51). These passages suggest a combination of control and manipulation very close to sadism, and this is confirmed in chapter fifty-three when Gride taunts the desperate Nicholas with promises to enjoy the sight of his "doting little wife" weeping, and to "beg" Nicholas's name from her "with kisses [. . .] Yes, and she'll tell me, and pay them back, and we'll laugh together, and hug ourselves—and be very merry" (an ambiguous phrase that conjures up distasteful pictures of Gride "enjoying" his young bride). Even after Nicholas has gone, Gride continues to refine his plans:

'If she ever turns pettish or ill-humoured, I'll taunt her with that spark
[. . .] She'll little think I know about him, and if I manage it well, I can
break her spirit by this means, and have her under my thumb." (*NN*,
804–05; ch. 53)

Thus Gride, the miserly money lender and follower of Ralph, embodies the ultimate danger to and degradation of the child in the world of the
novel, equating capital with the worst forms of child abuse. While Gride
owes some of his characteristics to stock-character depictions of misers and
old men lusting after young women, in his desperate, near-pornographic desire to consume, manipulate and control the commodified Madeline, and ultimately to "break her" if he wishes, as if she were a toy, we find a terrifying
vision. The system of financial capitalism, the novel says, destroys both the
social order and the moral fabric; it inserts contingency and risk in relationships (father and daughter) that should be predictably nurturing; it enables
dehumanization and cruelty; and it destroys—through the destruction of
childhood—the softening memories and imaginative power that allow us to
save ourselves.

NICKLEBY'S CASE AGAINST CAPITALISM:
THE TELEOLOGY OF CAPITAL IS DEATH

The third destructive effect of finance capitalism which I want to examine
is that of the teleology of capital in *Nicholas Nickleby*, the ultimate threat
the financial system poses to social order and to human life itself. This
theme becomes increasingly important in Dickens's critique of financial
capitalism as it develops. In *Nickleby*, as in Dickens's other works, "capital"
is associated with the exchange-value of money and implies the accumulation of money for its own sake. Such "capital" is sharply distinguished
from money used to acquire use-value—to purchase food, for example.
Marx characterizes these two uses of money as two "circulations": one, "C-
M-C" is based on consumption; the other, "M-C-M," on accumulation.
Marx states that one kind of circulation, " C-M-C, " denotes "the transformation of commodities into money and the reconversion of money into
commodities; selling in order to buy [. . .] But alongside this form we find
another form, which is quite distinct from the first: M-C-M, the transformation of money into commodities, and the reconversion of commodities
into money; buying in order to sell" (*Capital*, vol. I, 247–48).[15] Marx also
refers to these circulations, after Aristotle, as "economics" and "chrematistics,"[16] respectively, and these terms shed additional light on how capital
may be regarded in *Nickleby*:

Now chrematistics can be distinguished from economics in that 'for chrematistics, circulation is the source of riches. [. . .] And it appears to revolve around money, for money is the beginning and end of this kind of exchange. [. . .] Therefore also riches, such as chrematistics strives for, are unlimited. Just as every art which is not a means to an end, but an end in itself, has no limit to its aims, because it seeks constantly to approach nearer and nearer to that end, while those arts which pursue means to an end are not boundless, since the goal itself imposes a limit on them, so with chrematistics there are no bounds to its aims, these aims being absolute wealth. Economics, unlike chrematistics, has a limit [. . .] for the object of the former is something different from money, of the latter the augmentation of money.'[17]

Thus "chrematistics" is "boundless," and will forever seek an end that cannot be reached because it does not exist; "economics," on the other hand, is limited by its goals—to supply particular wants at particular times. Marx goes on to relate these concepts to the kinds of commercial and financial activities we find in *Nickleby*:

In merchants' capital the two extremes, the money which is thrown on the market and the augmented money which is withdrawn from the market, are at least mediated through a purchase and a sale, through the movement of circulation. In usurers' capital the form M-C-M' is reduced to the unmediated extremes M-M', money which is exchanged for more money, a form incompatible with the nature of money and therefore inexplicable from the standpoint of the exchange of commodities. Hence Aristotle says: 'Since chrematistics is a double science, one part belonging to commerce, the other to economics, the latter being necessary and praiseworthy, the former based on circulation and with justice disapproved (for it is not based on nature, but on mutual cheating), the usurer is most rightly hated, because money itself is the source of his gain, and is not used for the purposes for which it was invented. [18]

Merchants like the Cheerybles, according to this passage, at least "mediate" their capital by involving it in the exchange of commodities. Ralph's business, however, the accumulation of money for its own sake, is a doubly evil activity: first, it is "incompatible" with the true purpose of money itself (the exchange of necessary commodities); also, it is a form of "mutual cheating." This accumulation, then, which is the true engine of capitalism, is in reality an unnatural horror which society has come to call "usury"; it is hated because it is a destroyer, a force that creates only entropy.

"FROM HIM EXACT USURY WHOM IT
WOULD NOT BE A CRIME TO KILL"

As a usurer, in fact, Ralph is constructed to be the distillation of the case against capitalism, and in describing Ralph's activities the novel determinedly ignores any of the more benign aspects of financial capitalism which were commonplace in nineteenth-century financial writing. For example, the London money-market by the 1820s was arguably the most important source of capital in the world, and the true "engine" of British economic progress. Bagehot described the importance of this market later in the century:

> Money is economical power. Everyone is aware that England is the greatest moneyed country in the world; everyone admits that it has much more immediately disposable ready cash than any other country. But very fewer persons are aware how much greater the ready balance—the floating loan fund which can be lent to anybody for any purpose—is in England than it is anywhere else in the world [. . .] The bankers' deposits of London are many times greater than those of any other city—those of Great Britain many times greater than those of any other country.[19]

Yet Dickens chooses to make Ralph primarily a "usurer" (as he calls himself in chapter nineteen), and secondarily the swindling promoter of a bubble company. This choice excludes from the novel's consideration of finance capitalism activities like those Bagehot cites, which might help make the case that provision of capital is essential for an economy that can continue to support middle-class homes and hearths. Instead, the choice brings in an unspoken subtext of Jewishness, aloneness and "outsider" status which attach to Ralph and through him, to all financial activities.

More importantly, perhaps, the choice of usurer as Ralph's occupation helps us see him as the walking embodiment of all the evils in the "case" against capitalism that *Nickleby* is making. Ralph's ferocity and bristling, paranoid aggression stand out strongly, giving him—and through him finance—a peculiar kind of destructive power in the novel, and marking him (and it) as essentially irredeemable. The uncompromising harshness of Ralph's world-view is apparent in his reaction to the news of Smike's death:

> 'If you tell me,' said Ralph eagerly, that he is dead, I forgive you all else. If you tell me that he is dead, I am in your debt and bound to you for life. He is! I see it in your faces. Who triumphs now? Is this your dreadful news, this your terrible intelligence? You see how it moves me. You did well to send. I would have traveled a hundred

miles a-foot, through mud, mire, and darkness, to hear this news just at this time.' (*NN*, 886; ch. 60)

Although Ralph is unaware that Smike is his son, there is something beyond the pale in his terrible rejoicing, something (like the black cloud that follows him home in chapter sixty-two) that causes the rest of humankind—even his fellow-usurer Gride—to shun him.

In presenting Ralph in such an uncompromisingly antagonistic way, *Nicholas Nickleby* is indirectly accessing the underpinnings of the great and long-running debate on usury (alive in politics and business from the time of the Church Fathers down through the repeal of usury laws in England in 1854), and using concepts from this debate to add weight to its critique of financial capitalism. Much of the discussion of usury in England and elsewhere, as Benjamin Nelson notes, centered around two verses in the Book of Deuteronomy:

> Deuteronomy formed a cornerstone of the blood brotherhood morality of the Hebrew tribesmen. It assumed the solidarity of the *mishpaha* (clan) and the exclusion of the *nokri* (the foreigner, as contrasted with the *ger*, the protected sojourner, or the *toshab*, the resident stranger) from the privileges and obligations of the fraternity. It forbade the Hebrew to take *nesheck* (usury, interest) from his brother (*ah*), but permitted him to exact it from the *nokri:*

> XXIII: 19. Thou shalt not lend upon usury (*neshek*) to thy brother (*l'ahika*); usury of money, usury of victuals, usury of anything that is lent upon usury:

> XXIII: 20. Unto a stranger (*nokri*) thou mayest lend upon usury; but unto thy brother thou shalt not lend upon usury, that the Lord thy God may bless thee in all that thou settest thine hand to in the land whither thou goest to possess it. (Nelson, xv-xvii)

Thus Deuteronomy presented a marked contrast between the clan and those under its protection, to whom it was not permissible to lend upon usury, and the foreigner, to whom lending upon usury was permissible. As Nelson points out, debate about who was or was not a "foreigner" informed discussion of usury for centuries, and one strong branch of this debate held that usury, in a world where all were brothers before Christ, could never be justified (Nelson, xix). However, usury proved necessary when governments, for instance, had to borrow money to finance wars, and commerce was incapable of expansion without reliance on broad pools of capital. One of the commentators most influential in attempting to block reformers who wanted to move away from the Mosaic prohibition on usury was Church Father St. Ambrose. As Nelson notes, Ambrose's argument derived from the Jews' biblical position as an embattled people:

> Ambrose proposed to account for the Deuteronomic discrimination against the alien by an appeal to Biblical antiquities. The true meaning and limits of Deuteronomy xxiii: 20, he argued, were clear only in light of the authorized war of the Chosen People against the tribes inheriting the Promised Land. "The Law forbids you under any circumstances," Ambrose warned, "to exact usury from your brother." Who is he? Your brother is "your sharer in nature, co-heir in grace, every people, which, first, is in the Faith, then under the Roman Law." Who, then, was the stranger? The Amalekite, the Amorite, the Canaanite: the notorious foes of God's people, who illegally withheld the lands which the Lord had promised to Israel for a habitation:
> "From him, it says there, demand usury, whom you rightly desire to harm, against whom weapons are lawfully carried. Upon him usury is legally imposed. On him whom you cannot easily conquer in war, you can quickly take vengeance with the hundredth. From him exact usury whom it would not be a crime to kill. He fights without a weapon who demands usury: he who revenges himself upon an enemy, who is an interest collector from his foe, fights without a sword. Therefore, where there is right of war, there also is the right of usury." (Nelson, 4) [20]

Ambrose's pronouncements make usury a weapon, and, in an attempt to prevent usury among Christians, relegated the use of this weapon to "non-brothers"—the Jewish usurer, for example. By the nineteenth century, such views had moderated into a more liberal approach to financial freedom, in a world where rationality and "self-interest" were said to rule, as the passage from Bentham cited earlier suggests. But, says *Nicholas Nickleby*, what if the true capitalist is a man who is more aligned with St. Ambrose than with Bentham? A man who, incarnating Ambrose's view, is perpetually at war with his enemies, and who uses "the hundredth" as a most potent weapon? Ralph is such a man, certainly, and in the resolution of *Nickleby* he embodies a financial system "at war" with the rest of society. For Ralph, despite the accidents of biology, there are really no "brothers," no "sharer[s] in nature, co-heir[s] in grace." When he hears of his brother's death, Ralph comments, "My brother never did anything for me, and I never expected it; the breath is no sooner out of his body than I am to be looked to, as the support of a great hearty woman and a grown boy and girl. What are they to me? I never saw them" (*NN*, 77, ch. 3).

What makes Ralph doubly dangerous is that the "enemies list" in Ralph's "war," in the end, includes everyone—even (and perhaps most significantly) himself:

> Stern, unyielding, dogged, and impenetrable, Ralph cared for nothing in life, or beyond it, save the gratification of two passions, avarice, the first and predominant appetite of his nature, and hatred the second. [. . .] The only scriptural admonition that Ralph Nickleby heeded, in the letter, was 'know thyself.' He knew himself well, and choosing to imagine that all mankind were cast in the same mould, hated them. (*NN*, 656; ch. 44)

So Ralph, priding himself on his clear vision and measuring the world against himself, judges the world and all in it to be empty and worthless.[21] In his willingness to embrace entropy, he is a formidable foe for Bentham's "man of ripe years and of sound mind, acting freely and with his eyes open [. . .] with a view to his [own] advantage." Such a person would expect rationality and self-interest to drive Ralph's actions, which are in actuality driven by hatred, paranoia and self-loathing—the homicidal and suicidal logic of usury—and are directed inevitably toward destruction. To expect the "invisible hand" of the market to regulate Ralph and people like him, who are, after all, the true capitalists, the novel says, is childish fantasy. Ralph is a deadly foe (as Nicholas realizes instantly) and must be treated like one.

"BROTHERLY" CAPITALISM: "DICKENS APPEARS TO HAVE SEIZED THE DOMINATING ELEMENTS— GENIAL, HEALTHFUL, GENEROUS, AFFECTIONATE— IN THE CHARACTER OF THE GRANTS"

As I have argued, *Nicholas Nickleby* sets up an alternative to Ralph's brand of capitalism in the Cheerybles, a polar contrast between "chrematistic" entropy and "economic" order. Part of the project of the novel is to present the Cheerybles' capitalism as a viable alternative to Ralph's. To support this, I would note, first, that the Cheerybles are placed alongside Ralph at the end of a novel that has expended tremendous energy in radically raising the reader's level of dissatisfaction with the status-quo. In placing the Cheerybles side by side with Ralph, the novel is trying to capitalize on this dissatisfaction—to provide us (ostensibly—we will come to the contradictions later) with an alternative way of thinking about business and finance. Also supporting this notion of the novel's project as the creation of a serious alternative to capitalism are two other factors. First, as Dickens insisted the Cheerybles were "no

creations of the Author's brain; but are prompting every day [. . .] some mu-
nificent and generous deed."[22] That is, they were "real"—businessmen modeled on the famous Grant brothers, operators of a large and successful textile
business in Manchester, who were widely known to be both economically
successful and demonstrably humane.[23] Second, the model of individual
benevolence the Cheerybles illustrate was not a "radical" solution in the sense
that Chartism was, or that Communism would be. Instead, it was compounded of recognizable elements like personal benevolence, reverence for the
past, for family and for God, and social order and control. That is, it was a
"solution" that was perhaps achievable and safe: it would not replace the chaos
and violence of finance capitalism with chaos and violence borne of revolution. All these elements were present to some extent in the Grants' story, and
Dickens carefully chose his material to create an emotionally and morally (if
not commercially) attractive "alternative."

Dickens was introduced to the Grants by William Harrison Ainsworth
in 1838,[24] when he apparently had dinner at their house. As far as is known,
he had only the one encounter with the brothers, and it is not known
whether he had any correspondence or other communication with them
after the single dinner. However, Dickens was able to turn the meeting to
good account, finding material he could use and, according to William
Hume Elliot, Manchester minister and author of an enthusiastically positive
Grant biography, creating not "copies of the Grants," but

> exquisitely faithful ideal representations, touching sometimes, with
> wonderful delicacy and accuracy, the borderline of the real. Dickens ap-
> pears to have seized the dominating elements—genial, healthful, gener-
> ous, affectionate—in the character of the Grants. [25]

Later in his book, Elliot notes that, by the time Dickens met the Grants,
"William Grant would be bordering upon three score and ten, while Daniel
would be about fifty-six or fifty seven—thirteen years younger. The name
and salient characteristics of these brothers were at that time familiar as a
household word in Manchester and far beyond its limits" (Elliot, 221). Thus
Dickens chose to build his "good business" characters by "seiz[ing] the dom-
inating elements" of real models, and models who were well-known for the
positive characteristics he intended to give the Cheerybles.

The core of the alternative model presented via the Cheerybles in
Nickleby can be found in a story that became both a family legend and an
example the Grants tried to follow in their lifetimes. Eliot reports that when
the young Grants and their parents arrived in England from Scotland they

were penniless; that night, after praying for help,[26] they slept on a hill over-looking Ramsbottom, where they later established their successful business:

> Remarkable to say, the next morning two gentlemen, shooting on the hill happened to see them, and having approached the unwonted group, questioned [William Grant, the father] as to how they came to be there. William's frank and manly answer to the questions and the strangely pathetic picture before their eyes, so impressed them that they thrust two sovereigns into his hand, and, wishing him good morning and better luck, with moistening eye and quickened step hastened from the scene. The "wilderness" now lay behind. Unconsciously Pisgah was reached, and the fair land of coming, yet unknown, conquest lay before the family. (Elliot, 84–85)

Several tropes here link the Grants to the kind of individualized charity *Nickleby* is advocating through the Cheerybles: the coincidental meeting that provides succor when it is most needed; the open, "manly" discussion of the situation; the reliever hurrying away with "moistening eye" before thanks can be offered; the ability of charity to turn the "wilderness" into "Pisgah," or, in *Nickleby*'s case, London into "Eden." All these tropes occur in *Nickleby*, forming elements of a model for how charity should be given. In addition, this family legend links to another vital element of power against the destructive force of finance capitalism—the softening power of memory that returns us to our childhoods, and prompts us to do good in the world. For the Grants, Elliot reports, the hilltop scene was a touchstone to which they returned all their lives:

> The anxious praying group beneath the wing of night on the lone hilltop and the timely answer so strangely brought next morning, formed a sacred tradition in the family circle to the end of their lives—seldom expressly spoken of, but, like an atmosphere, always there, and in their impressive filial reverence, their ready sympathy with the friendless and the needy and their cheerful and abounding generosity always operative. (Eliot, 85)

Eliot and T. H. Hayhurst, another "appreciative" biographer, both note the formative quality of this experience on the Grants' business and charitable practices in later life. Such an anecdote, living proof of the softening power of memory even on these shrewd businessmen, had to have been compelling to Dickens, who recreates it in the Cheerybles' recollections of their arrival in London as penniless youths (which prompts Charles's initial interest in Nicholas) and in their memories of their mother, who, like the Grants' mother, is positioned as a guiding moral force in their lives. The outcome of these experiences, in the view of the Grants' biographers, was an "economic" use of money. Eliot writes of Daniel Grant:

> One of those who knew him best—a relative who had been brought up with him—told the writer, in a letter received from a distant land, some years ago—"No one will ever know what Daniel Grant has done for hundreds of people. He considered that God had given him the wealth, not to hoard and use for self-gratification, but for good to the poor and needy; and many who had seen better days, and were in trouble, were helped and raised up again by him. He was very sensitive himself, and when he gave to help others, he did it in such a way that no one could feel in the least uncomfortable in receiving assistance from him." (Elliot, 162–63)

In stark contrast to Ralph, the Grants appear to enact the *first* part of Deuteronomy's pronouncement on usury, treating people like brothers, "sharer[s] in nature, co-heir[s] in grace," in Ambrose's words, in general, and in dealings involving money in particular. Their capitalism produces "ready sympathy with the friendless and the needy and [. . .] cheerful and abounding generosity" in place of psychological trauma. In their world children are "helped and raised up" rather than debased or destroyed. And instead of entropy, their capitalism has a productive end-point: it yields "impressive filial reverence," and "sacred tradition[s]"; it leads to "Pisgah" rather than emptiness, providing the necessaries of life for the Grants as well as those around them.

    Given the material above, the model represented by the Cheerybles appears to have some substance—at least to have worked to mitigate capitalism's excesses at a particular time and place. However, this model is beset by a number of contradictions which undercut it, and in so doing expose some of the knottier problems with which Dickens was grappling. At the most basic level, compared with accounts of the Grants, which dwell in detail upon their business, its technologies, its selling process and other details, the presentation of the Cheerybles seems to lack substance. While we know they are "German Merchants,"[27] we see none of their financial or commercial activity beyond scenes in which Tim Linkinwater and/or Nicholas are updating the books. Significantly, as the embodiments of "good" business, they are seen to do no business at all, thus affirming poor Belling's unintentional parody of Squeers's "teaching" in chapter 4: "Never—perform—business!" (*NN*, 98; ch. 4). The implication of this omission—perhaps the question with which Dickens was contending—is that any contact at all with capital is tainting; that money can be handled only for purposes of charity or to acquire a commodity for its use-value. Just as Ralph's makeup as a financier is "edited" to include only the most destructive aspects of financial capitalism, so the Cheerybles as merchants are "edited" to remove even more benign aspects of financial capitalism, such as the "merchant's capital" described by Marx above. This description of their business amounts to, as Steven Marcus says, "a combined visiting and burial society"[28] rather than a business model that could challenge Ralph's, and one is left wondering why the novel omits the kind of detail that might authenticate Cheeryble Brothers as a "going concern" rather than a private charity. While we could refer this lack of business substance to Dickens's ignorance or lack of interest, his own business shrewdness argues against this. Instead, we are reminded of his letter to Forster quoted above, and the inability suggested there to conceive of a "bargain" that did not include the destructive elements of capitalism. In the Cheerybles' case, Dickens was asking the right questions about a kinder capitalism, but was unable to fill in the answers.

There are contradictions, too, if we dig deeper into the Grants' story. For one thing, like the Cheerybles,' the Grant's charity, though liberally given, was paternalistic, even controlling. For example, T. H. Hayhurst notes:

> At Springside [one of the Grants' major fabric-printing plants] , as we have said, the poor were perpetually feasted. [. . .] Occasionally, however, when national events called up the festive instinct of the people, the Brothers would indulge in hospitalities which for extent, substance, and heartiness did something to recall the baronial excitements of olden days.[29]

And Elliot, quoting from the *Manchester Guardian*'s "reference to William's decease" (1842) notes that Grant "by industrious exertion and unsullied integrity, had acquired an independent fortune, which he was ever disposed to make subservient to the calls of poverty and misfortune; not dispensing his charities indiscriminately, but under the control of discretion" (Elliot, 203–04).

Such "baronial" paternalism makes the modern reader uncomfortable, as does the forelock-pulling toast proffered by the Cheerybles' "sturdiest and jolliest subordinate" in chapter thirty-seven. But underneath the discomfort, we must examine the contradiction inherent in this blithely accepted paternalism. On one hand, these acts take place in a world in which the implacable Ralph, symbolizing "capital [which] comes dripping from head to toe, from every pore, with blood and dirt" (*Capital*, vol. I, 925) is waging total war on humanity. Seen in this light, the Grants' and Cheerybles' condescension may be read more the way Scrooge reads Fezziwig's generosity in Stave II of *A Christmas Carol*:

> He has the power to render us happy or unhappy; to make our service light or burdensome; a pleasure or a toil. Say that his power lies in words and looks; in things so slight and insignificant that it is impossible to add

and count 'em up: what then? The happiness he gives, is quite as great as
if it cost a fortune.[30]

In this sense, the Grants' is a "power" to treat others with generosity or the
reverse, and their treatment of their people is a sign of their respect at some
level, for the essential humanity of those in their employ—a refusal to make
every transaction a "mere matter of bargain and sale," as Mr. Dombey says.[31]
However, the Grants' very power—their "discretion"—comes not from familial relationship but from money. Their money gives them effective control over others, and this implies, at some level, commodification of those
others, who, in this case, are hardly "sharer[s] in nature, co-heir[s] in grace,"
but mere employees. Here the "brotherly" aspect of the new-model capitalism breaks down in favor of a relationship mediated by money, and this
breakdown is strongly echoed in *Nickleby* in the Cheerybles' controlling,
money-based paternalism. As Joseph Childers has noted:

> In a way, the Cheerybles have entered the friends and family free-agent
> market and put together the best set of acquaintances money can buy.
> Their cherished domestic space is run just as their business is. Indeed,
> there is no distinguishing between the two and the intersection between
> public and private is no intersection at all, but rather the shape of the
> Cheerybles' ontology. They, and because of their influence all those for
> whom they care, always exist both privately and public [sic], domesti-
> cally and commercially.[32]

Again, one gets the sense of Dickens grappling with an intractable
problem and answering it more with a wish than a true "solution." In a
money-based society, is there truly "no distinguishing" between personal and
business relations? Clearly, "capitalists" like Fezziwig can try to mitigate the
impact of money on relationships, but even in Dickens's own life, the impact
of money appeared inescapable, as we can see from another letter he wrote to
Forster (15 November 1838) during *Nickleby*'s serialization:

> How is the tooth-ache? I have the heart-ache, for I paid fifty-seven
> pounds, two and six pence for Edward Barrow this morning [the editor
> notes: "Probably to honour a bill Edward Barrow had signed for John
> Dickens in Dec 34."]. And so it always is;—directly I build up a hun-
> dred pounds, one of my dear relations comes and knocks it down again.
> (*Pilgrim Letters*, vol. I, 454)

The frustration in this letter matches the one I quoted earlier, but this time the object is not Dickens's publisher, but his father. The "heart ache" over his inability to "build up a hundred pounds" foregrounds the real problem here—that John's actions are making Charles (and his family) less secure. In a world where even the most intimate relations can easily turn into a "matter of bargain and sale," where money mediates literally every relationship, Dickens is unable to see a way out, so instead he forcefully wishes for one, and creates one, if only in his imagination.

There is another anecdote of the Grants that suggests an even more radical breakdown in the new-capitalism model we have been discussing—a breakdown that involves the kind of disorder against which Dickens and many of his contemporaries viewed benevolence as a safeguard. As Humphry House notes, a Benthamite "righteous [. . .] indignation" at injustice and inefficiency was driven both by the desire to improve things and by fear, and "[e]very subscription to a benevolent scheme was in part an insurance premium against a revolution or an epidemic."[33] But the failure of the hoped-for linkage between benevolence and social order can be seen in an anecdote Hayhurst tells of William Grant's experience as a magistrate in 1826 during the "power loom riots" when "he was called upon to exercise his magisterial functions in an extraordinary and (to him) exceedingly painful manner." When a mob bent on destroying the power looms approaches a town near Ramsbottom, the troops (the Queen's Bays) are called out. As Magistrate, Grant is summoned to read the Riot Act, but first he tries to solve the problem using reason and the promise of benevolent aid:

> Mr. William Grant [. . .] rode out a few yards in front of the soldiers to address the mob which fell back respectfully. He told the men that His Majesty (George IV.) had been exceedingly liberal in donations to the various communities in distress, and that his Majesty's Ministers were doing everything in their power to alleviate the prevailing distress. "And lads," continued Mr. Grant, "I can assure you there has been a meeting of gentlemen of this county for the sole purpose of seeing how they can relieve you, and you may rest assured that something will be done for you almost immediately. We are going to send people round to enquire into your condition, to inspect your habitations, and to see what you stand in need of; and not one of you here this day, or your families, but shall be relieved."

The paternalistic appeal, however, does not work:

The mob [. . .] heeded no counsel, and as they expressed a determination to destroy all the looms at Chadderton, Mr. Grant read the Riot
Act. Men and women ran off in haste down the hill toward the mills of
Messrs. Ashton [. . .] Several [of the mob] were killed and many
wounded before the mob was dispersed by the joint action of the
Queen's Bays and a small body of sharp shooters of [sic] greenjackets
(volunteers) organised by the Messrs. Ashton from among their
workpeople. (Hayhurst, 42)

This passage is not so much an indictment of Grant's personal benevolence
(it was not, after all, his plant that was being attacked) as a depiction of how
quickly the possessors of capital will turn from an attitude of "brotherhood"
to the use of coercion and even force: "not one of you here this day, or your
families, but shall be relieved" turns almost instantaneously into "Several
were killed and many wounded" when capital is at risk. Thus the fragility of
the new model is exposed—a fragility that paradoxically increases in times of
economic stress when "brotherhood" is more than ever needed.

In the case of the Cheerybles, this breakdown is perhaps more implicit
than explicit: it may be the obverse of the obsession with order in the count-
ing house, and it is implied in the scene in chapter thirty-seven when the
workers are brought in for the toast: "We're allowed to take a liberty once a
year, gen'lmen, and if you please we'll take it now" (*NN*, 563; ch. 37). More
significantly, we might cite the Cheerybles' need for iron control over the
marriage arrangements at the end of the novel, their insistence on making
decisions for all those in their sphere, and their subtle but constant moves to
ensure social control throughout their sphere.[34] Joseph Childers points out
"the incredible power that accrues to [the Cheerybles] through the effects of
their philanthropic steamrolling as they gleefully force their good will on
everyone who lies in their path, power that is always connected to the agency
of other characters" (Childers, 62)—in other words, power that subsumes
the autonomy of others. This mania for control is the reciprocal of the reading of the riot act: if iron control is the norm in good times, what kinds of
coercion are not possible in hard times? And again, we see Dickens at this
point grappling with the same intractable problem: if disorder threatens
one's financial security, what is the "brotherly" (or filial) response? In the case
of the Cheerybles, wishful thinking is again operative; perhaps benevolence
(and, to be fair to Dickens, real reform) *will* stave off disorder, and the decision to read the riot act will not have to be made.

There is no telling how much Dickens knew of this history (the biogra-
phies I have been citing were both published after his death), but his faithful
portrayal (even down to the characteristically abrupt speech of Daniel) would

indicate that he absorbed much of the history and lore surrounding the Grants. One other incident in their lives resonates for us as readers of Dickens. Eliot describes the death of their young sister in 1784, when William was four and Daniel an infant, as "a great never-forgotten family sorrow [. . .] Mary, who was rather lame, and eight years old" did not return from her factory job and

> on inquiry, it was found she had never reached the works [. . .] Great indescribably was the distress of the family, still comparatively strangers, when this was ascertained. Search, immediate and persistent, was made. Neighbourly sympathy and prompt and willing help were not lacking. But in vain. Mary had not been seen by anyone since she left home, and not a trace of her could be found. A night or two afterwards a workman dreamt that "Mrs. Grant's daughter was lying in the Irwell," at a particular place. When he awoke he told his wife, and forthwith search was made, and little Mary's body was found at that spot. It was a stormy day on which she was lost, and it was believed that a sudden gust of wind had blown her into the river. (Elliot, 91–92) [35]

A child named "Mary," lame, also a child laborer and perhaps even a murder victim—her story does not figure in the presentation of the Cheerybles, and there is no certainty that Dickens knew it. But there is a connection, in any case, to the contradictions with which *Nickleby*'s alternative model of capitalism is riddled. Mary went out to work, as the young Dickens did, to assist in providing her family with financial security; she was allowed, even welcomed, into the factory because her labor was cheaper than that of adults. Thus the child is commodified—"sold" by her parents for money and "bought" by the factory owner for the surplus value she would generate. Her labor benefits everyone but her—"fills their pockets" as Dickens would say— and in the end she dies on her way to fulfill these functions. Here, the exemplars of this kinder, brotherly capitalism have in their past seen one of their own siblings killed, in a sense, by capital itself.

In the end, Mary's story and the anecdote about the riot-act remind us of another, anything but utopian, subtext of "brotherly" relations: the fratricide and violence represented by Cain and Abel and Jacob and Esau. In the novel, this subtext is mainly connected with Ralph's role as brother and uncle. But the subtext is apparent, too, in the coercive aspects of the Cheerybles' "management," and suggests, even as a muffled echo of the Old Testament stories, that the irrationality and stubborn self-interest at the basis of brotherly or familial violence is a major—perhaps fatal—contradiction in the "brotherly" capitalism represented by the Cheerybles. Alexander Welsh comments on such "motiveless malignity":

Cain, according to Augustine, had no readily understandable motive in
slaying Abel:
"The founder of the earthly city was a fratricide. Overcome with envy,
he slew his own brother, a citizen of the eternal city, and a sojourner on
earth. [. . .] Now these brothers, Cain and Abel, were not both ani-
mated by the same earthly desires, nor did the murderer envy the other
because he feared that, by both ruling, his own dominion would be cur-
tailed,—for Abel was not solicitous to rule in that city which his brother
built,—he was moved by that diabolical, envious hatred with which the
evil regard the good, for no other reason than because they are good
while themselves are evil."[36]

Unreasoning violence, psychological control rather than physical destruction, seems to color even the familial relations which form the basis of the
better kind of capitalism the Cheerybles represent. Such violence, real and
potential, seems inescapable; it infects even the benevolent relationships
upon which *Nickleby*'s "brotherly" capitalism is based, and undercuts the
more benign form of capitalism even as it is being proposed.

POISED BETWEEN GOOD AND EVIL:
COMPETING "MARKETING STRATEGIES"

Having examined the opposing models of capitalism, one can easily conclude that whatever "victory" the new model of capitalism claims at the end
is forced and unconvincing, as are the Cheerybles themselves. As I will argue,
it is certainly true that Ralph's dark version of capitalism dominates *Nickleby*,
and shadows even Nicholas's Edenic retirement. But more interesting than
whether the "good guys" or the "bad guys" win is the "marketing" of each
model during the course of the novel—the overt as well as the perhaps unin-
tentional attempts to "sell" one or the other type of capitalism to the reader
as the "better" one. In my view, this is a struggle for the heart and mind of
the reader that says much about the struggle within Dickens himself to come
to terms with his own position inside a capitalist society—a position in
which he was at once a shrewd capitalist, a producer of commodities, and an
acute critic of the system.

First, *Nickleby* consciously attempts to "sell" the reader on the possibility
and viability of the Cheerybles' new-model capitalism. Dickens's insistence on
the realism of the Grants in his prefaces anticipates his defenses of Krook's
spontaneous combustion as "real" in his *Bleak House* prefaces, and signals his
concern that the reader take the Cheerybles seriously at some level.[37] More importantly, perhaps, *Nickleby*, like Dickens's later novels, attempts to engage us

in the moral judgements of issues presented in the text, as Edgar Johnson notes when he cites "the intensity with which [Dickens] demanded the sympathies of his readers for the emotions and sufferings of actual people."[38] But while in later works like *A Christmas Carol* or *Dombey and Son* we as readers are exhorted, guided in fact as to where and how to engage our sympathies, *Nickleby* offers far less overt direction. Instead, the novel often presents us with "cases" in the form of spectacles which implicate us in the making of value judgements about what is going on in *Nickleby.* These spectacles interpellate us, as Audrey Jaffe notes, by foregrounding a lack which we are then invited to fill. [39] For example, when Nicholas and Smike return to London in chapter thirty-two, we see a lengthy description of the goods on display in the great "emporium" of London. The description ends with a series of spectacles, framed in shop windows:

> The rags of the squalid ballad-singer fluttered in the rich light that showed the goldsmith's treasures, pale and pinched-up faces hovered above the windows where there was tempting food, hungry eyes wandered over the profusion guarded by one thin sheet of brittle glass—an iron wall to them; half-naked shivering figures stopped to gaze at Chinese shawls and golden stuffs of India. (*NN,* 489; ch. 32)

At one level the sumptuous commodities interpellate the "half-naked shivering figures" who want but cannot have them. But in this scene the spectacle does not affect us in the same way. Instead, we are made to feel the "lack" depicted by the framed picture of the poor barred from the goods, and are asked, in effect, how (or even whether) we might want to fill *that* lack—the lack of charity and even human dignity in the world unfolding before us. This interpellation is made morally more resonant later in this same scene, where "clothes for the newly-born" and "coffins for the dead" are placed side by side and where "repletion and starvation laid them down together": the ending of the scene, a *memento mori* for participants in a commercial society, reminds us of the ultimate futility of selfishness and uncharity—the ultimate teleology of the capitalist system which produces the "lack" from which the figures of the poor are seen to suffer.[40] Similarly, other spectacles demand our attention and ask us to fill the "lack" in each case with moral outrage. For example, Nicholas wakes up on the morning of Smike's disappearance to a spectacle of commodified and destroyed children:

> Little could be distinguished but the sharp outlines of pale faces, over which the sombre light shed the same dull heavy colour, with here and there a gaunt arm thrust forth: its thinness hidden by no covering, but fully exposed to view in all its shrunken ugliness. There were some who,

> lying on their backs with upturned faces and clenched hands [. . .] bore
> more the aspect of dead bodies than of living creatures [. . .] A few—and
> these were among the youngest of the children—slept peacefully on with
> smiles upon their faces, dreaming perhaps of home. (*NN*, 212; ch. 13)

Here again we are interpellated—shamelessly, in fact—by the irony and
pathos of the smiling faces of the innocent younger children lying in what
amounts to a mass grave. We are called upon to fill the "lack" here with
moral outrage, even, in the case of Dickens's original readers, to be moved
enough to take some action against the evil described. Certainly Dickens's remarks in his 1848 Preface indicate that mobilizing such outrage was his intent in 1838, and that this intent was successful: "There were [in 1838] a
good many cheap Yorkshire schools in existence. There are very few now.
[. . .] I was always curious about them—fell [. . .] into the way of hearing
more about them—at last, having an audience, resolved to write about
them" (*NN*, 47–48).

Such conscious "marketing" of the novel's stance against capitalism is
highly effective, and convinces us, as readers, of the destructiveness of the
system, as I have described above. But even this creation of moral outrage,
located as it is within the capitalist system and within a capitalist product, is
not without contradiction. Spectacle, as Thomas Richards has pointed out in
his analysis of the Great Exhibition of 1851, is closely identified both with
the process of creating "want" for capitalism's commodities, and with the
ideology of capitalism itself:

> The Great Exhibition began by creating an official rhetoric of public repre-
> sentation of the commodity and ended by making the commodity into the
> one rhetoric of all representation. That rhetoric, which has been designated
> spectacle, adumbrated an emerging commodity culture and contributed
> materially to fashioning, for the first time in history, a dominant machin-
> ery of specific capitalist representation. Commodity representation now
> became synonymous with the phenomenology of possession guided by the
> presence of bourgeois authority. In the Crystal Palace, capitalism was not,
> as the classical economists had claimed, a natural state of affairs; it was a
> sanctioned state ideology affirmed by representatives from all walks of Vic-
> torian life. Led by Prince Albert, the nation joined together to proclaim a
> new dominion of things.[41]

Admittedly, Richards is describing the emergence of a commodity culture twelve years after Dickens finished the novel, but if we think of the spectacles in *Nickleby* as reflecting the same set of emerging cultural forces that

would come into focus at the Great Exhibition, we cannot help but think that *Nickleby's* "marketing," as I have described it, is compromised. One might argue that a writer of Dickens's acuteness might be using such techniques in order to criticize them, or parody them, as he does, certainly, with the meaningless signs generated on behalf of the Muffin Company. But the spectacles we have been considering (and many others, especially those featuring Kate and Madeline) are surely serious and straightforward attempts to generate moral outrage, and not clever criticisms of marketing itself. One could also argue that *Nickleby* may be attempting to "co-opt" the techniques of capitalistic marketing—to use them against itself. This may even be true, but it still leaves the novel on dangerous ground, for the use of these techniques requires the commodification of those about whom we are supposed to feel moral outrage—requires, that is, immersing them in the stream of commodities which is at the root of the problems the novel is trying to attack. Thus Dickens is left, at best, commodifying the poor in order to protest their commodification; at worst, *Nickleby* subtly endorses the capitalist ideology it is protesting against by adopting its most effective, and destructive, marketing techniques. Again, we see Dickens wrestling with a problem in which he and his work are inextricably tangled, and falling back on wishful thinking (in this case wishing away the connection between his spectacles and commercial ones) rather than providing a solution outside of the capitalist framework.

Nickleby's attempt to outrage us with the capitalist system is effectively accomplished, compromised as it may be. But the other portion of the novel's project, to "sell" the Cheerybles' "brotherly" capitalism as a better alternative, fails utterly. What is interesting about the failure, though, is not that the Cheerybles themselves are unsatisfactory (though they are), but that the attempt to "sell" their capitalism is eclipsed by another "marketing campaign" occurring simultaneously in the novel. This campaign, perhaps unintended, but obvious and powerful, is an attempt to "sell" Ralph's brand of capitalism. Before considering the details of this "campaign," we should look more closely at the concept of marketing, which I have loosely linked with "selling" up to this point. In defining "marketing" the authors of *Problems in Marketing* (1977), a business-school textbook, comment:

> [M]arketing is considerably broader in its purposes and activities than is generally recognized by the lay person or casual observer. While marketing is very much concerned with such specific functions as advertising, personal selling, distribution, and pricing, it is equally involved in determining what products or services the firm should offer,

how they should be designed, and to whom they should be directed.
[. . . T]he marketing process is used to develop detailed marketing
programs: What specific combination of product features, information (advertising and personal selling), convenience [. . .] , attendant
services [. . .], and price will cause a specific customer or group of
customers to purchase a particular product or service from us rather
than from our competitors [. . .]?[42]

Thus marketing, like much of Dickens's writing, is aimed at producing specific behavior (i.e., "buy my product," "help the poor"); in fact the definition
above uses language ("determining," "directed," "cause") that blurs the line
between marketing as a form of persuasion and a form of coercion. I think
this line is blurred in *Nickleby* as well—in the use of spectacle to promote
moral outrage against capitalism, as I have noted above; but more significantly, perhaps, in the use of rhetoric, imagery and the whole considerable
arsenal of Dickens's art to promote (unconsciously, perhaps, but vigorously)
Ralph's brand of capitalism Moreover, such promotion is as coercive as any
other marketing activity, since it seeks to match its presentation of the product with our needs as consumers in a way that will cause us to accept, to
"buy," the product. By this I do not mean that *Nickleby*'s intent is to undercut the "brotherly" capitalism it is trying to promote, but that, through its
"marketing" of Ralph, its effective and forceful presentation of him as a commodity calibrated to our needs, it all but forces us to accept him as real and
inevitable, and to dismiss the Cheerybles as hollow.

The marketing campaign focusing on Ralph operates at the level of entertainment, whereas the campaign to position the Cheerybles' capitalism as
better operates at a more conceptual and moral level. As consumers of entertainment, our needs may be for excitement, interest, suspense, detail, surprise—a set of needs perhaps quite different from the logical and moral needs
we might exhibit as consumers of economic arguments. It is on this level—a
level of supreme importance to Dickens the producer of "product," if not to
Dickens the reformer—that Ralph's capitalism is so effectively marketed: the
novel expends more time and words on, and consistently offers much more
striking images of, the entropic force of "chrematistics" than the healing force
of "economics."

For example, the premises of Cheeryble Brothers is a marvel of "economy." It is, first, a temple of order: situated in a "quiet, shady little square," it is
"the oldest and cleanest-looking house of business in the square"; Nicholas notices the "respect which had been shown [Charles Cheeryble] by the ware-
housemen and porters whom they passed"; Tim Likinwater sits in "a little,

partitioned-off counting-house like a large glass case" (*NN*, 535; ch. 35). Money here is used "economically," too—exchanged for commodities to meet the needs of the "six poor children" of the man who has been "smashed by a cask of sugar" (536) for example, or to build the almshouses and supply the charities noted on the bills "[a]mong the shipping-announcements and steam packet lists which decorated the counting-house wall" (*NN*, 554; ch. 37).

This is all well and good, we think as readers; but it is far less memorable than the picture of Gride's premises we get in chapter fifty-one—an "old house, dismal, dark and dusty," which appears to be "hoarding" Gride as he hoards his money, among its "[m]eagre old chairs and tables of spare and bony make, and hard and cold as miser's hearts" (*NN*, 763; ch. 51). We notice immediately that these objects have life, or at least a kind of personality, in them—a spark of the same "moral aptitude" (as Dorothy van Ghent put it)[43] as Gride himself. These humanized objects are in sharp contrast to the rather strained symbolism of the "rusty and shattered" blunderbuss and the "broken and edgeless" swords on the Cheerybles' walls, which, if they convey a "moral aptitude" at all, signal impotence as strongly as pacifism (*NN*, 554; ch. 37).

Gride's actions and his speech, too, come loaded with meaning about the kind of man he is. When attempting to choose a wedding suit, he "never took two articles of clothing out [of the wardrobe] together, but always brought them forth singly, and never failed to shut the wardrobe door and turn the key, between each visit to its shelves (*NN*, 764; ch. 51)." Such actions are in sharp contrast, in terms of meaning something, to the Cheerybles' pointless (nervous?) hand-rubbing. Gride's speech, too ("It was a lucky suit, too, this bottle-green. The very day I put it on first, old Lord Mallowford was burnt to death in his bed, and all the post-obits fell in" [765]) is surprising in its juxtapositions and rich in its linkage to what we know of him; the Cheerybles' speech, on the other hand, strikes the reader either as eccentric and disconnected ("'Eh?' cried the old man [. . .] 'What! Dear me! No, no. Well-behaved young gentleman reduced to such a necessity! No, no, no" [*NN*, 553; ch. 35]) or queasily sincere platitudes recited as in chorus ("'For these and all other blessings, brother Charles,' said Ned. 'Lord, make us truly thankful, brother Ned,' said Charles" [*NN*, 550; ch. 37]).

This constant "marketing" through language and imagery is stepped up considerably in power when we consider Ralph himself. Certainly the attractive power of the Cheerybles' "economic" capitalism pales in comparison to the power embodied in Ralph. The Cheerybles' hand-rubbing and tut-tutting is completely eclipsed, for example, by the black cloud that seems to follow Ralph on his last frantic walk though London—a melodramatic trope

that both tantalizes the reader with the uncanny, and adds weight and meaning to the scene by implicating even the sky above him in his death.[44] Moreover, Ralph is a persuasive "product" because he is a villain who will neither
change, nor leave the stage. Ralph brings the issue of entropy back into the
sharpest possible focus when, about to commit suicide, he hears "the sound
of a deep bell":

> 'Lie on!' cried the usurer, 'with your iron tongue! Ring merrily for births
> that make expectants writhe, and marriages that are made in hell, and
> toll ruefully for the dead whose shoes are worn already. Call men to
> prayers who are godly because not found out, and ring chimes for the
> coming of every year that brings this cursed world nearer to its end. No
> bell or book for me; throw me on a dunghill, and let me rot there to in-
> fect the air!' (*NN*, 906; ch. 62)

Such rhetoric depicts a man for whom none of the rituals or passages of life
have meaning; the life of accumulation, we are reminded again, leads only to
emptiness and the entropy of a rotting corpse on a dunghill. But Ralph's suicide, unlike Merdle's in *Little Dorrit*, does more than signal the (just) end of
the financier and his swindles. We hear nothing from Merdle about his suicide, which is portrayed as an almost impersonal event, part of a vast system
rather than the action or statement of one person. Ralph's suicide, on the
other hand, is vehemently, intensely personal; his final speech functions as a
curse, extending out into the future and infecting it, just as he hopes his
corpse will. In his final speech, Ralph underlines the danger he has come to
represent as he picks out and reverses the values of the key elements (the
weddings, the families, the reverence for the dead Smike etc.) of the novel's
happy ending and its "solution." In effect, Ralph ends by declaring war on
the novel, and us as readers; he provides a "parody" of the novel's resolution
that is more memorable (and perhaps more in keeping with the world
Nicholas Nickleby is trying to depict) than the actual resolution itself.[45]

Thus Ralph's power as an embodiment of capitalism grows as he steps
out of his frame at the end of the novel, devaluing the events that are about
to provide a conventionally happy ending, overshadowing the ending and
the beneficence of the Cheerybles who make it possible. Even from the
grave, he is still able to make his point: "Ralph having died intestate," the
novel tells us, Nicholas, Kate and Mrs. Nickleby would have become "in
legal course his heirs. But they could not bear the thought of growing rich on
money so acquired, and felt as though they could never hope to prosper with
it. They made no claim to his wealth; and the riches for which he had toiled
all his days, and burdened his soul with so many evil deeds, were swept at last

into the coffers of the state, and no man was the better or happier for them" (*NN,* 931; ch. 65). At one level, the usurer, who has worked so hard for nothing, is foiled, proven to have lived in vain. But at another level, the man who wants to "ring chimes for the coming of every year that brings this cursed world nearer to its end" (*NN,* 906; ch. 62) actually triumphs—his money does no good, helps no one, descends into the entropic state to which he has consigned himself and all life. "Choke on it," Ralph seems to say, as he has the last laugh after all.

In the end, Ralph's combination of intensely personal hatred and completely consistent ideology—extending entropy out into the future and even beyond the page to include us as readers—is simply more arresting and appealing—better able to meet our "needs" as consumers of entertainment—than the hand-rubbing alternative. At some level, despite its inherent contradictions, the "brotherly" capitalism of the Cheerybles is a better, more humane alternative than that embodied by Ralph. But it does not come across to us as readers as real in the sense of being detailed and pungent, or realistic, in the sense of being economically viable, even if we ignore the contradictions I have noted. At the same time, Ralph's capitalism carries with it the weight of our own and Dickens's experience, and of our and his fish-in-water inability to see beyond it, and so seems to represent the "real" world with which we struggle, while the language and imagery render it vital and snarlingly real on the page.

The idea of Dickens's own art working against the ideological project of the novel seems an appropriate emblem for this complicated and contradictory novel. The novel itself is a battleground on which Dickens's own conflicting attitudes about capitalism, and the inherent contradictions of his positions as artist and capitalist, entertainer and reformer, benevolist and provider of economic security for his family, were starting to crystallize, and where he tries, but fails, to come to terms with them. In the end, *Nickleby's* project is undermined because Dickens himself must operate within the capitalist system his novel says it opposes. Dickens's livelihood depends not on another's benevolence, but on his "product's" sales; his relationship with the world around him, even with his own relatives, is mediated by cash, and he is a "player" in the system of which *Nickleby* is a critique. This position provides clarity and pointedness to the novel's portrayal of competitive, self-interested capitalism. More significantly, Dickens's role as an author—a producer of signs—within the system suggests an equation between his work and the often debased, sometimes even meaningless, stream of signs (beginning with money itself) that is the lifeblood of financial capitalism. In the end, the novel presents a clear picture of the evils of financial capitalism, but is unable to resolve the contradictions inherent in its and its author's positions within the capitalist system to present a clear, unencumbered alternative: instead, *Nickleby* ends with a desperately wished-for and skillfully drawn picture of a fragile Eden, funded by benevolence, but walled off from the world and, wishfully, at least, protected from the forces the novel has so clearly described.

Chapter Two

"With what a strange mastery it seized him for itself": The Conversion of the Financier in *A Christmas Carol*

Writing and publishing *A Christmas Carol* in the fall of 1843 was a project of urgency and importance for Dickens, as we learn from Forster's account of the story's creation:

> [B]efore the end of November [1843] he had finished [. . .] his memorable *Christmas Carol*. It was the work of such odd moments of leisure as were left him out of the time taken up by two numbers of his *Chuzzlewit;* and though begun with but the special design of adding something to the *Chuzzlewit* balance, I can testify to the accuracy of his own account of what befell him in its composition, with what a strange mastery it seized him for itself, how he wept over it, and laughed, and wept again, and excited himself to an extraordinary degree, and how he walked thinking of it fifteen and twenty miles about the black streets of London, many and many a night after all sober folks had gone to bed. (Forster, *Life*, vol. I, 325–26)

Forster's comment about the story's "strange mastery" of Dickens is highly appropriate: the *Carol* is a tale of obsession with money, the lack of money, and the effects of money; and at the same time the *Carol* itself is an obsessional narrative structure, in which doublings and redoublings, returnings and refigurations both emphasize the circular nature of life in a society based on financial capitalism, and infect "redemption" itself with doubleness and ambiguity.

The complexity of the *Carol's* obsessional nature and its overall project are suggested in Dickens's varied reasons for writing it in late 1843, as he was

laboring to make *Martin Chuzzlewit* a financial success. As Dickens told
Southwood Smith, the conversion story was intended to strike "a sledgehammer blow for the poor man's child"[1] and to forestall the "doom" prophesied
by the appearance of Ignorance and Want in Stave Three—that is, the story
was meant to provoke action. At the same time, the *Carol* was meant to be a
specific remedy for Dickens's growing money-troubles in late 1843; thus it
was meant to function both as a "weapon" against the values of financial capitalism, and as a money-making commodity for its author. This dual function reflects Dickens's own position astraddle the line dividing art and
commerce and suggests that the *Carol* is a project divided in fundamental
ways between its role as a critique of financial capitalism and its status as a
"product" under that system. In this chapter I will argue that this rift goes
even deeper—that there is indeed a redemptive *Carol* which attempts to
strike Dickens's sledgehammer blow, but that this *Carol* is significantly, even
systematically, undermined by an "anti-*Carol*" that suggests that Scrooge's
(and society's) redemption is problematical—an act of authorial will rather
than a "solution" to the social problems the *Carol* deplores.

THE HEART OF THE "ANTI-*CAROL*"

By "anti-*Carol*" I mean a set of subversive influences undercutting the narrative and meaning of the *Carol* itself. These forces derive from the nature,
structure and ubiquity of financial capitalism itself, and insinuate obsessive
self-interest and ambiguity into all societal relations based on money. In *Capital,* as we have seen, Marx describes financial capitalism as a form of circulation that is itself circular and self-referential: "the transformation of money
into commodities, and the reconversion of commodities into money; buying
in order to sell." In Marx's view, the formation of capital is nothing but a circular "exchange of money for money"; this circulation, where "the whole
process vanishes," is really nothing more than entropy—a self-contained,
self-sealed process leading only to emptiness and decay (*Capital,* vol. I,
247–48). And to nail down the obsessional, self-referential nature of the
technical process of accumulating capital, Marx also notes the obsessional
nature of the psychology of the capitalist:

> As the conscious bearer [*Träger*] of this movement, the possessor of
> money becomes a capitalist. His person, or rather his pocket, is the
> point from which the money starts, and to which it returns. The objec-
> tive content of the circulation we have been discussing—the valoriza-
> tion of value—is his subjective purpose, and it is only in so far as the
> appropriation of ever more wealth in the abstract is the sole driving

force behind his operations that he functions as a capitalist, i.e. as capital personified and endowed with consciousness and a will. Use-values must therefore never be treated as the immediate aim of the capitalist; nor must the profit on any single transaction. His aim is rather the unceasing movement of profit-making. This boundless drive for enrichment, this passionate chase after value, is common to the capitalist and the miser; but while the miser is merely a capitalist gone mad, the capitalist is a rational miser. The ceaseless augmentation of value, which the miser seeks to attain by saving his money from circulation, is achieved by the more acute capitalist by means of throwing his money again and again into circulation. (*Capital*, vol. I, 254–55)

In this passage we see the motive of the capitalist is an obsessive drive to augment the capital he or she already has. The capitalist is reduced to a monomaniacal entity—"capital personified and endowed with consciousness and a will," whose "boundless drive for enrichment" requires ceaseless repetition—"throwing his money again and again" into a circulation that is itself circular, self-referential, obsessional. Importantly, the only difference in Marx's formulation between the unbalanced if not aberrant "miser" and the successful, socially-accepted "capitalist" is methodology, and the implication is that an exchange-value-based society rests, in reality, on a foundation of instability—even madness—and danger.

Finally, in a note to the above passage, Marx suggests an ambiguity in both the structure and psychology of finance that is highly relevant to the *Carol*: he points out that the same Greek expression can mean both "saving" and "hoarding," and he adds in English that 'to save' means both *retten* [to rescue] and *sparen* [to save]. This duality concerning motives for accumulation of capital is worth noting. "Saving," "rescuing" and "hoarding" are different, and carry different moral subtexts—the prudent habit of saving, for example, versus miserly hoarding. But Marx's note suggests that such concepts blur or mix at some point, and elsewhere in the same chapter he notes that such confusion is all but inherent in modern economics. He points out in an earlier note on Aristotle that "with the discovery of money," trade focusing on use-values "of necessity developed into [. . .] trading in commodities, and this again, in contradiction with its original tendency, grew into chrematistics, the art of making money" (*Capital*, vol. I, 253).[2] He adds a page later that "in the circulation M-C-M both the money and the commodity function only as different modes of the value itself [. . .] it is constantly changing from one form to the other" (*Capital*, vol. 1, 255). Thus finance itself is slippery and ambiguous: it is based on the constant shape-shifting of money and commodities, and it turns inevitably from "economics" to "chrematistics." This ambiguity seems to be an inescapable part of the system of financial capitalism; the very word "economics" implies "use-value" to Aristotle, but is inescapably intertwined for us (and for Dickens's readers, well aware of the philosophy of "political economy") with exchange-value. Thus the ambiguity Marx is getting at provides a hint that even use-value itself is unreliable—can be transformed at any moment, in a commodified, capitalistic society, into exchange-value. As I will argue, the obsessional accumulation and fundamental ambiguity built into the world of financial capitalism operate in the *Carol* as a powerful counterweight—an "anti-*Carol*"—to the redemptive forces the story deploys in Scrooge's conversion.[3]

THE "ANTI-*CAROL*" AT WORK

To begin to examine the function of this "anti-*Carol*," I would like to provide an alternate reading of a scene in the *Carol* which has been the focus of thought-provoking analysis by Audrey Jaffe—the scene in Stave Three where Scrooge and the Spirit of Christmas Present visit the poulterers' and fruiterers' shops. Jaffe's reading of this scene and of the *Carol* stresses importance of visual detail in the spectacles the story offers:

> An emphasis on visuality, whether literary or cinematic, promotes spectatorship as a dominant cultural activity. [. . .] *A Christmas Carol* (1843) is arguably Dickens's most visually evocative text. In its detailed attention to and elaboration of surfaces, in its reliance on contrasts between darkness and light, its construction as a series of scenes (a structure reproduced in the images the spirits exhibit to Scrooge), and particularly in its engagement with a dynamic of spectatorial desire, the story is an artifact of, and an exemplary text for understanding, the commodity culture Guy Debord terms a "society of spectacle"; the mechanism of Scrooge's conversion is, after all, spectatorship.[4]

Jaffe's argument links spectacle and sympathy, presenting the *Carol* as a means of reinforcing acceptance of and participation in a Victorian mass culture of consumption:

> The story's ideological project—its attempt to link sympathy and business by incorporating a charitable impulse into its (male) readers' self-conceptions—underlies its association of charitable feeling with participation in cultural life. [. . .] Dickens's text situates its readers in the position of the man without feeling in a narrative whose function it is to teach him how to feel, and it appeals to them by manipulating visual effects in a manner that mirrors Scrooge's own interpellation

through spectacle. [. . . T]he story focuses chiefly on objects, persons, and scenes that are already spectacular in Victorian culture: invested with cultural value and desire. As the story seems to spectacularize the real, that is, it in fact reinforces the desirability of a series of culturally valorized images and contributes to a sense that nothing exists—at least nothing worth looking at—outside those images. (256)

Jaffe demonstrates both the importance of spectacle as a mechanism of conversion, and the fact that Scrooge is essentially being converted into a participant in middle-class consumer culture. However, upon close examination, the spectacle of the shops in Stave Three seems to contain elements that incite the spectator in ways that go beyond the rather benign list of dominant cultural values ("youth, boyhood, heterosexual desire, and familial pleasure") Jaffe notes. In the *Carol,* the "speaking commodities" (Jaffe, 260) in the poulterers,' fruiterers' and grocers' shops seem "impregnated" with a strong and particular "moral aptitude" (Van Ghent, 30):

> The poulterers' shops were still half-open, and the fruiterers' were radiant in their glory. [. . .] There were ruddy, brown-faced, broad-girthed Spanish Onions, shining in the fatness of their growth [. . .] and winking from their shelves in wantonness at the girls as they went by, and glanced demurely at the hung-up mistletoe [. . .] there were bunches of grapes, made [. . .] to dangle from conspicuous hooks, that people's mouths might water gratis as they passed; [. . .] there were Norfolk Biffins [. . .] in the great compactness of their juicy persons, urgently entreating and beseeching to be carried home [. . .] and eaten. [. . . At the Grocers'] the almonds [were] extremely white, the sticks of cinnamon so long and straight [. . .] the figs were moist and pulpy, [and] the French plums blushed in modest tartness.[5]

Jaffe notes that these objects are "erotically charged," and that this spectacle interpellates Scrooge and renders him a subject: "Visual representation inscribes the spectator as absence or lack, and these images, in their fullness, emphasize that lack. But the relation between spectator and image is reversed, as these commodities call out to the spectator to complete them" (Jaffe, 259). But Jaffe's view that this spectacle merely presents the observer with the value of "heterosexual desire" does not take into account the insistently, repetitively sexual nature of the objects presented, nor the almost crazily insistent tone of the narrator in this passage. It may be more accurate to say that this spectacle presents a world crammed with sexual references, one in which sexually-charged objects, commodities following their natural tendency to come alive in a commercial culture, are "urgently entreating and beseeching" the spectator's (sexual) participation.

Considered more closely, these images become more unsettling: they depict commodities portrayed as sex objects in a parody ("long and straight [. . .] moist and pulpy") of the way human beings and their bodies are often commoditized by market place values. This is a world of sexual confusion, a world of pan-sexuality, where the piling on of images and the narrator's nearly hysterical tone ("The Grocers'! oh the Grocers'!") blur the boundaries between the commodities and human sexuality. This blurring creates a sense of the "polymorphous perverse," an indiscriminate, unfocused sexuality perhaps illustrated by the behavior of "the customers [. . .] so hurried and eager [. . .] that they tumbled up against each other at the door, clashing their wicker baskets wildly, and left their purchases on the counter" (*ACC*, 91). Moreover, this insistent suggestion of the polymorphous perverse forces the reader to recall the indiscriminate, pan-sexual interests and pleasure-seeking activity of childhood. Certainly such a scene does recall the "value" of "heterosexual desire" as Jaffe says. But it also unsettles because it so insistently undermines the values it appears to be advocating. This spectacle interpellates both Scrooge and us, but not in a simple way; we are forced to see and experience abundance and heterosexual fertility, but we are also forced to experience a kind of eroticism we as adults are supposed to have given up. This is a non-generative, self-replicating eroticism (a purposeless accumulation of pleasure for its own sake) akin to the chrematistic accumulation Marx describes, rather than the generative eroticism of adult heterosexual desire.

Reading these passages one feels that running underneath the conversion narrative of the *Carol* is an undercurrent of danger. First, the passages contain a subtext of fear of the immense power and inevitability of the commoditizing marketplace, which appears to infect even use-value itself ("the fetishism which attaches itself to the products of labor, *as soon as they are produced as commodities*"—*Capital*, vol. I, 165; my emphasis). More startlingly, the passages signal to us that there are in childhood itself hidden threats. As I noted, the marketplace scene gives us the overpowering sense of the underlying seductivity of the "polymorphous perverse"—a direct challenge to the familial, heterosexual value-set the scene seems to represent. Moreover, this pan-sexuality also represents a kind of lawlessness—another direct challenge, this time to the self-mastery adults (especially adult males) in an ordered, civilized society were supposed to have been educated into embracing. Leonore Davidoff and Catherine Hall note the "general advocacy of mastery over self as well as the external world" in describing the values middle-class education was supposed to inculcate:

As Isaac Taylor said in his handbook for youth, *Self Cultivation Recommended*, 'men do not play like children.' Regularity was the life of business and the regularity of school helped create the willingness to undergo dull routine, to produce steady application to a task. Above all, the education necessary to train a youth to 'act rightly' would lead him to attain the 'emulated epithet' of *manly:* 'a man must act, whether to earn his living or even if not, yet he must act.' His education should rest on 'self-instruction, self-command and self-acting energy.'[6]

As Davidoff and Hall suggest, "labour discipline" (234) was necessary for the middle-class (the employers) as well as for the working class (the employed). But in the marketplace passage in the *Carol*, we see this ideal of self mastery (both the sexual discipline and the labor discipline of society—the ideal of the "manly" and the ordered society of "dull routine" and steady application") at risk.

In effect, the very force the story sets up as the vehicle for our redemption—childhood and its point of view—carries within it the seeds (planted and nurtured by the commodification and exchange-value focus that are the motive forces of financial-capitalist society) of the destruction of the order on which society depends. In my view, this pattern of doubleness—of hope and redemption undermined by powerful and dangerous forces—runs throughout the *Carol*. In the rest of this chapter I will examine this doubleness as it occurs in four aspects of the *Carol*: in the structure of the tale itself; in the presentation of childhood and its point of view as the primary motive power behind conversion and change; in the violence that is the price of Scrooge's conversion in the story; and in the equivocal position of Dickens as businessman-author.

THE *CAROL* AND FIGURAL PROPHECY

The *Carol's* narrative structure—the Stave-by-Stave description of Scrooge's conversion—partakes of the obsessional tone with which I began this chapter. It is a tissue of doublings, repetitions and refigurations, from the past into the present and on into the future, that is a driving force in the story's redemptive project. The *Carol's* narrative presents a continuum in which past, present, and future are interpenetrated, and one in which patterns of replication and repetition are ubiquitous and seemingly inevitable. This structure can be seen as an example of what Erich Auerbach calls "figural interpretation." This is a view of history as prophecy, in which

the individual earthly event is not regarded as a definitive self-sufficient reality, nor as a link in a chain of development in which single events or

combinations of events perpetually give rise to new events, but viewed
primarily in immediate vertical connection with a divine order which
encompasses it, which on some future day will itself be concrete reality;
so that the earthly event is a prophecy or *figura* of a part of a wholly divine reality that will be enacted in the future. But this reality is not only
future; it is always present in the eye of God and in the other world,
which is to say that in transcendence the revealed and true reality is
present at all times, or timelessly.[7]

Auerbach is talking about figures in scripture representing both Old Testament events (i.e., the sacrifice of Isaac) and New Testament events (the cruci-
fixion of Christ), as well as mankind's future salvation—all real
events—while, at the same time, being represented by real actors on a real
stage in a medieval Mystery play. Auerbach explains that some of the power
of figural representation comes from its peculiar kind of inevitability—the
reverse of what a modern sensibility might expect:

> Whereas in the modern view the event is always self-sufficient and se-
> cure, while the interpretation is fundamentally incomplete, in the fig-
> ural interpretation the fact is subordinated to an interpretation which is
> fully secured to begin with: the event is enacted according to an ideal
> model which is a prototype situated in the future and thus far only
> promised. (Auerbach, 58–59)

The inevitability of such a system depends, of course, on belief in a "true
reality," "an ideal model [. . .] situated in the future," and implies faith in
God, who designed the system and has made the promise upon which the system depends. As a description of the *Carol's* narrative structure, such an
avowedly religious model helps to explain the patterning inherent in the story;
rather than demonstrating a linear development the story presents young
Scrooge figuring the converted Scrooge, who returns to his childlike state at
the end of the story (figuring, in turn, the reader's return to such a state after
reading the *Carol*). The relevance of this medieval and Christian model to the
Carol receives at least a hint of justification in Dickens's description of the story
as "a whimsical kind of masque [. . .] to awaken some loving and forbearing
thoughts" (*ACC*, Prefaces, xxix). As Robert Tracy points out, Dickens's description of the *Carol* as a masque locates it in a theatrical tradition rooted in medieval drama and linked with behavior change (or "conversion"):

> The important thing about the masque, as Dickens adapted the term,
> is that it is a literary form that both demonstrates and inculcates

virtue; and that the demonstration of virtue is usually the method of inculcation. The Stuart courtier, watching a masque of sovereignty, sees the power and virtue of his master allegorically demonstrated, and is presumably strengthened in his loyalty. [In *The Tempest*,] Ferdinand and Miranda glimpse the rewards of a chaste marriage and are strengthened in their commitment to pre-marital restraint. Ebenezer Scrooge watches a triple masque about Christmas and charity, staged for him by the three Spirits. [. . .] What Scrooge sees reforms him. He changes from an opponent of Christmas to a keeper of Christmas, or, more accurately, from a selfish man to a man of charity—the lesson Dickens wished to teach. It is clear that the story describes the wakening—or re-awakening—of social morality and fellow-feeling in Scrooge[.] [8]

But in the end this figural narrative requires faith and a "promise" like that of mankind's redemption through Christ's sacrifice. Given the *Carol*'s relatively secular posture, this "promise" is not identical with the Christian promise, although it comes dressed in similar clothes. The motive power behind the figural prophecy in the *Carol*, as I hope to show, is Dickens's abiding obsession with and faith in the power of the child's imagination, sensibility and point of view, and the faith inherent in the *Carol* that, once we are forced back into the child's mind-set, individual benevolence can emerge and flower in the world.

THE FIGURAL PROMISE: CHILDHOOD'S REDEMPTIVE FORCE

Rather than presenting an economic or ideological philosophy to motivate Scrooge, the *Carol*, I think is offering a powerful alternative: a philosophy that stresses a return to the values inherent in the child's point of view, and that, for added emotional appeal, wraps these values in the trappings of Judeo-Christian religion. This emphasis on the virtues of childhood comes in part from emerging views of the value of childhood in the mid-nineteenth century, especially in contrast with the commercial virtues of the middle class, as Malcolm Andrews points out:

> The mid-century idea of childhood—principally male childhood—to which Dickens responds and which his writings help to shape, is assembled largely from the human material that has been rejected as unsuitable for the fully efficient functioning of the mature model citizen. Earnest single-mindedness has no room for charming capriciousness; a trained intelligence and breadth of knowledge finds no place for anarchic imagination and intuitive wisdom; the stiff upper

lip is incompatible with emotional candour. Success in the aggressive, new commercial world depends on erasing the 'old fashioned' values associated with, say, little Paul Dombey.[9]

Such a view of childhood meshes well with the emphasis on the value of "fancy" in Dickens's writing, and the idea of the child's virtues as the opposite of the adult's commercial virtues supports the notion of a return to childhood as a remedy for commercialism. Andrews also cites the growing tendency at mid-century to view children as "different in *kind*" from adults (Andrews's emphasis); in this view, the child, Andrews says,

> has equal claims to cultural maturity because, for a while, it possesses powers that will be lost with maturity. Adults may reach back for those lost powers, but they are irretrievable. Ruskin observed in *Modern Painters,* 'childhood often holds a truth with its feeble fingers, which the grasp of manhood cannot retain, which it is the pride of utmost age to recover.' (Andrews, 24) [10]

The fact that this notion was current in the 1840s also helps to support the assertion that childhood may offer a powerful remedy for the ills produced by society's fixation on financial capitalism. But even with all this in the air, shaping Dickens's thinking or being shaped by it, the deeper roots of the power of childhood in the *Carol* must lie with Dickens's own obsessional preoccupations—especially his sense of the power of childhood imagination and play to redeem adults and children from the ill effects of financial capitalism, just as he had been redeemed from the blighting effects of his time in the blacking warehouse.

We can see the motivating and redemptive power of imagination at work in Stave Two, as Scrooge observes himself reading:

> [A] lonely boy was reading near a feeble fire; and Scrooge sat down upon a form and wept to see his poor forgotten self as he had used to be. [. . .] The Spirit touched him on the arm, and pointed to his younger self, intent upon his reading. Suddenly a man, in foreign garments: wonderfully real and distinct to look at: stood outside the window [. . .] "Why, it's Ali Baba!" Scrooge exclaimed in ecstasy. (*ACC,* 72)

As I noted above, the trope of the neglected child reading is powerful and frequent in Dickens's work, and one closely identified with his own life. This scene offers Scrooge and us the pathos of the bright child sitting alone in sordid surroundings, and the redemptive function of "fancy" in such a child's life.[11] In this scene, Scrooge doubles the Dickens of the "Autobiographical Fragment" in his "reading as if for life" (Forster, *Life,* vol. I: 10) and in his choice of reading matter, making the power of the values being exhibited suddenly highly personal. To the young Scrooge Ali Baba is almost literally real: "[W]hen yon solitary child was left here alone, he did come, for the very first time, just like that. Poor boy!" (*ACC,* 72). But the adult Scrooge "had as little of what is called fancy about him as any man in the City of London, even including—which is a bold word—the corporation, aldermen, and livery" (*ACC,* 54). As Jaffe notes, this scene uses spectacle to interpellate Scrooge (who watches himself watching Ali Baba, a concrete marker of the child's imaginative potential) with forceful evidence of the value he has lost. Perhaps the scene also interpellates the businessman Dickens of 1843, reminding him of the importance of what is at risk in the world of financial capitalism. And we stand outside the frame Scrooge stands in, with the spectacle of his interpellation interpellating us, inducing us to recall the power of childhood imagination in our own lives, and making us part of the redemptive pattern.

Along with imagination, a value-set associated with childhood play is presented as a superior alternative to a merely economic or philosophical one. This occurs light-heartedly in Stave One when Bob, despite having almost been fired and "boast[ing] no great coat," goes "down a slide on Cornhill, at the end of a line of boys, twenty times, in honour of its being Christmas Eve, then [runs] home to Camden Town as hard as he could pelt, to play at blindman's buff" (*ACC,* 53). This scene highlights Bob's purposeless (in any economic sense) play despite his troubles, reminding us that economics is not the whole of life. The point is more telling when we realize where Bob's childish fun is taking place: a contemporary reader would know Cornhill as an archtypical business street, home to important private banks and other commercial concerns. Later, this scene's emphasis on play is recalled and reinforced much more seriously as Scrooge watches the adults play at Fred's Christmas party: "After a while they played at forfeits: for it is good to be children sometimes, and never better than at Christmas, when its mighty Founder was a child himself" (*ACC,* 104). This scene asserts the value of a return to childhood at times, and links childhood with Christ, thus adding to the attraction and motivating power of childhood and its point of view as the *Carol's* philosophy.

The positioning of childhood as embodying a set of values powerful enough to stand against the "values" imposed by financial capitalism continues in the presentation of Tiny Tim. The *Carol* explicitly connects Tim's goodness with Christ in Stave Three, as Bob reports:

'Somehow he gets thoughtful sitting by himself so much, and thinks the strangest things you ever heard. He told me, coming home, that he hoped the people saw him in the church, because he was a cripple, and it might be pleasant to them to remember upon Christmas Day, who made lame beggars walk, and blind men see.' (*ACC*, 94) [12]

Culturally, as Andrews' comments above indicate, an image like Tim's has the power to move Scrooge and the *Carol*'s readers. But this power is significantly augmented by the linking of Tim with the secularized Christ Dickens often portrayed. A similar linkage can be seen in "A Christmas Tree," written in 1850, when the narrator describes the Christmas memories, including religious images he has retained from childhood:

a baby in a manger; a child in a spacious temple, talking with grave men; a solemn figure, with a mild and beautiful face, raising a dead girl by the hand; again, near a city gate, calling back the son of a widow, on his bier, to life; [. . .] with a child upon his knee, and other children round[.] [13]

In this excerpt, as in the *Carol*, Christ, childhood and children are linked, and reciprocally strengthen each others' value. Christ lends the weight of divine order and "promise" to childhood's virtues, while childhood renders Christ an acceptable, accessible divine figure for Dickens and readers in a time when humankind found itself at an increasing distance from God. Thus the *Carol*'s conversion mechanism is supplied with an attractive motive power in the values embodied in childhood; and the references to Christ provide the figural prophetic narrative structure with an anchor in a quasi-divine order and "promise" of future redemption: here on earth via benevolence—modelled by Christ in the miracles cited above—and perhaps in heaven as childlike souls sitting at Christ's feet.

SUBVERSION: THE COMPETING STRUCTURE OF THE "ANTI-*CAROL*"

At one level, this figural structure carries the day: Scrooge is converted and enacts a rational, individual form of benevolence. But at another level, the "figure" of childhood is deployed in an almost desperate attempt to fend off the forces of exchange-value—an attempt that succeeds more through an act of authorial will than through any logic inherent in the story. While Tiny Tim may profit from Scrooge's newfound charity, Ignorance and Want still huddle disquietingly on the London streets and another model—if not of narrative structure, at least of the motive force which informs relations between people and things and creates narratives in the world of the *Carol*—is distressingly visible in the text. This model is suggested in Marx's passage on commodity fetishism:

> [There is] a physical relation between physical things. [But] the commodity-form, and the value-relation of the products of labour within which it appears, have absolutely no connection with the physical nature of the commodity and the material [*dinglich*] relations arising out of this. It is nothing but the definite social relation between men themselves which assumes, here, for them, the fantastic form of a relation between things. In order, therefore, to find an analogy, we must take flight into the misty realm of religion. There the productions of the human brain appear as autonomous figures endowed with a life of their own, which enter into relations both with each other and with the human race. So it is in the world of commodities with the products of men's hands. This I call the fetishism which attaches itself to the products of labour, as soon as they are produced as commodities, and is therefore inseparable from the production of commodities. (*Capital*, vol. I, 165)

Here Marx portrays another kind of patterning, replication, and "refiguration," but the effect of commodity fetishism is not to produce the ordered, destined world Auerbach's model describes. If Auerbach's model demonstrates the clear and inevitable links between things and events in a divinely-ordered world, Marx's commodity fetishism demonstrates links between things and people that obscure and undermine our sense of universal order and hierarchy, replacing a rigid world with a plastic one where the relationship between a thing that represents or replicates another is problematized. For example in the figural world Auerbach describes, Isaac's pyre, an instrument made of wood used by a father to sacrifice his son, is morally a fair equivalent to Jesus's cross. But does Bob Cratchit really "equal" fifteen shillings ("fifteen copies of his Christian name" [*ACC*, 93])? In the world Marx describes, he does; and he also may "equal" anything else that costs fifteen shillings, even though he is a man and the other 15 shilling item is a quantity of wool or some bushels of corn. In contrast to the stability of value in the figural world, the value of any given thing in the economic world Marx describes is debased—unanchored from any universal objective standard, since value has no connection with "physical properties"—and linked instead with exchange-value, with money. This linkage is the root of the problem; it recalls Marx's discussion of money "as a radical leveller, [which] extinguishes all distinctions," even those involving the structure of society.

From this, we must infer that the modern commodity, represented by money, is in a real sense dangerous: "Ancient society [. . .] denounced [money] as tending to destroy the economic and moral order"(*Capital,* vol. I, 229–30).[14]

In this Marxian model, then, we find destabilizing forces that can blur distinctions between things, and between things and people, threatening both the moral and economic order of things and even the individual's own identity and internal order. These forces, located, we should recall, inside the obsessional structure of financial capitalism, run underneath the action of the story. That is, while Scrooge is being "redeemed" by reconnecting with his past, or by connecting with the abundance and joy of living in the present, the forces represented by the relationship between money and commodities are also in operation, offering a destabilizing, almost parodic, counterpoint to what is happening on the surface of the story.

CHILDHOOD IN THE "ANTI-*CAROL*"

Despite the power of childhood values, the straightforward conversion narrative of the *Carol* is counterbalanced and undermined in the "anti-*Carol*" for two reasons. First, childhood and the values it embodies are particularly vulnerable in the world Dickens creates in the *Carol* and in other writings. Second, childhood itself, enmeshed in a world of financial capitalism, seems to have been infected with the values it is positioned in the *Carol* to counteract.

Childhood's basic vulnerability is easily seen in "A Christmas Tree," where some of the items on the tree of memory are portrayed as highly threatening: the narrator describes, for example,

> that infernal snuff-box, out of which there sprang a demoniacal Counsellor in a black gown, with [. . .] a red cloth mouth, wide open, who was not to be endured upon any terms, but could be not put away either; for he used suddenly, in a highly-magnified state, to fly out of Mammoth Snuff-boxes in dreams, when least expected. ("A Christmas Tree," 4)

This vulnerability is reinforced by repeated use on the same page of terms like "horrible," "sinister," "ghastly," "intolerable," and "all perspiration and horror." Some of this is simply childhood imagination and fears of the monster under the bed, but the emphasis on such things reminds us that the state of childhood is fragile, despite its value.

Childhood's vulnerability is portrayed as more serious and deep-rooted in another image seen on the tree:

When did that dreadful Mask first look at me? Who put it on, and why
was I so frightened that the sight of it is an era in my life? It is not a
hideous visage in itself; it is even meant to be droll; why then were its
stolid features so intolerable? [. . .] Perhaps that fixed and set change
coming over a real face, infused into my quickened heart some remote
suggestion and dread of the universal change that is to come to every
face, and make it still? The mere recollection of that fixed face, the mere
knowledge of its existence anywhere, was sufficient to awake me in the
night all perspiration and horror, with, "O I know it's coming! O the
mask!" ("A Christmas Tree," 4–5)

Both the positioning of this scene in a Christmas article and the unex-
pected intensity and simplicity of the language (contrasted with the rather
droller, more elaborate and yet more distanced treatment of the "demoniacal
Counsellor" earlier) suggest the residue of real vulnerability and fear. The
basis of the fear is the same kind of metonymic shape-shifting we observed in
the marketplace scene in the *Carol,* and which we have associated with
money, commodities and finance. While the mask is linked conventionally
with death, it appears to be the change itself—the unexplained shift—from a
mobile face to the fixed mask, from living being to undifferentiated, commodified object, that is most unsettling to the child recalled by the narrator.
The child's hysteria recalls that of the narrator in the marketplace scene; this
reaction to the interaction and confusion between an object and the human
face suggests an extreme susceptibility within childhood itself to ambiguities
like those introduced into life by the system of financial capitalism.

The vulnerability of childhood is, of course, one of the things the
Carol's "hammer blow" was intended to ameliorate. But even with this in
mind, the impact of the system of financial capitalism on children's lives
seems, at best, a problem which the *Carol's* "solution," Scrooge's new-found
individual benevolence, will scarcely dent. Tiny Tim dies, in Stave Four,
without Scrooge's help, a result explicitly linked to the political-economical
mindset used by Scrooge and others like him to justify their self-interest.
"Say he will be spared," Scrooge begs the Spirit of Christmas Present in Stave
Three, but the Spirit says: "If these shadows remain unaltered by the Future,
none other of my race [. . .] will find him here. What then? If he be like to
die, he had better do it, and decrease the surplus population" (*ACC,* 97).
This message, that the philosophy behind financial capitalism murders children, is driven home a little later by the appearance of Ignorance and Want.
The narrator takes pains to describe these children in language that emphasizes unnaturalness and horror. Scrooge asks what is protruding from the
Spirit's robe, "a foot or a claw!"

'It might be a claw for the flesh that is upon it,' was the Spirit's sorrow-
ful reply. [. . .] From the foldings of its robe, it brought two children;
wretched, abject, frightful, hideous, miserable. [. . .] They were a boy
and girl. Yellow, meagre, ragged, scowling, wolfish; but prostrate, too, in
their humility. Where graceful youth should have filled their features
out, and touched them with its freshest tints, a stale and shriveled hand,
like that of age, had pinched and twisted them, and pulled them into
shreds. Where angels might have sat enthroned, devils lurked. [. . .] No
change, no degradation, no perversion of humanity, in any grade,
through all the mysteries of wonderful creation, has monsters half so
horrible and dread. (*ACC*, 108)

The ferocity and insistence of this description—starker here in allegorical
form than the depiction of the similarly twisted young Smallweeds in *Bleak
House*—suggests both the vulnerability of the child and horror and outrage
that childhood could be so perverted. And again, Scrooge is forced to eat his
own words when he wonders that there is no recourse for such children:
"'Are there no prisons,' said the Spirit, turning on him for the last time with
his own words. 'Are there no workhouses?'" (*ACC*, 109). Certainly the
image is intended to work on Scrooge and the reader to produce both outrage at a system that could allow this (child angels being remanufactured
into devils) to happen, and the desire to act to prevent such degradation.
But at the same time, the repetition of Scrooge's political-economic language undermines the redemptive project because it reminds us of how easily and habitually that language rolled off Scrooge's tongue, and of how
widely such rhetoric was used to dismiss the problems the *Carol* is presenting. Continuing this undermining, the allegorical images of Ignorance and
Want and the absolutist rhetoric in which they are presented ("No change,
no degradation, no perversion of humanity, in any grade, through all the
mysteries of wonderful creation, has monsters half so horrible and dread")
suggest intractable problems unalterable by the individual, unorganized
remedies the *Carol* is suggesting.

At a deeper level, childhood, vulnerable in the *Carol*, is downright dangerous in the "anti-*Carol*." We saw some evidence of this in the marketplace
scene discussed earlier. Another, more pointed example occurs earlier in Stave
Three, as Scrooge is observing Belle's family. Again, the narrator's tone seems to
take us "over the top" if the spectacle is merely meant to make Scrooge (or the
reader) more attracted to family values, heterosexual love, or simple intimacy:

Near to the winter fire sat a beautiful young girl [. . . who], soon beginning to mingle in the [other children's] sports, got pillaged by the young

brigands most ruthlessly. What would I not have given to be one of them! Though I never could have been so rude, no, no! I wouldn't for the wealth of the world have crushed that braided hair, and torn it down; and for the precious little show, I wouldn't have plucked it off, God bless my soul! to save my life. (*ACC,* 81)

The narrator's delight in telling us, in detail, what he would *not* do soon gives way to a recital of what indeed he *would* like to do:

To have touched her lips; to have questioned her, that she might have opened them; to have looked upon the lashes of her downcast eyes, and never raised a blush; to have let loose waves of hair, an inch of which would be a keepsake beyond price: in short, I should have liked, I do confess, to have had the lightest license of a child, and yet been man enough to know its value. (81–82)

True enough, immediately following this interesting aside we observe the arrival of "the father" and "The joy, and gratitude, and ecstasy!" of the family's Christmas—both a reminder of the moral order inherent in the family structure and a spectacle that underlines Scrooge's missed opportunity and bachelor status. But our main impression of this sequence is of moral *dis*order—the unsettling feeling that we have been caught doing something we shouldn't, as if we were children caught playing "doctor." The prior passage commodifies the young girl as effectively and obviously (and sexually) as the fruits and vegetables in the marketplace. Moreover, the leering tone of the passage (perhaps more blatant for a modern reader), as it forces us to review the catalogue of the girl's physical charms, reminds us of the "polymorphous perversity" of the market scene and implicates us with the "young brigands" (young children, we should recall) who want to "pillage" the girl. The violence here is done to the girl, who is commodified, to Scrooge and to us, who are turned from responsible adults of the sort Isaac Taylor wanted to foster ("Men do not play like children")[15] into "pillaging," pan-sexual children, chrematistically accumulating pleasure for its own sake. This transformation adds to the complexity of the use of childhood in the *Carol;* it suggests that, while childhood is vulnerable to economic forces within society, "society" in terms of social mores and conventions—in terms of moral order—is vulnerable to the disruptive, entropic effects of childhood as well. Thus childhood itself becomes dangerously subversive, but in a lawless way—not in the more constructive way, perhaps, that Andrews intends when he discusses childhood's "anarchic imagination," "charming capriciousness" and "emotional candour" in the passage quoted above (Andrews, 69).

All this suggests that redemption in the *Carol* is ultimately undermined in the "anti-*Carol*" by the idea of childhood itself, since childhood is shown to be inescapably infected with a sexuality linking it with the non-generative, self-referential dynamics of exchange-value. And this undermining is made all the more striking when we realize that the narrator himself is implicated in it. Prior to this passage, the narrator has avowed his affinity with Marley's Ghost: "I am standing in the spirit at your elbow," he says (*ACC*, 68), while Marley has "sat invisible beside [Scrooge] many and many a day" (*ACC*, 63).[16] In other words, the Narrator doubles Marley's role as teacher and, in a sense, redeemer. The fact that such a teacher or redeemer so forcefully injects the lawlessness of the "polymorphous perverse" into the story at this point creates a dissonant note, almost a parody of the expected function of a religious teacher or redeemer, that undercuts the power of the Christ-childhood linkages noticed above, and reinforces the "anti-*Carol*'s" constant, subsurface undermining of the redemptive power of childhood (or any other value-set) against financial capitalism.

THE PRICE OF CONVERSION: VIOLENCE IN
CAROL AND "ANTI-*CAROL*"

The dualism of *Carol* and "anti-*Carol*" continues in the story's treatment of the violence usually associated with conversion. In the *Carol*, violence in the form of psychological invasion supports the conversion project because it seems both appropriate and in proportion to the magnitude of the gulf between the "unnatural" Scrooge and the "natural" state to which he is to convert. These invasions take the form of the forced viewing of poignant memories, being made to fly over the ocean and terrifying abysses, being made to hear himself described as an "odious, stingy, hard, unfeeling man" by Mrs. Cratchit, and as "a disagreeable [. . .] savage animal" during the game at Fred's (*ACC*, 98 and 106). The culmination of these "appropriate" psychological invasions occurs, of course, in Stave Four, where Scrooge is made to witness the aftermath of his own death. The truly terrifying moment for Scrooge comes not when he visits his own grave, for by then he is already trying to "sponge away the writing on this stone" (*ACC*, 126). Rather, it comes as he views what he fears is his own corpse in his own bedroom:

> He recoiled in terror, for the scene had changed, and now he almost touched a bed: a bare, uncurtained bed: on which, beneath a ragged sheet, there lay something covered up, which, though it was dumb, announced itself in awful language. (*ACC*, 117–18)

The uncertainty and bare anonymity of the scene ("unwept, uncared for was the body of this man" [118]) drive home the lesson, and reinforce the values of human connection and intimacy that stand in opposition to the exchange-value system he has lived by:

> [Scrooge] thought, if this man could be raised up now, what would be his foremost thoughts? Avarice, hard dealing, griping cares? They have brought him to a rich end, truly! (118)

With a certain justice we see that the psychological violence of Scrooge's encounters with the Spirits has so shaken his psyche that it has unseated the psychological, obsessive "nervousness" of financial and commercial life—and so Scrooge can now be self-critical, and critical of the system to which he had adhered so blindly and for so long. (And so, on Christmas morning, the "fog [. . .] so dense without, that [. . .] the houses opposite were mere phantoms" [*ACC*, 47] is replaced with "No fog, no mist; [. . .] Golden sunlight; Heavenly sky; sweet fresh air" [128].) The violence administered by the Spirits thus seems appropriate because Scrooge can respond to it—it is a wake-up call he can heed and, by taking action, improve the situation and become more "natural."

Thus the violence of conversion in the *Carol* seems to further the Spirit's aim: redemption or "your reclamation," as the Spirit of Christmas past puts it (*ACC*, 69). But there is other violence—belonging to the "anti-*Carol*," so to speak—and this violence again serves to counterbalance the possibility of real change in society, to undermine the *Carol's* "act of faith." At a general level, such violence is inherent in the instability and shape-shifting in a commodity-based society, as we have seen in the market scene in Stave Three, where the commodities' sexuality forces itself on the spectator. This is violence as a kind of intrusion on the identity and integrity of another—not dissimilar from a mental form of rape. Such violence is not a consequence of conversion; on the contrary, it seems so pervasive as to be in operation constantly and without regard to any individual's moral mind-set. It is based ultimately in the seemingly inevitable tendency of a society devoted to financial capitalism to view human beings as commodities, and to debase and manipulate them by "valuing" them in commodity or money terms.

More directly, the violence in the "anti-*Carol*" revolves around Scrooge's role as a petty financier, and casts doubt on the validity of his conversion, and of conversion in general. In being portrayed as a usurer, as Jonathan Grossman notes, Scrooge also partakes in the "unnatural" and outsider status traditionally accorded to the Jewish financier or moneylender.[17]

Scrooge, of course, is not a Jew, and is in fact portrayed quite realistically as a low-level, "retail" financier;[18] but as a usurer a Jewish subtext is inescapably attached to him and directly affects the viability of the conversion project. The backdrop for Scrooge's position as usurer is, Dickens's 1843 readers would have understood, a long history of aversion and disgust. Aristotle says:

> Usury is most reasonably hated, because its gain comes from money itself and not from that for the sake of which money was invented. For money was brought into existence for the purpose of exchange, but interest increases the amount of the money itself; consequently this form of the business of getting wealth is of all forms the most contrary to nature.[19]

Aristotle is talking about the same "chrematistics" we have seen Marx use as a synonym for the financial capitalist's desire to accumulate money for its own sake, rather than for its use-value. (In a note to the above passage, Marc Shell says "interest is money born of money" [94].) Thus usurers (often Jews or characterized as Jews) appear at the root of the problem Scrooge's conversion is meant to solve. As "contrary to nature," usury was often heavily punished, especially where Jewish usurers were involved. Carlyle's discussion of Abbot Samson's financial reforms in *Past and Present* provides the example of the "insatiable Jew" to whom the Abbey owed £1200, much of which was interest:

> [O]ne hopes he never got satisfied in this world; one almost hopes he was one of those beleaguered Jews who hanged themselves in York Castle shortly afterwards, and had his usances and quittances and horse-leech papers summarily set fire to! For approximate justice will strive to accomplish itself; if not one way, then in another. Jews, and also Christians and Heathens, who accumulate in this manner, though furnished with never so many parchments, do, at times, 'get their grinder teeth successfully pulled out of their head, each day a new grinder,' till they consent to disgorge again. A sad fact,—worth reflecting on.[20]

The virulence of this description is remarkable—an almost visceral reaction of hatred for those who "accumulate in this manner," mixed with a large measure of anti-Semitism. Of course, the hypocrisy of this hatred was visible in the City, where Jewish bankers like the Rothschilds and Goldsmids were knighted for lending—at interest—to the government to finance wars and other expenditures.[21] But "retail" usurers, like Scrooge, were not so esteemed—and seemed, in fact, to draw the lightning of hatred the larger lenders escaped.

Along with this aversion, conversion of the Jews, as Michael Ragussis
has noted, was a topic that carried with it a large measure of distrust in the
early to mid-nineteenth century. Conversionist societies, tracts and novelistic
literature focused attention on the conversion of Jews, and intense debate occurred over whether or not Jews could truly be converted. Ragussis's book
displays woodcuts of violent eighteenth and nineteenth century conversion
scenes where the Jew must either eat pork—thereby renouncing Judaism—
or be thrown into a fiery cauldron, for example. These woodcuts demon-
strate the traditional mistrust of Jewish conversions (the victim must
physically "prove" his conversion by eating the pork) and the long history of
the link between conversion of the Jews and violence.[22]

This Jewish subtext and the mistrust and violence that traditionally go
with it operate under the surface of Scrooge's conversion in the "anti-*Carol.*"
First, as Grossman points out (51), reactions to the reformed Scrooge are
also incredulous and his acceptance into the world of humanity is far from
unqualified: Bob Cratchit believes the reformed Scrooge has gone mad and is
ready to defend himself with a ruler (*ACC*, 133). While no one offers physical violence to Scrooge, he must still buy his place in society, by raising Bob's
salary, paying Tiny Tim's medical bills, perhaps offering Fred a partnership.
Scrooge himself realizes that his route to acceptance in Society—not unlike
that of the Rothschilds and the Goldsmids—is through his money. When he
meets the "portly gentleman" in the street on Christmas Day, he whispers
some presumably large amount in his ear: "Not a farthing less," he says. "A
great many back-payments are included in it, I assure you" (*ACC*, 131).
While there is justice in this, it also suggests that Scrooge still views (and perhaps must view) morality on a financial scale—that the ability of the financial capitalistic system to insinuate its "values" into the deepest moral zones
of human interaction continues unabated, both within Scrooge and within
the society into which he is trying to gain acceptance, but which can only see
him in financial terms. All this casts unmentioned doubt on the realness
(and indeed on the possibility) of Scrooge's conversion, since, although it is
claimed that he has changed, he still seems, at bottom, enmeshed in the old
values, as does the rest of society. In addition, if Scrooge is an "everyman" or
proxy for us in the story, the attachment of the Jewish subtext to him casts
doubt on our—or anyone's—ability to work free from the ubiquitous entan-
glements of a society based on financial capitalism.

This subtext of anti-Jewish mistrust and violence, finally, connects back
to the vulnerability and danger associated with childhood, wrapping the
themes together in a way that again unsettles us and continues to undermine
the story's conversion project. After he awakens on Christmas morning,

Scrooge enlists the "boy in Sunday clothes" to purchase the prize turkey from "the Poulterer's, in the next street but one":

> "What, the one as big as me?" returned the boy.
> "What a delightful boy!" said Scrooge. "It's a pleasure to talk to him. Yes, my buck."
> "It's hanging there now," replied the boy.
> "Is it?" said Scrooge. "Go and buy it." (*ACC*, 128–29)

This dialogue suddenly equates boy and turkey (as well as suggesting an image of boy as "buck" "hanging" in a butcher shop), implying that children and the food of religious or festive rites are interchangeable commodities; this implication, in turn, reminds us of the ancient "blood libel" accusing Jews of eating the flesh of Christian children and drinking their blood. Thus the story's insistence on the importance of protecting children and the child's point of view is turned on its head. The "redeemed" Scrooge doubles as a child-eating Jew whose dialogue ("What a delightful boy [. . .] a pleasure to talk to him") seems to mark the boy as a commodity—a delicacy to be enjoyed. A little later, we learn that the turkey is "twice the size of Tiny Tim," again equating the child as a commodity with food, but this time bringing with it parodic associations of Christ as the "food" consumed in a redemptive sacrifice (and in the Anglican communion service itself). Here the child-eating Jew is thrust into a context stressing the protection of children and the redemption of humankind; in effect, financial capitalism is consuming the very weapon the *Carol* is trying to use against it. Such an image anticipates Marx's link between commodity fetishism and religion and undercuts our faith in the ability of *any* redemptive force (even the most powerful) to prevail over the powers of money and commodification in a society based on financial capitalism.

AN ACT OF WILL VS. THE FORCES OF ENTROPY

The *Carol* seems to see only too clearly how fragile and vulnerable the saving grace of childhood is, despite its being the only thing that can save us. The story does not dwell on Ignorance and Want; any succor for them from Scrooge's conversion—where most of the benevolence is showered on the lower middle-class Cratchits—is so indirect as to be invisible. Instead, the *Carol* moves rapidly and forcefully through Scrooge's conversion and turns him quite emphatically into a child before our eyes, with multiple references. He says, "I will live in the Past, the Present, and the Future! [. . .] The Spirits of all Three shall strive within me" (*ACC*, 126); then we see him as "merry as a school-boy" (127) and stating that he is "quite a baby. [. . .] I'd rather be a baby" (128). At this point, I believe the *Carol's* effort turns into an act of faith, as opposed to any kind of a believable, programmatic solution to social ills. The forces inherent in capitalism can destroy the childhood that is our only hope, but the story presents Scrooge's conversion as an exemplum and an assertion—the enacting of one redemption in spite of all the opposing forces. It is a hoped-for instance of the kind of divine order Auerbach refers to—a way of prompting the change than can come if we embrace the child within us, and a prophecy that more of us will do so. And it gains in power because it mirrors the real redemptive process that saved the young Dickens—whose story is a kind of "evidence" that the forces we have been discussing can be overcome.

But at the same time the images of Ignorance and Want linger in the background, and we recall the "polymorphous perversity" of the marketplace scene, and these things continually chip away at any optimism we may harbor for significant change in society. This constant undermining, the distinguishing feature of the "Anti-*Carol,*" seems to attain its climax in the Scene in Stave Four where Scrooge visits Joe's rag and bone shop. Here we see the charwoman, the laundress and the undertaker's man turning Scrooge's possessions into cash. This scene functions in two ways to undermine the strength of the conversion narrative and its act of will. First, the scene is a dark analogue to the later scenes of Scrooge's benevolence. Here, his assets are stripped from him to benefit others, the suggestion being that the autonomous value in his goods will move inevitably, in the form of money, whether he wills it or not. This scene, likened to "obscene demons, marketing [a] corpse" [*ACC,* 117], is supposed to disgust, and to picture a fate Scrooge can avoid if he changes his heart. But the scene's very clear illustration of the rapid and autonomous movement of value in a modern, money-based economy (the bed curtains come down and are converted into cash before the body is even cold, seemingly) casts doubt on any individual's ability to control those movements, ubiquitous and tidal as they are, in any meaningful way. In such an economy, individual benevolence as a way of channeling value where it is most needed may be benign, even beneficial in some limited way; but it is also, more or less, beside the point given the scope and power of the money-based system opposing it.

The setting for this scene also undermines the story's assertion that, given the right point of view and enough individual good will, things can be made right in a society based on money and commodities. This setting, another spectacle that calls out to us, demonstrates that, in the end, all commodities are essentially rubbish—and offensive, reeking rubbish at that:

> Far in this den of infamous resort, there was a low-browed beetling
> shop, below a pent-house roof, where iron, old rags, bottles, bones and
> greasy offal, were bought. Upon the floor within were piled up heaps of
> rusty keys, nails, chains, hinges, files, scales, weights, and refuse iron of
> all kinds. Secrets that few would like to scrutinise were bred and hidden
> in mountains of unseemly rags, masses of corrupted fat, and sepulchres
> of bones. (*ACC*, 114)

This spectacle produces horror because, anticipating *Our Mutual
Friend*'s fundamental imagery, it graphically displays the inevitable dissolution of all commodities—it tells us that every *thing* we have accumulated
and cherished will eventually be no more than corrupting refuse. The scene
insistently equates commodities, and hence the system of exchange-value itself, with death and dissolution. Coming within a narrative which has repeatedly emphasized the slippage of identification between people and
commodities, between individuals (Bob, Belle) and their monetary value,
and even between aspects of childhood and the elements of financial capitalism, the scene suddenly offers a summary syllogism: if we as people accept that we are qualitatively equal to some quantity of commodities (a
proposition the story makes it impossible to refute logically), we must also
accept that we are therefore qualitatively equal to "masses of corrupted fat,
and sepulchres of bones."

Thus Joe's rag and bone shop is the stripped-down epicenter of a
world dominated by exchange-value—it is a working demonstration of
Marx's point that money essentially devalues all commodities by making
them alike.[23] At one level, this scene functions as a warning of the dangers
of a society based on exchange-value. But the rag and bone shop scene turns
the fact of the ubiquity of the system of exchange-value ironically on us
when we remember our participation in a culture in which the commodity
has become the object of desire, the seductive object powerful enough to interpellate us from within the shop window. And the scene makes the same
ironic comment on *any* participant in the system, including Dickens himself, the author and worried man of business in 1843. The rag and bone
shop scene, in fact, identifies the problems inherent in the *Carol* very
clearly: the financial-capitalistic system, the *Carol* tells us, leads only down-
ward, to "masses of corrupted fat, and sepulchres of bones"—to entropy and
the true horror of meaninglessness. But at the same time, just as Tiny Tim
could not be saved without access to Scrooge's money, we (and Dickens)
cannot live without money. We can neither control nor extricate ourselves
from the system which is destroying us. In the end, the rag and bone shop

spectacle, ironically doubling that of the speaking commodities in Stave Three, interpellates *us* as subjects and points out the danger we ourselves face, while increasing our pessimism that these dangers—excepting the success of the "act of faith" underpinning the *Carol*—can be overcome.

CONCLUSION: THE TWO *CAROLS* AND DICKENS THE BUSINESSMAN-ARTIST

Having explored the tensions and doubleness at the heart of the *Carol*, we can also see doubleness in its outcomes as a redemptive project. At one level, the *Carol* fulfills its mission. As figural prophecy, it provides the redeemed Scrooge as fulfillment of the promise of his younger, imaginative self, and of the benevolent Fezziwig. Scrooge is also a figure of the reformed capitalist reader—the individual who, after consuming the *Carol*, would go on to enact the "fulfillment" of individual benevolence in the real world. It appears, in one sense at least, that this prophetic project was successful; as Forster notes, Dickens's contemporaries found the *Carol* a force for positive change:

> [M]ention must [. . .] be interposed of the success quite without alloy that also attended the little book, and carried off in excitement and delight every trace of doubt or misgiving. 'Blessings on your kind heart!' wrote Jeffrey to the author of the *Carol*. 'You should be happy yourself, for you may be sure you have done more good by this little publication, fostered more kindly feelings, and prompted more positive acts of beneficence, than can be traced to all the pulpits and confessionals in Christendom since Christmas 1842.' 'Who can listen,' exclaimed Thackeray, 'to objections regarding such a book as this? It seems to me a national benefit, and to every man or woman who reads it a personal kindness.' (Forster, *Life*, vol. I: 345)

The book was predictive and productive of change among Dickens's less literary and more capitalistic readers as well. Phillip Collins recounts

> a memorably pleasant anecdote about a consequence of [Dickens's] reading [the *Carol*] in Boston Christmas Eve, 1867. In puritan New England, as in presbyterian Scotland, Christmas was not a recognized holiday, was indeed looked upon askance by the most pious; but a local manufacturer was so moved by Dickens's performance that next day he closed his factory and from next year he inaugurated the custom of giving all of his employees a turkey.[24]

Collins also notes that, on Dickens's reading tours in the 1850s and '60s, the "unique status [of the *Carol*] led many audiences to feel that it provided not merely a glorious entertainment, but also a spiritual tonic: they came away from it 'better' persons" (Collins, 172).

But none of this responds logically to the obsessional forces embodied in financial capitalism and their undermining effect. In the end, money is a necessary evil—without it, children like Tiny Tim die. The need for money despite its destructiveness brings us back to Dickens's uncertain position as author and "manufacturer" of commodities. Clearly, Dickens viewed writing as a business and, as Robert L. Patten comments, "[w]riting for money was not only a necessity for Dickens: it was also a principle. Throughout his career he thought of himself as a professional writer, an identity which an older generation deplored."[25] But just as clearly, Dickens also thought of himself as an artist,[26] and the latter calling was problematized by the former. Catherine Gallagher describes the blurry boundary between artistic creation and capitalism, focusing on the analogy between authorship and prostitution:

> It has been noted that Aristotle was uncertain about whether writing most remembered the natural generativity of plants and animals or the unnatural generation of money, which, in usury, proliferates through mere circulation, but brings nothing qualitatively new into being. At times, Aristotle speaks of poetic making as a method of natural reproduction; at other times, he speaks of the written word as an arbitrary and conventional sign multiplying unnaturally in the mere process of exchange. The former idea of language promotes the metaphor of literary paternity; the latter the metaphor of literary usury and, ultimately, literary prostitution. [27]

Importantly, Gallagher links literary (and physical) prostitution with usury, thus connecting Dickens's dilemma with Scrooge's:

> Like money, the prostitute, according to ancient accounts, is incapable of natural procreation. For all her sexual activity, she fails to bring new substances, children, into the world. Her womb, it seems, is too slippery. And yet she is a source of proliferation. What multiplies through her, though, is not a substance but a sign: money. Prostitution, then, like usury, is a metaphor for one of the ancient models of linguistic production: the unnatural multiplication of interchangeable signs. (Gallagher, "George Eliot and *Daniel Deronda*," 40–1)

Gallagher's insight, applied to the *Carol*, suggests a tension, unresolved and perhaps unresolvable, between authorial production of the "unnatural multiplication of interchangeable signs" or meaningless writing produced for money, and the production of something new, generative, and useful—in other words, between literary whoredom and literary art. Dickens's intense hopes for the *Carol* seem to position it as a vehicle to strengthen the generative, artistic and moral side of his authorial practice. He wrote to Southwood Smith on 10 March 1843 to explain his decision to put off publishing the "pamphlet" (which later became the *Carol*) he had promised to write in response to the *Second Report of the Children's Employment Commission:*

> I am not at liberty to explain [the reasons for postponing the proposed pamphlet], just now; but rest assured that when you know them, and see what I do, and where, and how, you will certainly feel that a Sledge hammer has come down with twenty times the force—twenty thousand times the force—I could exert by following out my first idea. (Pilgrim *Letters*, vol. III, 423)

The passionate hopes expressed here are striking, and support the notion of the *Carol* as an act of faith—a prophecy which, with enough faith behind it, could change the world. However, even as Dickens was writing to Southwood Smith, he was facing increasing money anxieties. Forster commented:

> [Dickens's] temperament of course coloured everything, cheerful or sad, and his present [late 1843] outlook was disturbed by imaginary fears; but it was very certain that his labours and successes thus far had enriched others more than himself, and while he knew that his mode of living had been scrupulously governed by what he believed to be his means, the first suspicion that these might be inadequate made a change necessary to so upright a nature. [. . .] Much of his present restlessness I was too ready myself to ascribe to that love of change which was always arising from his passionate desire to extend and vary his observation [. . . but t]he money difficulties on which he dwelt were also, it is now to be admitted, unquestionable. Beyond his own domestic expenses necessarily increasing, there were many, never-satisfied, constantly-recurring claims from family quarters, not the more easily avoidable because unreasonable and unjust. (*Life*, vol. I: 333–34)

Forster's picture of Dickens blends insistence on the moral nature of Dickens's attitude to and relationship with money with real and painful needs involving money, "never-satisfied, constantly-recurring" troubles that suggest the obsessional component of capitalist life, and inevitable infection of even the purest motives with the taint of exchange-value. Dickens's letters of the period, too, are full of language combining business and nervousness—certainly as preoccupied with the minutiae of "bargain and sale" in the moment of writing as any of his businessman characters. For example, here is Forster quoting a letter from Dickens, 1 November 1843; on his proposed alliance with Bradbury and Evans:

> I am afraid of Bradbury and Evans's desire to force on the cheap issue of
> my books, or any of them, prematurely. I am sure if it took place yet
> awhile, it would damage me and damage the property, *enormously*. It is
> very natural in them to want it; but since they do want it, I have no faith
> in their regarding me in any other respect than they would regard any
> other man in a speculation. I see that this is really your opinion as well;
> and I don't see what I gain, in such a case, by leaving Chapman and Hall.
> If I had made money, I should unquestioningly fade away from the public
> eye for a year, and enlarge my stock of description and observation by see-
> ing countries new to me; which it is most necessary to me that I should
> see, and which with an increasing family I can scarcely hope to see at all,
> unless I see them now. (Forster, *Life*, vol. I: 330; Dickens's emphasis)

The emphasis here on "damag[ing] the property, *enormously*" suggests Dickens's worries over the "capital" he was accumulating through his writing, and the desire to preserve and grow that capital. In this regard, Dickens's financial hopes for the *Carol* were as strong and passionate as the artistic and moral hopes he communicated to Southwood Smith, as we can see in disappointed retrospect, from a letter Dickens wrote to Forster on 10 February 1844:

> Such a night as I have passed! [. . .] I really believed I should never get
> up again, until I had passed through all the horrors of a fever. I found
> the *Carol* accounts awaiting me, and they were the cause of it. The first
> six thousand copies show a profit of £230! And the last four will yield as
> much more. I had set my heart and soul upon a Thousand, clear. What
> a wonderful thing it is, that such a great success should occasion me
> such intolerable anxiety and disappointment! My year's bills, unpaid,
> are so terrific, that all the energy and determination I can possibly exert
> will be required to clear me before I go abroad; which if next June come
> and find me alive, I shall do. Good heaven, if I had only taken heart a
> year ago. [. . .] I am not afraid, if I reduce my expenses; but if I do not,
> I shall be ruined past all mortal hope of redemption. (Forster, *Life*, vol.
> I, 343)

In effect, this letter shows the invasive, infective power of the chrematistic circulation M-C-M in Dickens's own life and relationship with the *Carol*. Even Dickens, its creator, cannot help turning from the avowed value of the story (its "use-value" being the "sledgehammer blow" for the "poor man's child") to its value in terms of money (its "exchange-value" as a commercial commodity). The tone of the letter and the power of the phrase "I shall be ruined past all mortal hope of redemption" elicit our sympathy; but the letter's content should make our spines tingle: exchange-value, laden as it is with entropy, chaos, death, has been able to substitute itself for use-value even in the mind and heart of the writer of one of the most powerful popular advertisements for individual benevolence ever written.

* * * * *

These letters and comments paint a picture of a man whose life was beset by the dualism we see in the *Carol*—passionate hopes for real change undermined, or at least threatened by powerful and ubiquitous economic forces. This picture, too, invokes Dickens's descent into poverty as a child, the shame produced by that descent, and his determination never to allow the same thing to happen again. We see Dickens positioned, if only in his imagination, perhaps, on the brink of the familiar abyss of poverty, and creating the *Carol* both as a means of denouncing the causes of that abyss, and as a tactical means of avoiding it. I have said that in the end, the *Carol* relies on faith to accomplish its mission—faith in the imagination, vision and sensibility of childhood. These values, after all, had enabled Dickens, in his view, to survive the traumas of his childhood, and had "kept alive [. . .] my hope of something beyond that place and time" (Forster, *Life*, vol. I, 9). They had served him once as bulwarks against the economic forces that threatened to degrade and destroy him, and they seemed, perhaps, the best weapons available to fight the forces he saw so clearly in the 1840s. But even in the 1840s, these values seem under siege. Scrooge's conversion is more of an act of bravado, a technical tour de force and a declaration of faith, than a lasting solution to the problems of Ignorance and Want. While Dickens's writings continue to stress the value of childhood and the child's point of view, childhood itself becomes problematized in the *Carol*, vulnerable to and even implicated in the economic system from which it is to redeem us. Similarly, while the importance of the benevolent individual never diminished for Dickens (who, after all, continued to enact this role until he died), his vision of the viability of individual benevolence as a counterweight to financial capitalism is diminished after the *Carol*, while his vision of the obsessive power and reach of financial capitalism (in novels like *Dombey and Son* and *Little Dorritt*) grows darker and more sweeping.

Chapter Three

"Terribly wild rang the panic cry": Finance, Panic and the Struggle for Life in *Little Dorrit*

Nineteenth-century, City of London-based financial capitalism was largely an unregulated, laissez-faire-driven and highly-concentrated financial system which produced tumultuous ups and downs—a regular cycle of booms and busts from the joint-stock mania of the 1820s through the railway mania of the 1840s to the panic of 1866, bringing riches to some and ruin to many more. Critics of Dickens, and of *Little Dorrit* in particular, have studied the economic impact of nineteenth-century capitalism and its effects on society, and have examined Dickens's radical criticism of nineteenth-century capitalism primarily in economic terms, using Marxian concepts like the commodity, exchange- and use-value, and others.[1]

But Marx sometimes moves beyond the economic and technical in describing capitalism and its effects on people. For example, toward the end of a discussion of the ill-effects on society of industrial capitalism, Marx uses language that implies a positively murderous side to the financial system of which capital is the heart: "If money, according to Augier, 'comes into the world with a congenital blood-stain on one cheek,' capital comes dripping from head to toe, from every pore, with blood and dirt" (*Capital,* vol. I, 925). Here, capital appears anthropomorphized and bearing the stains of its gritty, obviously destructive, origin. But it is also portrayed more intensely than mere "money": "dripping from head to toe, from every pore" suggests complete involvement with violence and even death, and presents capital as kind of specter or ghoul, perhaps seen in the act of rising from a meal. The meal, of course, is made up of capitalism's victims—children, women, and slaves—described in the preceding pages. Marx quotes one account of child-workers in Lancashire, John Fielden's *The Curse of the Factory System*, 1836:

> In many of the manufacturing districts, but particularly, I am afraid, in
> the guilty county to which I belong [. . .] cruelties the most heart-rend-
> ing were practiced upon the unoffending and friendless creatures [child
> laborers from 7 to 14 years old] who were thus consigned to the charge
> of master-manufacturers; they were harassed to the brink of death by
> excess of labour [. . .] were flogged, fettered and tortured in the most
> exquisite refinement of cruelty: [. . .] they were in many cases starved
> to the bone while flogged to their work and [. . .] even in some in-
> stances [. . .] were driven to commit suicide [. . .] The profits of man-
> ufacturers were enormous, but this only whetted the appetite that it
> should have satisfied.[2]

The impact of this passage, along with the image of capital "dripping [. . .] with blood and dirt," is profound in terms of the realization of the economic exploitation that is being described, of course. But the images of child-slavery, cruelty and even torture produce a more visceral reaction; the reader is given a sudden unwanted glimpse into profound psychological depths created by the seemingly abstract subjects of capital, finance, productivity and economic growth.

Again, critics of Dickens and of *Little Dorrit* have explored psychological themes from Clennam's depression to Freudian aspects of the relationships between Little Dorrit and her father.[3] However, the psychological impact of living under the capitalist system—for example, the impact that has made Frederick Dorrit live in his unwashed, fugue-like state for twenty-five years—has been fully explored neither by Dickens's economic nor his psychological critics. While Dickens's fiction often presents personal and societal nervousness and "dis-ease" juxtaposed with money, as I noted in earlier chapters, in *Little Dorrit,* this nervousness becomes true madness on a societal scale.

Certainly we have seen that financial "madness" exists in works like *Nicholas Nickleby,* where it affects both individuals and society profoundly. But in *Nickleby* and other earlier works, this kind of madness is at least contained; for example, much of it flows from and returns to Ralph, an ultimate outsider and a pungent combination of melodramatic malevolence and ego at "war" with humanity. Ralph is a representative, perhaps, of a class of capitalists (misers, moneylenders and Jews), but is always "other," and his reach is ultimately limited. In *Little Dorrit,* by contrast, the "madness" is presented as something more profoundly dangerous. It is uncontained, highly invasive and seemingly able to affect individuals all across society *from within themselves*—that is, through humanity's own inherent weakness for the temptation of chrematistic accumulation, through our own human nature. Financial madness here is associated with Merdle, who is, after all, an absolute nullity of a character who serves only as an enabler and a figure for a whole society's generalized capitalistic greed. In *Little Dorrit*, as I argue below, madness, in the form of a generalized, ingrained "mania" for chrematistic profit, has moved from the background to center stage; thus, in my view, this novel provides both a summation of many of the anti-capital themes of Dickens's earlier fiction, and a prefiguration of the even more pervasive "biological" roles given to capital, exchange-value and chrematistic accumulation in *Our Mutual Friend.*

FINANCE AND PSYCHOLOGY: FROM "DIS-EASE" TO MADNESS

To start with, it would be useful to consider the question of how the psychological impact of living in a world dominated by financial capitalism was viewed in Dickens's time. Clearly Marx understood that madness was often found at the intersection of capital and psychological trauma ("even driven to commit suicide"), but did participants in finance? Did the middle-class reader who was Dickens's primary audience? To understand how much of the connection between financial capitalism and psychology was or was not a part of the *zeitgeist* from which Dickens, perhaps the nineteenth-century's finest reporter, took his observations, I want to digress for a short time to the work of David Morier Evans, a financial journalist who served as City correspondent for the *Times* and later the *Morning Herald* and the *Standard*,[4] and who wrote several books detailing financial history in the period we are considering.[5] Reading Evans is much like watching CNBC or reading the *Wall Street Journal* today— his accounts of the financial world are those of a professional of that world, a "fan" of the system in some respects, but an able observer as well.

In *The Commercial Crisis 1847–1848,* Evans wrote of the atmosphere surrounding the collapse of the Railway Mania bubble in April 1847:

> The "week of terror" will long linger in the remembrance of those who witnessed its career. [. . .] The intensity of the alarm; the measures to which London and Country bankers resorted in order to strengthen their own resources; and the tremendous decline which was daily quoted in all kinds of produce marked in rugged, but intelligible lines the fearful precipitancy of the retrograde movement. There was no relief, and no prospect of it, and hence terribly wild rang the panic cry. Previous commercial revulsions were considered by many not at all analogous to the course of ruin in operation[.][6]

Evans describes the breakdown of the commercial system, and the anxiety, building to panic, which arose from it. Evans' language describes a society in extremis—"terror" and "the intensity of the alarm" have bankers scrambling. There is "no relief" in sight, and the crisis is sending produce prices lower, threatening a general collapse of trade in which many more than bankers will suffer. The "terribly wild" "panic cry" that rings out signals "bankruptcy and ruin": "so great was the madness of all classes, that from peer to peasant, few ultimately escaped unscathed" (Evans, *Commercial Crisis*, 52).

Evans's position in describing the progress of the mania is a moral one—an attempt to illustrate the role of human frailty in the workings of an otherwise admirable capitalist system. To delineate his position, Evans first endorses the overall value of the system and carefully distinguishes between different meanings of the word "speculation." In the positive sense, he refers to "the daring spirit of speculation, which at all times distinguishes a nation like the English in the cherished pursuit of commercial adventure" (Evans, *Commercial Crisis*, 52), and states that finance is the means, via its railroad investments, of extending civilization's "socializing influence." Over against the value of "speculation" as business and financial activity leading (not without risk, and hence an "adventure") to tangible benefits like economic growth and jobs, Evans lays a second definition of "speculation" typified by "the folly and sin of railway gambling" illustrated in the warnings he quotes from the *London Times* in November, 1845:

> The mischief has gone too far already. With so fearful a testimony to the speculative madness of our countrymen as that which we this day display to our readers, we may apprehend almost anything. [. . .] It is the ridiculous amount of premium on worthless scrip, and the gullibility, or rather the voracity, of the multitude, which have prompted the crowd of adventurers to bait their hooks and cast their nets for prey.[7]

In pointing out that the "gullibility" and the "voracity" of the multitude do indeed open the way for the preying "adventurers," Evans's reportage describes a system in which the simple moral expedient of avoiding the "folly and sin" of speculation (*Commercial Crisis*, 23–24) is problematical, if not impossible. Certainly, England cannot give up the factor which "distinguishes" it in its pursuit of "commercial adventure," the engine of its economic growth. Yet the human factors making people easy prey for the second kind of speculation—to speculative manias and consequent collapses (the "commercial revulsions" occurring roughly every ten years from the 1820s though the 60s)—seem ingrained in human nature, unchangeable, and inseparable from every state of humanity "from the peer to the peasant": "Men without houses or homes, clerks at small salaries in banks and merchants' establishments, have as openly proclaimed themselves buyers and sellers of their favourite shares, as if they represented their employers" (*Commercial Crisis*, 6–7). As Dalhousie said in Parliament in 1846, discussing the then-burgeoning railway mania, "speculation [. . .] pervaded every class, high and low, rich and poor, young and old, and I am sorry to be obliged to say that it exerted its influence upon one sex as much as upon another."[8]

Thus, in *The Commercial Crisis* and in his other books, Evans describes a world in which speculation-driven financial crises, with their attendant panics and collapses, are all but inevitable. He also depicts, sometimes in almost allegorical language befitting the moral warning it his project to deliver, the psychological costs of living under such a system:

> Gaunt panic, with uncertain gait and distorted visage, stalks hurriedly through the land. Like the leper of old, downcast in mien and paralysed in limb, his presence is the signal for immediate apprehension, lest his contagious touch should strike with disease sound constitutions, and bleach white the bones of living men.[9]

Notable in this description is the word "apprehension," a state of anxiety rendered universal and therefore more troubling by its links with leprosy and contagion—with the notion that the "disease" in question can spread far and wide, "from the peer to the peasant," like a physical disease. Evans's reportage of commercial crises is studded, in fact, with stark reminders of the (primarily aberrant) psychological states inherent in living under such a system. These states run the gamut from "apprehension" or simple dis-ease to mania ("phrenzy," "phantasy" and "furor") to a kind of insanity ("speculative madness," "rage," "a spasmodic rush known as panic"). The ultimate end-point of the mind ruined by speculation is obsession and madness, revealed in Evans's description of an old City operator named Perez, who is "ill":

> "Ah!" remarked my companion, looking at the row of small tenements toward which we were directing our steps, "this is what a great number of them come to. It is a desperate game; but some fare even worse, distressing as the case may be—suicide, expatriation—all the fearful consequences of this kind of life!" [In one of the tenements, on a low trestle bed, delirious, is Perez.] Talking in his native tongue, the motion of his hands and his significant gesticulations seemed to indicate that he was impressing advice upon an imaginary acquaintance. I could distinguish at intervals something of what he said, but from my imperfect

knowledge of Spanish, I was unable to catch everything. The strongly and oft repeated exclamation, as he raised his head, of *"Si, senor, vende tu camisa y comprate los vales"* ("Yes; sell your shirt, and buy the bonds"), was sufficient to inform me that he supposed he was in his accustomed haunts, surrounded by the associates of his former periods. (Evans, *Speculative Notes*, 54–59)

And again, this ruinous aspect of life under the financial system of "the greatest commercial country in the world" is not confined to financiers or the rich: "I was brought into contact with many [speculators]," Evans reports, "and had opportunities rarely enjoyed, of watching the ravages of the cankerworm that has eaten to the core of many an honest heart, and blighted the most brilliant prospects of many a happy family. Old and young, rich and poor, have I seen drawn into this inextricable vortex, each struggling with his own particular views to obtain the one grand object, but never in reality getting it; and when disappointed and heartbroken, sinking into decrepitude, and at last the grave" (Evans, *Speculative Notes*, 53–4). The language here implies universality, but it is undercut by ambivalence injected by Perez's Spanishness. This nationality provides, of course, a whiff of exoticism reflective of the traditional outsider status of the financier (originally "Jews and goldsmiths");[10] but more strikingly, Perez's otherness plants a face-saving suspicion that perhaps this speculative madness is more natural to Latins, Jews or others not Anglo-Saxon. Thus, Evans can acknowledge the universality of the "ravages" of speculation, but can also provide the English reader with some comfortable distance from it.

Evans's portrait of the financial system—of "the London money market, which certainly is the central pivot of the financial transactions of the entire world" (Evans, *Speculative Notes*, 156)—depicts a world underpinned and determined by ebbs and flows of money, where exchange-value dominates, and where individuals' access to even the most basic commodities ("produce"), the necessities of life, can be affected by those ebbs and flows, creating a life or death struggle among bankers and peers for solvency, among clerks and peasants for survival. Moreover, this physical struggle is mirrored in a psychological struggle; Evans's financial world is a "nervous" world at best, and at worst a world where "madness" can spread like a disease into even "an honest heart."

Thus Evans, who wrote for outlets with which Dickens was familiar, and who probably expressed the point of view of a thoughtful, middle-class insider, described the financial world as he knew it, and painted a picture of a "nervous" world—a world of anxiety, even psychosis. How representative is this picture? The picture seems stronger when we supplement it with some of the evidence Walter Houghton provides in *The Victorian Frame of* Mind, in his discussion of the Victorian age as an era of transition and anxiety. For example Houghton quotes Newman on "the commercial sprit": "that low emotion which sets everyone on the look-out to succeed and rise in life [. . .] to triumph over his hitherto superiors." Houghton also describes the "bourgeois dream" "of retirement from work into idleness": "The middle-class businessman longed to escape from drudgery in hideous surroundings into a world of beauty and leisure [. . .] from which sordid anxieties were shut out."[11] These references suggest a world where "dis-ease" has become even more pervasive and corrosive than it was in *Nicholas Nickleby* or the *Carol*—a world of watchful competitiveness, of anxieties ignored at one's peril, and from which refuge was heartily desired. In his book *American Nervousness, 1903,* Tom Lutz describes a "cultural complex" he associates with neurasthenia, or chronic nervous excitement. Lutz makes the point that this societal condition proceeded from economic pressures and produced a range of "advice and anecdotes" from "artists, intellectuals and other 'experts' on subjectivity and morality" for "that group which identified itself as the middle class."[12] Evans's texts provide us with the suggestion that such a "cultural complex," perhaps similar in impact and linked closely with financial causes, was part of the material available to Dickens in writing about the world of *Little Dorrit* and the impact of financial capitalism ("dis-ease" or nervousness for some, actual disease and even death for others) on that world and its inhabitants.

FINANCE AND PSYCHOLOGY IN *LITTLE DORRIT*

From this brief review, it is clear, at least, that connections between finance and nervousness, panic and psychological pathology, were part of the middle-class insider's view of finance as Dickens was writing, and that the threat of financial instability—societal, institutional, or personal—was never far away. From this base, we can now examine how these (more or less orthodox) ideas about the financial world and its impact on people play out from within the imaginative vision presented in *Little Dorrit.*

Like all of Dickens's novels, *Little Dorrit* is full of characters who, through grotesque or exaggerated outward signs like gestures and "signature" words, body forth their subjectivity; but in this novel the emphasis, in character after character, is on outward forms of inner nervousness, past psychological trauma, and even pathologies. This nervousness is even apparent, as Brian Rosenberg points out in *Little Dorrit's Shadows,* in "the general hesitancy" of the narrator's voice, suggesting "inconsistencies, anxieties, and contradictions"; Rosenberg quotes Susan Horton, who "notices in Dickens's fiction a 'profusion of forms of expression such as seems, perhaps, if, and might have been' that altogether conceal 'a multitude of evasions in the midst of Dickens's rhetorical stance of certainty.'"[13] One root of the undercurrent of nervousness or "dis-ease" in the novel's language is the sense it gives us that the worlds of business and finance on the one hand, and humanity and love on the other, are interpenetrated somehow—not easily separable even by the incomparably sharp eye and pencil of the Dickensian observer. I will deal with this "interpenetration" on a structural level below, pausing here simply to notice how the novel's language contributes to its general atmosphere of "dis-ease" and nervousness because it seems unable to prevent commercial and financial terms, and their attendant anxieties, from forcing their way into passages where they do not seem to belong. For example, Maggy's "reading lesson" early in *Little Dorrit* consists solely of prices and advertising slogans:

> She could read after a sort; and picked out the fat figures in the tickets of prices [. . .] She also stumbled [. . .] through various philanthropic recommendations to Try our Mixture, Try our Family Black, Try our Orange-flavored Pekoe, challenging competition at the head of Flowery Teas; and various cautions to the public against spurious establishments and adulterated articles.[14]

Here the emphasis of the passage, that the environment is pervaded by the language of commerce, competition, and money, is consonant with the novel's implication that such influences are negative—tainting even a "child's" reading practice. But this emphasis is quickly overwhelmed by the barrage of language itself, which immediately forces us as readers into the commercial act of considering the advertising slogans as if we were consumers—"playing" them in our heads like radio commercials—and requiring us to participate in the commercial world ourselves for a moment. In a world where commerce can interpellate us, the readers, so easily and forcefully, nervousness and dis-ease are not out of place.

If commercial influences in the environment can force their way into our psyches, they also seem imbedded in those psyches and constantly forcing their way out. This interpenetration, reversing and emphasizing the one discussed above, can be seen during Arthur's reunion with Flora, as the narrator describes Clennam's romantic history:

> Such was Clennam's case. In his youth he had ardently loved this woman, and had heaped upon her all the locked-up wealth of his affection and

imagination. That wealth had been, in his desert home, like Robinson Crusoe's money; exchangeable with no one, lying idle in the dark to rust, until he poured it out for her. (*LD*, 152; bk. I, ch. xiii)

Again the emphases of the passage on Clennam's solitary, Crusoe-like past, his loneliness, the waste of his youthful love, all consonant with the scene the novel is presenting, are quickly clothed in the language of wealth and exchangeability—of mid-Victorian finance and commerce—language and images, significantly, all coming from within Clennam, not forced on him from outside. The "wealth of affection and imagination" rusting away is not in itself a remarkable image; but the Robinson Crusoe reference, for readers aware of the subtext, goes off like a bomb (a bomb buried inside the reader) that greatly emphasizes the interpenetration of finance and commerce with other aspects of life. When Crusoe finds money in the wreck of his ship he calls it a "drug," and asks "'What art thou good for? Thou art not worth to me, no, not the taking off the ground.' [. . .] But on second thoughts, I took it with me."[15] Suddenly, a passage wistfully describing Clennam's lost past is transformed by financial and commercial language, reinforced by the inevitability of Crusoe's "I took it with me." Again, we are interpellated—financial capitalism taps us on the shoulder and forces us to deal with it—but this time from within.

Another form of this general nervousness, mental "disease" to complement the various kinds of "dis-ease" we see in the novel, extends to pathology in the behavior of many characters; both the Dorrit brothers, for example, enact what behavioral psychologists call "leaving the field," the behavior that results when laboratory rats literally leap out of the maze (as both brothers depart from their own versions of reality) because there is no single spot where they will not receive a shock. In the Dorrits, this syndrome may be more akin to the kind of "inner emigration" undertaken by people living under a totalitarian regime from which they cannot escape—in any case, a striking psychological effect of living under tremendous, inescapable stress.

One might go so far as to say that characters' (and narrator's) nervousness, anxieties, obsessions and even psychoses are paralleled by the world of the novel itself, where frequent, nervous shifting of the shapes, names and identities of people and things are sometime interrupted with a burst of real psychosis—seemingly erupting through the fabric of the world itself. One example of this "psychosis" is the striking passage that comes just before Merdle's suicide as Fanny, from her balcony, watches him going down the street, penknife in his pocket, to the warm baths:

Fanny passed into the balcony for a breath of air. Waters of vexation filled her eyes, and they had the effect of making the famous Mr. Merdle, in going down the street, appear to leap, and waltz, and gyrate, as if he were possessed by several devils. (*LD*, 672; bk. II, ch. xxiv)

Here, Merdle's image seems to become a picture of demonic possession. The narrator's "as if" and the lens of Fanny's frustrated tears are hardly enough to allow us to dismiss the sight as an optical illusion. Instead, the uncertainty adds to the image's power to startle, as if one had seen something horrifying from a passing car or train, but had no chance for a second look. The effect is almost as if the psychological pressure of Merdle's financial situation bursts out of him, transforming him for a wild instant into an emblem of what he really is—not a lumpish, common-looking man who is also the premier embezzler and forger of his time, but an embodiment of societally-sanctioned evil, an abscess of contagion about to burst. The novel shows us this image through Fanny's eyes, when, presumably, it would have been equally easy for the narrator to show us the picture of Merdle dancing without reference to Fanny at all. We are led to think that Merdle's true self is bursting through the sensory and psychological fabric of the world itself—as indeed it is, since the ruin within him is just about to be set loose—so strongly that even Fanny, perhaps one of the least willing to accept it, must see it.

CAPITAL FORMATION AND MURDER: MARX'S VIEW

The extreme nervousness inherent in the world of *Little Dorrit* is driven materially by the financial system, which serves as the kind of moral "engine" in this novel that Chancery does in *Bleak House,* pervading society, shaping characters' personalities and destinies, and involving them, in the end, in a struggle for survival. To support this hypothesis, some of Marx's key financial insights, providing a framework with which to analyze the novel's treatment of financial capitalism, must be recalled. First, the world of *Little Dorrit* is dominated by money. As I noted earlier, Marx points out that such money-focus is fraught with problems for any society:

> Just as in money every qualitative difference between commodities is extinguished, so too for its part, as a radical leveler, it extinguishes all distinctions. But money is itself a commodity, an external object capable of becoming the private property of any individual. Thus the social power [money is "the universal equivalent form of all other commodities, and the directly social incarnation of all human labour" (230)] becomes the

private power of private persons. Ancient society therefore denounced it as tending to destroy the economic and moral order. (*Capital,* vol. I, 229–30)

In such a situation, money's "leveling" function extends to all commodities—to everything, in fact: "Everything becomes salable and purchasable," Marx says. "Circulation becomes the great social retort into which everything is thrown, to come out again as the money crystal. Nothing is immune from this alchemy, the bones of the saints cannot withstand it" (*Capital,* vol. I, 229). In *Little Dorrit,* this effect of money is so pronounced that the presentation of commodities differs from presentations of commodities in earlier novels—most often a two-term proposition where people become things, while things take on the attributes of people. But *Little Dorrit* has far fewer of the "speaking commodities" noted by Audrey Jaffe, for instance, in her discussion of *A Christmas Carol:* "The objects Scrooge sees in the 'real' world [. . .]—such as the Norfolk biffins that ask to be 'carried home in paper bags'—are conscious of the spectator, and they explicitly invite participation in the form of possession" ("Spectacular Sympathy," 259). Instead, the presentation of commodities in *Little Dorrit* much more often revolves around only the other term of the proposition: people turning into commodities. We see this in Pancks, who becomes both a steam tug and Casby's "grubber"; in Mrs. General, who is both "an article of that lustrous surface which suggests that it is worth any money" and a machine with "a little circular set of mental grooves, or rails, on which she started little trains of others opinions" (*LD,* 435; bk. II, ch. ii); Mrs. Merdle, who is largely a bosom; Miss Wade, who believes she was "bought" for her looks, by those who "were curious to ascertain what [her] full value was" (*LD,* 639–40; bk. II, ch. xxi); Casby, who appears in his ticking parlor like a machine designed to project an image of benevolence, with "his thumbs slowly revolving over one another" (*LD,* 147; bk. I, ch. xiii). In each of these cases, and in many others, we can make a direct link between the character's commodification and anxiety about or desire for money or financial security.

Marx goes further in his discussion of capital, positing two types of circulation. As I noted earlier, one of these, which he labels C-M-C, is "the transformation of commodities into money and the reconversion of money into commodities; selling in order to buy" (*Capital,* vol. I, 247):

But alongside this form we find another form, which is quite distinct from the first: M-C-M, the transformation of money into commodities, and the reconversion of commodities into money; buying in order to sell. Money which describes the latter course in its movement is transformed into capital, becomes capital, and, from the point of view of its function, already is capital. [. . .] The result, in which the whole process vanishes, is the exchange of money for money, M-M. If I purchase 2,000 lb. of cotton for £100, and resell the 2,000 pounds of cotton for £110, I have in fact exchanged £100 for £110, money for money. (*Capital,* vol. I, 248)

The importance of this second form of circulation for this chapter lies in the impact of the M-C-M form on those who live under the financial system it typifies. Marx goes on:

> The path C-M-C proceeds from the extreme constituted by one commodity, and ends with the extreme constituted by another, which falls out of circulation and ends with consumption. Consumption, the satisfaction of needs, in short use-value, is theretofore its final goal. The path M-C-M, however, proceeds from the extreme of money and finally returns to that same extreme. Its driving and motivating force, its determining purpose, is therefore exchange-value. (*Capital,* vol. I, 250)

The "final goal," then, the teleology of capital is, in the most obvious sense, exchange-value, and the idea of exchange-value brings with it several problems clearly visible in *Little Dorrit.* First, a world dominated by exchange-value, like this novel's, is a world in which people and commodities are fungible, where a worker's "worth" and his or her salary are equivalent, and where the individual's humanity is devalued. Second, in such a world, work done to satisfy needs is devalued, and work done solely to accumulate money is overvalued, as is clear in this description of the popular view of Mr. Merdle's business enterprises:

> Mr. Merdle came home from his daily occupation of causing the British name to be more and more respected in all parts of the civilized globe, capable of the appreciation of the world-wide commercial enterprise and gigantic combinations of skill and capital. For, though nobody knew with the least precision what Mr. Merdle's business was, except that it was to coin money, these were the terms in which everybody defined it on all ceremonious occasions, and which it was the last new polite reading of the parable of the camel and the needle's eye to accept without enquiry. (*LD,* 382; bk. II, ch. xxxiii)

In such a world, the narrator's sarcasm makes clear, it is quite impossible to determine true "worth," since exchange-value is an artificial construction, a societal judgement call, whereas use-value is real—producing real benefits for society. The narrator's strong feelings on this point are reinforced by his reference to the parable of the needle's eye, which is a reverse echo of the earlier use of the parable of the talents to anchor Doyce firmly in the world of use-value. When Arthur asks Doyce whether "a man" might not be better to "let [his invention] go" rather than suffer as Doyce has, the inventor replies emphatically: "He can't do it. [. . .] It's not put into his head to be buried. It's put into his head to be made useful. You hold your life on the condition that to the last you shall struggle hard for it" (*LD*, 191; bk. I, ch. xvi). The problem with this stance in *Little Dorrit* is that, although Doyce is morally right, as the parables emphasize, the "good guys" are losing. The world has turned to exchange-value as its primary measure of worth, and even in the end, when many things are arranged happily, Doyce and Clennam make no progress with the Circumlocution office.

Finally, an additional problem with a world dominated by exchange-value arises from capital's tendency to replicate itself autonomously and single-mindedly. Marx's technical description of this capital formation process quickly takes on language that emphasizes the significance of the process:

> [I]n the circulation M-C-M, value suddenly presents itself as a self-moving substance which passes through a process of its own, and for which commodities and money are both mere forms. But there is more to come: instead of simply representing the relations of commodities, it now enters into a private relationship with itself, as it were. It differentiates itself as original value from itself as surplus-value, just as God the Father differentiates himself from God the Son, although both are of the same age and form, in fact one single person; for only by the surplus-value of £10 does the 100 originally advanced become capital, and as soon as this has happened, as soon as the son has been created and, through the son, the father, their difference vanishes again, and both become one £110. (*Capital*, vol. I, 256)

This circular movement, compared with the mystery of the Christian Trinity, is striking enough, seeming to describe a process which operates with a larger-than-life force—a kind of destiny, and not a particularly positive one. Earlier, Marx points out that "the circulation of money as capital is an end in itself, for the valorization of value takes place only within this constantly renewed movement. The movement of capital is therefore limitless" (253), suggesting an endless, self-replicating cycle constantly moving around, over, under and through the world and its inhabitants. Such a transformative, self-replicating process is productive of some of the nervousness we have noticed above—especially when its rootedness in exchange-value is remembered. But the situation is worse, Marx notes, when we add in the capitalist and his motives:

> [T]he valorization of value [. . .] is his subjective purpose, and it is only in so far as the appropriation of ever more wealth in the abstract is the sole driving force behind his operations that he functions as a capitalist, i.e. as capital personified and endowed with consciousness and a will. Use-values must therefore never be treated as the immediate aim of the capitalist; nor must the profit on any single transaction. His aim is rather the unceasing movement of profit-making. This boundless drive for enrichment, this passionate chase after value, is common to the capitalist and the miser; but while the miser is merely a capitalist gone mad, the capitalist is a rational miser. (*Capital*, vol. I, 254–55)

The capitalist, "capital personified with consciousness and a will," is completely uninterested in the positive benefits of use-value, but is committed only to the "passionate chase" after exchange-value.[16] And if capital is "dripping from head to toe, from every pore, with blood and dirt," so is the capitalist. In the same discussion with the "blood and dirt" characterization of capital, Marx quotes an even more chilling evaluation of the amorality of capital by T.J. Dunning, a writer on unionism:

> Capital is said by a Quarterly Reviewer to fly from turbulence and strife, and to be timid, which is very true: but this is very incompletely stating the question. Capital eschews no profit, or very small profit, just as Nature was formerly said to abhor a vacuum. With adequate profit, capital is very bold. A certain 10 per cent will ensure its employment anywhere; 20 per cent certain will produce eagerness; 50 per cent positive audacity; 100 per cent will make it ready to trample on all human law; 300 per cent, and there is not a crime at which it will scruple, not a risk it will not run, even to the chance of its owner being hanged. If turbulence and strife will bring a profit, it will freely encourage both. Smuggling and the slave-trade have amply prove all that is here stated."[17]

Thus in Marx's view capital formation is a continuous, self-referential process, voracious in its appetite and utterly amoral (and quite willing to be immoral) in its relations with individuals and society. In "Imaginary Capital: The Shape of the Victorian Economy and the Shaping of Dickens's Career," Tatiana Holway points out that City writers like Evans tended to postulate the cause of the recurrent manias and panics as a national propensity to gamble—the inevitable flip side of the commercial spirit said to make the country great, while political economists threw up their hands and said that recurrent manias were "in accordance with natural law."[18] But *Little Dorrit*'s vision cuts deeper than either of these groups.' The novel directly equates financial madness with the dynamics of capital formation itself—painting a "Marxian" picture of a voracious process which, once begun in the essentially unregulated Victorian marketplace, develops its own momentum, "even to the chance of its owner being hanged." In *Little Dorrit*, we never really know why Merdle does what he does—we learn nothing of his motivation beyond his desire to serve society, which is as much a business strategy as anything else. But we really do not need to know anything else if we view Merdle as "capital personified and endowed with consciousness and a will." He is capital on legs, acting according to his nature.

"THE WAY THE WORLD WORKS": THE TELEOLOGY OF CAPITAL IN *LITTLE DORRIT*

The process of capital formation, always in action, is seen and accepted, if not embraced, by much of the world in *Little Dorrit*—certainly by Society and its hangers-on, and by less exalted personages like Pancks and the Ruggs, who believe they must work within its system to survive—as "the way the world works." We can see this clearly in the following exchange between Henry Gowan and Clennam before Gowan's marriage to Pet:

> "Buy one of my pictures, and I assure you, in confidence, it will not be worth the money. Buy one of another man's—any great professor who beats me hollow—and the chances are that the more you give him, the more he'll impose on you. They all do it."
> "All painters?"
> "Painters, writers, patriots, all the rest who have stands in the market. Give almost any man I know, ten pounds, and he will impose upon you to a corresponding extent; a thousand pounds—to a corresponding extent; ten thousand pounds—to a corresponding extent. So great the success, so great the imposition. But what a capital world it is!" cried Gowan with warm enthusiasm. "What a jolly, excellent loveable world it is!" (*LD*, 303; bk. I, ch. xxv)

Gowan's remarks, interestingly, echo Dunning's, and suggest the extent of the penetration of this process of capital formation into all parts of the world—even among intellectuals and patriots, people very much outside the business world of the City. Gowan, of course, is cynical and habituated to a "leveling" mindset that exalts the low and debases the high, much as money itself does—an effect re-echoed and reinforced by the pun linking "capital" with "jolly, excellent [and] loveable." However, his remarks resonate as a true description of the forces people like Doyce (if we accept him as an exemplar of use-value) and Little Dorrit (if we accept her as an exemplar of all that is true and good in humanity) are up against. I will return to Gowan later, too, to consider how Dickens's own "stand in the market" as a successful author puts him into a position where he must, like his characters, consider how best to live in the world I have just described.

Thus far, we have seen that *Little Dorrit* presents a financial world that produces psychological damage—even psychosis—in those who live in it, even those, like Pancks, for example, who do not wholly embrace it. But living under financial capitalism is even more problematic than this. Jeff Nunokawa points out that the laws of the marketplace in *Little Dorrit* make stability in a commodity-based system all but impossible:

> [I]n *Little Dorrit* [. . .] it's not just that property fit to circulate in the market might be parted from its owner, it must be [. . . S]uch grave losses result less from accident or avarice than from laws of the marketplace situated beyond human error [. . . Dickens's] economic imagination [. . .] locates the origin of such losses in the nature of the market and of marketable property rather than in the will or weakness of individuals (Nunokawa, 8).

Recalling Marx's view of the teleology of capital reinforces Nunokawa's point: "[T]he circulation of money as capital is an end in itself, for the valorization of value takes place only within this constantly renewed movement. The movement of capital is therefore limitless" (*Capital*, vol. I, 253). These views help us see that the system being described in *Little Dorrit* is a closed movement of accumulation of exchange-value—a sterile, inhuman accumulation of a sign which has become so debased it no longer stands for anything but itself, and a system that is unstoppable, inescapable. In other words, for human beings, for the human part of them (a life as something other than a fungible, money-denominated commodity) at least, the teleology of capital is death.

We can see the implications of this teleology at work in the way the novel ironically reverses the spectacle of the desirable commodity, inviting the observer into a relationship with a "commodity" that combines the attraction of the commodity in the shop window with the repulsion of the physical details of death. It is worth recalling here that Thomas Richards describes the spectacle as the presentation—for consumption—of the meaning inherent in commodities, echoing Baudrillard's "if we consume the product as product, we consume its meaning through advertising."[19] Thus spectacle is meant to affect the viewer, as Audrey Jaffe has noted: "Spectacle depends on a distinction between vision and participation, a distance that produces desire [for the product on display] in a spectator" ("Spectacular Sympathy," 256).

As we have seen, business is often represented by spectacle in Dickens. "Good" businesses are involved with use-value and generative wealth-creation; their spectacles contain anthropocentric representations of commodities as objects of desire and real use—like the objects cited by Jaffe in *A Christmas Carol* (for example, the "speaking" biffins cited above). The desire is heightened by a temporal distance in many cases, heightening desire or at least nostalgia for what has been.

Spectacles of this sort are common in Dickens's novels and journalism, as Jaffe and others have noted. But perhaps more important for the purposes of this discussion is another type of spectacle, an ironic reversal of the kinds of spectacles referred to above. In May of 1856 Dickens wrote in *Household Words*:

> I am thinking of the Moonian [Parisian] Morgue, where the bodies of all persons discovered dead, with no clue to their identity upon them, are placed to be seen by all who choose to go and look at them. All the world knows this custom, and perhaps all the world knows that the bodies lie on inclined planes within a great glass window, as though Holbein should represent Death, in his grim Dance, keeping a shop and displaying his goods like a Regent Street or Boulevard linen-draper.[20]

This spectacle also produced a desire or "lack" in the narrator, an immediate attraction that later mixes with repulsion, desire tinged with disgust. We are told "all the world" knows that "the bodies lie on inclined planes" and other details of the functioning of the morgue as if all the world were as enthusiastically familiar with such details as the narrator is—a familiarity bred by numerous visits to a place of obvious attraction. In a later sketch ("Some Recollections of Mortality" [1863]), the Dickensian narrator reveals how powerful this attraction can be. He tells of arriving at the morgue in the wake of a procession bearing a newly deceased person on a litter. As he stands in the crowd, which had been required to leave the viewing area while the new body was prepared and is waiting to be readmitted to view it on display, the narrator tells us:

> We [the assembled crowd] had been excited in the highest degree by seeing the Custodians [morgue attendants] pull off their coats and tuck up their sleeves as the procession came along. It all looked so interestingly like business. Shut out on the muddy street, we now became quite ravenous to know all about it.[21]

The "commodities" in this particular shop-window are, of course, dead bodies which, in "Railway Dreaming:" are presented ironically *as* commodities, and as commodities like fashionable "Regent Street" articles of clothing, subject even to fickle public tastes. The narrator discusses the impatience with which the crowd, once admitted to the morgue, awaits the unveiling of the newest corpse, and ignores the three bodies "that had drawn exceedingly [. . .] ten minutes [before:]"

> Three lately popular articles that had been attracting greatly when the litter was first descried coming dancing around the corner by the great cathedral, were so completely despised now, that nobody save [. . .] two little girls (one showing them to a doll) would look at them. Yet the chief of the three, the article in the front row, had received jagged injury to the left temple; and the other two in the back row, the drowned two lying side by side [. . .] were furtive of appearance [. . .] (in their puffed way). ("Some Recollections of Mortality," 105)

Language here mixes everyday commercial terminology ("It all looked so interestingly like business") matter-of-factly with the horrors of "jagged" wounds and "puffed," "drowned" bodies. The "articles" seem to have passed into the stream of commerce—the system of exchange which is so powerful the little girl appears to be "training" her doll to participate in it; yet the "articles" are repellent. They are "anti-commodities" which attract like the commodities in the Great Exhibition, yet also repel because they are stripped of their humanity, extreme examples of the way living people are reified under the system of financial capitalism. To us as onlookers, the bodies are emblems of our own deaths, of course, but they also imply the living death of a world where exchange-value predominates.

In *Little Dorrit,* spectacle is used to incite similar emotional connections with "objects" by making palpable for the observer the inevitable link between exchange-value-based finance and death. Here, spectacle has shifted from a representation of commodities inducing attraction and the desire for possession to a representation of "anti-commodities" inducing other emotions—attraction followed by repulsion, uneasiness, fear, disgust; its demonstration of the empty values of non-generative financial activity also reflects a lack of, and a need for, an opposite set of values.

One such spectacle, the discovery of Merdle's dead body in his bath, forces the observer to confront the link between non-generative financial activity and death, and to recognize, with at least a certain degree of pessimism, the seemingly all-pervasive nature of this kind of financial activity.

This spectacle is framed by the structure of the warm-baths building and by the door frame itself:

> The messenger hurried before [Physician], along a grove of little rooms, and turning into one at the end of the grove, looked round the door. Physician was close upon him and looked round the door too. (*LD*, 675; bk. II, ch. xxv)

When we do get to see Merdle's corpse, visuality and detail, along with the "box" and wrapping, present him as a commodity. It is worth noting that we have seen him presented this way before—enclosed with Mr. Dorrit in his carriage, "this public car of triumph," "[riding] into the City [. . . where] the hats [. . .] flew off grey heads [amid] the general bowing and crouching" (*LD*, 591; bk. II, ch. xvi). Mr. Dorrit, both a participant and observer of this spectacle, feels "rapture" as he bathes in "the light of Mr. Merdle." But the spectacle of Merdle dead in his bath, not the desirable commodity he was thought to be, does not provoke rapture:

> There was a bath in that corner, from which the water had been hastily drained off. Lying in it, as in a grave or sarcophagus, with a hurried drapery of sheet and blanket thrown across it, was the body of a heavily-made man, with an obtuse head, and coarse, mean, common features. A skylight had been opened, to release the steam with which the room had been filled; but it hung, heavily upon the walls and heavily upon the face and figure in the bath. [. . .] The white marble at the bottom of the bath was veined with a dreadful red. On the ledge at the side were an empty laudanum-bottle and a tortoise-shell handled penknife—soiled, but not with ink. (*LD*, 676; bk. II, ch. xxv)

Here the commodity in its nest of boxes and wrappings is not only "a heavily-made man, with an obtuse head, and coarse, mean, common features," but an explicit figure of death and self-extinction. The "dreadful red" veining of the marble echoes Merdle's opened veins, and the comparison turns him into a kind of stone, like the "jewels" he used to hang upon the "capital bosom" of Mrs. Merdle (*LD*, 224; bk. I, ch. xxi). Merdle has become an "anti-commodity" like the bodies in Paris. Like that of Merdle in his coach, this spectacle of one of the great objects of attraction in *Little Dorrit* again invites emotions—but this time of aversion, disgust, even shame. Physician, having pronounced Merdle dead and read his confessional note, leaves the warm-baths: "Physician was glad to walk out into the night air—was even glad, in spite of his great experience, to sit down upon a door-step for a little while; feeling sick and faint" (*LD*, 676; bk. II, ch. xxv). Merdle's body, framed, packaged and presented as an ironic "anti-commodity," is as powerful an attraction as the commodities in the Great Exhibition; but this commodity attracts only to shock and repel. This spectacle functions like a mousetrap, drawing the viewer in close enough, then snapping shut. The values embodied in a commodified way of life, the spectacle of Merdle's body declares, end "in a grave, or sarcophagus."

The details of this spectacle paint a shocking still-life of the financier, stripped of the trappings that have created his image, and self-extinguished, just as any capital given to him has self-extinguished. Moreover, for its power, this spectacle draws culturally on many other images of decadence and emptiness, from archtypical Roman suicides to recent financial scandals. The most important of these images is that of the notorious 1856 suicide of financier John Sadlier whose connection with Merdle is "hinted at" in Dickens's preface to the 1857 edition of *Little Dorrit*, as Barbara Weiss points out in "Secret Pockets and Secret Breasts: *Little Dorrit* and the Commercial Scandals of the Fifties."[22] Sadlier's suicide would have been in the minds of many readers of the original monthly parts, and his resemblance to Merdle is more than casual. For example, Evans comments that "the name of Mr. John Sadlier at the head of the board was, by many shareholders, considered to be equivalent to a rise of at least one per cent. in the market value of their shares; no wonder, then, that he speedily found himself installed as Chairman of the Royal Swedish Railway Company, Director of the East Kent, and joint manager of half a score of other enterprises."[23]

Sadlier's attraction as a financier was a real-world equivalent to Merdle's, as were his crimes of forgery and embezzlement. His suicide is worth considering more carefully for a moment because it, too, was a widely publicized spectacle. Evans describes Sadlier's death scene:

> On Sunday morning, the 17th of February [1856], as a labouring man was crossing Hampstead Heath, immediately at the back of the tavern known as Jack Straw's Castle, he discovered the body of a gentleman, cold and stiff. He had evidently been dead some hours, and was lying on the rise of a small mound, in a spot which seemed to have been carefully selected. His clothes were undisturbed; by his side was lying a bottle labeled in several places "Essential Oil of Almonds," "Poison," and still containing a small portion of the fatal liquid. At a short distance from him was a silver cream ewer, empty, but smelling strongly of the same drug. To mark his identity he had written his name and address on a piece of paper, which was found in his pocket. He was removed to

Hampstead Workhouse, where the inquest was held. (Evans, *Facts, Failures, and Frauds*, 235)

As much as Merdle's, Sadlier's death scene is a carefully crafted spectacle, so much so that it seems the only thing missing is a store-window (or proscenium arch). In a "spot which seemed to have been carefully selected," Sadlier is found surrounded by props. There is the bottle melodramatically labeled "Poison," and the silver cream ewer denoting luxury even in extremis. The label, a counter to anonymity, both underlines the commodification of the dead man, and advertises exactly what is "on display"—so that the full import of this particular commodity would be understood. Sadlier's body, "cold and stiff," prefigures the anti-commodity—attracting and then sharply repelling—that Merdle becomes. Dickens and his middle-class readers were well acquainted with the details of Sadlier's death,[24] and the fate of suicide for Merdle intensifies the impact of the moral meaning of the financier's activities by linking them with the widespread, universally recognized "ruin" caused by Sadlier (Evans, *Facts, Failures and Frauds*, 236, 253). That the spectacle of the financier's suicide was a common trope in financial writing and in novels with financial focuses only reinforces the power of the Merdle spectacle.[25] Thus, the depiction of Merdle's suicide turns the attraction of the commodity in upon itself to present a powerful picture of the certain end of all speculation, and a figure of the cycle of attraction and desire followed by ruin and destruction that speculation has brought to the world of the novel. "Like a heat-seeking missile or the teleological subject of History or Therapy, capital never fails to realize its potential, " as Jeff Nunokawa notes (Nunokawa, 9).

FINANCIAL CAPITALISM AS A SOCIAL DISEASE

But despite the power of such spectacles (echoing Sadleir's highly-publicized suicide in the real world, and the spectacle of the drawn-out inquest upon his body) and the emotions they evoke, the financial system and its speculative promise are almost impossible for even the most morally upright characters to turn away from, as Clennam shows us. This means that the outlook for any kind of use-value-based life, for a human identity free from the taint of financial capitalism, for life itself as opposed to commodification, extinguishment and death, is at best highly uncertain. This near-inevitability of "contagion" by the financial system—and thus the pessimism inherent throughout *Little Dorrit*—is constantly reinforced by the way finance is presented linguistically in the novel.

Dickens's novels use specific kinds of language to talk about finance—particularly speculation. This language is rarely direct, and this indirectness stems from the sense (both in the novels and in nineteenth-century business literature) that finance itself is a "non-generative," somewhat shameful activity—the process of moving money around to produce more without actually creating anything. The language of finance mimics this aspect of its subject; it is at times an arbitrary stream of signs with problematic connections to what is signified. More specifically, this language is often metonymic—"slippery" in that one word may be substituted for another similar but not identical, word more or less opportunistically, rather than logically.[26]

The significance of the metonymic nature of the language of finance becomes apparent in the discussion about "investments" between Clennam and Pancks, as finance and speculation penetrate into what has become a warm personal relationship:

> '[I]s it not curious, Pancks, that the ventures which run just now in so many people's heads, should run even in little Cavalletto's?'
> 'Ventures?" retorted Pancks, with a snort. "What ventures?'
> 'These Merdle enterprises.'
> 'Oh, Investments,' said Pancks. 'Aye, aye. I didn't know you were speaking of Investments.'
> His quick way of replying caused Clennam to look at him, with a doubt whether he meant more than he said. (*LD*, 557; bk. II, ch. xiii)

The reader, having seen Merdle "evasively rolling his eyes" and giving "uncomfortable glances" in the previous chapter, has more than an inkling that Merdle's "greatness" may be problematical, and that he, in person, does not appear to be a man one would trust with a fortune. Yet when "Ventures" is suddenly replaced by "Investments" these activities—unthinkable in themselves—become more acceptable even to the sober Clennam; and this linguistic substitution takes place even in the safety of the home, before the hearth, perpetrated by a close friend.

Thus the opportunism and slipperiness of the language surrounding finance and especially speculation in the novel are significant because they give this language properties that enable it to mirror the levelling function of money itself, in which one commodity easily substitutes for another, regardless of use-value. This language mimics the action of capitalism, but also hints that the mechanism behind capitalism, money's ability to act as "the great social retort into which everything is thrown," is out of control. For example, the word "Merdle" is constantly and opportunistically equated with "Millions" (and becomes a metonym for "money") at all levels of society. But

"Merdle" is also, constantly, uncontrollably, equated with excrement—not only in its sound, but in its "sticky" nature: "Merdle [. . .] deposited on every lip, and carried into every ear [. . . the] name [. . .] in everybody's mouth." These phrases allow excrement to stand for money and put both in contact with "every lip," "every ear," "everybody's mouth," images reinforced both by the "black traces" around Merdle's lips and by Pancks's constant griminess: money, like the mud in *Bleak House,* seems stickily to pollute and violate everything (*LD,* 547, 549; bk. II, ch xiii, 588; bk. II, ch. xvi). This substitution hints at the metonymic chaos beneath the supposedly rational world of markets: "Merdle" equals money, but the process cannot stop there; if everything equals everything else (in the absence of use-value, that is) the process must continue and money eventually must equal excrement. In the end, everything is valueless.

In my view, *Little Dorrit* hints at this all-pervasive chaos—this fundamental sense that something is radically wrong under the surface of society—but does not explicitly explore this larger issue.[27] Rather, the novel focuses more narrowly—in effect mimicking the metonymic nature of finance itself by substituting the processes of sexual seduction and disease transmission for "speculation," and, at the same time demonstrating, as clearly as Marx does in *Capital,* the autonomy and opportunism inherent in the processes of capitalism. We can see an almost parodic mirroring of the process of selecting a speculative investment in the conversation cited above, as Pancks, the seducer, takes the lead: 'Yes. Investments is the word. [. . .] I am coming back to it, you see' (*LD,* 557; bk. II, ch. xiii). Later, speculation—the topic of their conversation—is referred to as an "infatuation." Finally, when Pancks "infects" Clennam with the speculative fever, the scene is couched in the language of seduction, "oriental" sensuality and sexual activity. Pancks ultimately says, "with an odd effect of having been from the commencement of the conversation loaded with the heavy charge he now fired off,"

'They're right, you know. They don't mean to be, but they're right.[. . .] I've made the calculations. I've worked at it. [Merdle's speculations are] safe and genuine.' Relieved at having got to this, Mr. Pancks took as long a pull as his lungs would permit at his Eastern pipe [. . .]

In those moments, Mr. Pancks began to give out the dangerous infection with which he was laden. It is the manner of communicating these diseases; it is the subtle way in which they go about. [. . . I]n this category [as trusted friend, "neither ignorant nor wicked,"] the infection he threw off was all the more virulent. (*LD,* 558–59; bk. II, ch. xiii)

The scene moves on, Clennam having been hooked, to its climax when Pancks "closes the deal" first by completing Clennam's seduction, then by making Clennam himself complicit in spreading the disease of speculation and the ruin it brings. First, Pancks says, in response to Clennam's surprise that he has invested in the Merdle schemes, "It's what you ought to do yourself. Why don't you do as I do?" Later, Pancks completes the seduction/infection by urging Clennam to invest Doyce's money as well as his own:

> 'Recompense him for his toils and disappointments. Give him the chances of time. He'll never benefit himself in that way, patient and pre-occupied workman. [. . .] Be as rich as you honestly can. It's your duty. Not for your sake, but for the sake of others.' (559, 561)

Pancks has seduced Clennam away from the generative uses of his money (providing for his future, building his business) and has even gotten him to divert the money of the "patient and pre-occupied workman" into speculation. Thus the metonymy here, this portrayal of "speculation" as a combination of seduction and the transmission of social disease, works at one level to allow the novel to comment on speculation's destructive power, while demonstrating the difficulty, for frail human beings, of avoiding it. But at the same time, this scene is more than a simple cautionary tale or exercise in social commentary. We see that Pancks himself, infected as *he* is with the speculative contagion, is only a vector for the speculative disease, a tool being used by capital itself—that autonomous, opportunistic force which, suddenly seeing the possibility of augmenting itself (by capturing Doyce's money as well as Clennam's), immediately takes action. Thus capital becomes a character in the novel, using the contagion of speculation to penetrate society completely, and even to "infect" those, like Doyce, who would never speculate themselves, and who explicitly warns Arthur against speculating.

    In the end the metonymic substitution of the term "Investments" for "speculation" is a figure of the ability of financial capitalism to penetrate society and seduce its (otherwise prudent) members. The use of this figure adds significant depth to the traditional depictions of speculation by contemporary commentators as a "plague" or "fever" by equating it, as Daniel Scoggin points out, with "social disease":

> Dickens presents an addition to the catalogue of so-called "social diseases" to compel the reader to reexamine the laissez-faire conception of financial reversal as necessarily rooted in personal shortcomings, such as avarice, laziness and luxuriousness. [. . . Disease, given its "democratic" ability to spread,] subtly refutes the notion that economic woes

(or natural tribulations) are based in the class-climbing prognostications (or moral transgressions) of the sick-poor as opposed to the healthy-rich.[28]

Scoggin points out rightly that one effect of the equation of "speculation" and "social disease" is to democratize the notion of financial reversal. But a more important effect of this equation, in my view, is to link the spread of financial obsession with the spread of venereal disease, which is both a product of individual moral choice and of the opportunistic autonomy, once it has penetrated a social body, of the disease itself. Such a comparison makes financial activity of this sort shameful both to the seducer and the seduced, while at the same time allowing the seduced some sympathy as a victim of sorts. This view of the "plague" of speculation is both subtle and realistic, accounting both for the attractiveness of speculation and for its devastating effects, and mirroring Dickens's own equivocal position as a critic of and a participant in the capitalist system. In addition, such a view accounts for the staying power of such infections, based as they are on a double metonymy linking sexual and financial obsession and autonomous sexual and financial "diseases," in the social body. This staying power is still apparent near the end of the novel; even as Pancks admits, "it was my misfortune to lead [Clennam] into that ruinous investment" the narrator adds, "Mr. Pancks still clung to that word, and never said speculation." (*LD*, 730; bk. II, ch. xxx)

AN ISLAND OF LIFE, A WORLD OF DEATH

Despite the grim picture of the possibilities for a decent life in *Little Dorrit*, versus the seemingly endless and very powerful opportunities to fall prey to the forces of exchange-value and death, Arthur and Little Dorrit are married in the end, and leave the church for a happy future:

> They went quietly down into the roaring streets, inseparable and blessed; and as they passed along in sunshine and in shade, the noisy and the eager, and the arrogant and the froward and the vain, fretted, and chafed, and made their usual uproar. (*LD*, 787; bk. II, ch. xxxiv)

In a sense, this ending conveys a sense of fitness; rhetorically, it satisfyingly nests the clause "inseparable and blessed" between "the roaring streets" on one side, and the broken—both rushing and stumbling—clauses that follow it. I would argue, too, that the ending seems to fit because both we, the readers, and Dickens, the author, want it to fit—we want a happy ending.[29] Before considering the role the reader's and author's desires might play in the fitness of the ending, though, we must step back and consider it in context. When considered against the backdrop of the financial and consequent psychological pressures I have been discussing, the ending certainly seems far too optimistic.

For one thing, Clennam, a double for Mr. Dorrit in our eyes, in his own, and in Amy's, might be expected to share the old man's fate of lengthy imprisonment and consequent mental deterioration—or at least might not be expected to be relieved by Doyce, acting as *deus ex machina*, as easily as happens in the novel. (When Doyce reappears he has been absent for more than 140 pages in the Penguin edition, and for months in the novel's time.) Also, just given the world of the novel, set sometime before the financial reforms of the 1840s that eased debtors' paths out of prison, Clennam might have been expected to suffer a harsher fate—might even have been expected, following Merdle's example, to commit suicide, a very common story in financial-press coverage of panics. It is clear from Evans's work and from other sources that sentiment and happy endings were not a common part of the emotional fabric of City life. In *The City of London*, David Kynaston quotes the observations of "moral scrutineer" Robert Hawker, clergyman, in his book, *The Royal Exchange* (c. 1808):

> I remarked a great number of advertisements [. . .] on the walls of the Royal exchange; many of them containing a sorrowful want; but, whether from their being considered commonplace things; or whether from the imperious demands which every man's own separate concern made upon him—it appeared that their tales of woe were not much regarded. Alas! I said, here is but little time for Charity of any description[.] [30]

This lack of charity Hawker finds in the businessmen on the Exchange even in the wake of the death of one of their own, as he reports in a passage reminiscent of what Scrooge hears on 'Change after his "death": "The enquiry at the Exchange, when [a merchant's] death is announced from every mouth, is, What did he die worth? Like a carcase at the shambles, the question only turns upon one point, doth he turn out well?" (Kynaston, 33).

But, while many of Merdle's infuriated victims, looking for a scapegoat, express similarly callous views of Clennam's fate, Doyce does not. "[N]ot a word more from you about the past," he tells Clennam. "There was an error in your calculations. I know what that is. It affects the whole machine, and failure is the consequence. You will profit by the failure, and will avoid it another time" (*LD*, 783; bk. II, ch. xxxiv). (Again, one could argue that Doyce, as the exemplar of use-value in the novel, might appropriately respond this way—especially as he had recouped at least some of the losses through his adventure in Russia. But in a world painstakingly painted as "dripping with blood and dirt," Clennam's salvation jars.)

Where does this ending leave Dickens, whose project, as Tatiana Holway rightly points out, has been to create a reality-based "economy" in *Little Dorrit* which, "from its conception, to its organization and narrative development, to its specific system of tropes [. . .] is not simply analogous to, but identical with the [actual mid-century] economy as a whole" (Holway, Imaginary Capital, 36)? What kind of a statement is made by a novel which insists on the relentless psychological and physical destruction wrought by the financial system, but allows Clennam, caught fast in the same web as Mr. Dorrit and the other debtors, to escape? I believe *Little Dorrit's* ending reflects a fundamental split in the novel's attitude toward financial capitalism.

On one hand, several elements of the novel's structure support its commitment to use-value and all that it implies, and its stand against exchange-value and all that that implies. For instance, Daniel Doyce, who "soberly" works on "for the work's sake" (*LD*, 495; bk. II, ch. viii), who exhibits a "composed and unobtrusive self-sustainment" (*LD*, 191; bk. I, ch. xvi), and who is "accustomed to combine what was original and daring in conception with what was patient and minute in execution" (190) serves as an exemplar of use-value in the novel, and is held up, by his one of his workers, as the very definition of a man: "Wherever you go, they'll find as they've got a man among 'em, a man as knows his tools and as his tools knows, a man as is willing and a man as is able, and if that's not a man, where is a man!" (*LD*, 646; bk. II, ch. xxii). The emphasis on tools echoes our first glimpse of Doyce, when he is described as

> A short, square, practical-looking man whose hair had turned gray, and in whose face and forehead were deep lines of cogitation, which looked as though they were carved in hard wood. He was dressed in decent black, a little rusty, and had the appearance of a sagacious master in some handicraft. He had a spectacle case in his hand which he turned over and over [. . .] with a certain free use of the thumb that is never seen but in a hand accustomed to tools. (*LD*, 123; bk. I, ch. x)

Unlike Merdle, Doyce is presented at no ironic distance, and his appearance and manner match perfectly with his inner nature. He is a creator and expert in "how TO do it," the antithesis of the emptiness of exchange-value. Doyce "doubles" Dickens in this creative role, his ability to "combine what was original and daring in conception with what was patient and minute in execution," and throws the weight of Dickens's own role as a generative artist, and successful middle-class entrepreneur, who lives, like Doyce, by the products of his personal labor, behind the case for use-value in the novel.

Similarly, Little Dorrit is another exemplar of use-value—in the form of pure love and truth—in the novel; she stands for all the things her father was not, yet she also stands for a complete and unquestioning love—both for him and later for Arthur. Untainted by the Marshalsea, except for the "speck" revealed by her feeling that Mr. Dorrit's years in jail should cancel out his debts, and unchanged by the family's riches, Little Dorrit represents one way of avoiding the ruin inherent in the financial system—divesting oneself of wealth and the desire for wealth (she changes back into her old dress to nurse Clennam in prison, and she has him burn the codicil of the will representing her inheritance), and replacing these with selfless love for another. The novel's commitment to what Little Dorrit represents is clear throughout, but especially toward the end of Book Two, when the narrator notes that "all the devotion of this great nature was turned to [Clennam] in his adversity, to pour out its inexhaustible wealth of goodness upon him" (*LD*, 725; bk. II, ch. xxix). Little Dorrit also doubles Dickens in the novel, in her role as the supportive and loving child of an improvident father; both as a figure representing the purity of the child, and as an echo of Dickens's own sense of himself as "worldly wise in hard and poor necessities" (*LD*, 86; bk. I, ch. vii), and as the provident provider in a family not entirely unacquainted with the kinds of "genteel fictions" that sustain Mr. Dorrit.

These characters and many other factors help make the case for use-value—the case for a kind of society, or at least a kind of individual life, which would not be dominated and distorted by financial capitalism and exchange-value. But even as this case is being made, other structural elements of the novel problematize it—not, of course, in the sense of discrediting it, but in the sense of demonstrating the difficulty, even the impossibility, of attaining this kind of society or individual life. We have already noticed Henry Gowan's remark about "stands in the market," a cynical pronouncement that puts art and creativity on the same level with Mr. Merdle's activities. Gowan, in this speech and elsewhere, embodies the "leveling" tendency of money emphasized by Marx—embodies the spirit of exchange-value, in a sense. Importantly, though, Gowan is an artist highly concerned with what his work will fetch in the marketplace, and highly attuned to the inner wants and needs of his audience. We can see this in his marketing pitch to Mr. Dorrit, which is typical of his leveling style:

> If you are going to throw away a hundred guineas or so, I am as poor as
> a poor relation of great people usually is, and I shall be very much

obliged to you if you will throw them my way. I'll do the best I can for the money; and if the best should be bad, why even then you may probably have a bad picture with a small name to it, instead of a bad picture with a large name to it. (*LD*, 488; bk. II, ch. vii)

Gowan's casualness here hides the precision of his pricing ("one hundred guineas or so" sets a very distinct "floor" to the pricing discussion, casual as the phrase seems) and his careful use of his connections to "great people"; his sales patter is perfectly calculated to win over its "upstart" audience, as he later terms Mr. Dorrit. In his concern with business and money, and his skill in "reading" his audience, Gowan doubles Dickens, to whom both of these issues were also supremely important. Clearly, Dickens the "creator" is largely embodied in Doyce, as we have seen, but Gowan's preoccupations as a "creator" are too close to Dickens's own to ignore. This doubling suggests a world in which exchange-value predominates, even in art. Gowan is not weighty enough as an artist for us to take his views as a serious statement about art and money, but, again, the juxtaposition of creativity (and other kinds of professionalism) with the indubitably powerful market-forces embodied in the rest of the novel causes us as readers to stumble—perhaps to think of Dickens's recreating Gowan, in a sense, in the final years of his life when, in his reading tours, he combined the urgent concern for profit with an uncanny ability to "read" his audiences.

Another character helps to undermine *Little Dorrit*'s ability fully and frankly to espouse the primacy of use-value, and all the anti-Mammonism that it implies. Amid the magnificence and decay of Italy, Mr. Dorrit bitterly reproaches Amy for her failure to become "one of us," meaning to adopt the "surface" offered by Mrs. General. That this is really a demand that Amy "convert" to the school of exchange-value is emphasized a page or two later when, hearing that the Dorrits have a prospective connection with the Merdles, Mrs. General is seen "raising her gloves and bowing her head, as if she were doing homage to some visible graven image" (*LD*, 465; bk. I, ch. v). As Mr. Dorrit is accusing Amy ("You—ha—habitually hurt me"), he offers a kind of justification for his desire to use her (to make her over, and even, prospectively, to "sell" her on the marriage mart as he had once tried to "sell" her to John Chivery to avoid straining his relations with Chivery's father, the turnkey):

There was a reproach in the touch so addressed to him that she had not foreseen, or she would have withheld her hand. He began to justify himself; in a heated, stumbling, angry manner, which made nothing of it.

'I was there all those years. I was—ha—universally acknowledged as
the head of the place. I—ha hum—I gave my family a position there.
I deserve a return. I claim a return. I say, sweep it off the face of the
earth and begin afresh. Is that much? I ask, is *that* much?'(*LD*, 461;
bk. II, ch. v)

Mr. Dorrit's specific use of financial language conceptualizes his relationship
with his own life as "a matter or bargain and sale," a contract much like one
Mrs. Clennam thinks she has made with God. Although he claims the return
on his supposed efforts on behalf of his family, the claim is really for a return
on "that quarter of a century behind prison bars" mourned by Little Dorrit
(*LD*, 460; bk. II, ch. v). Such a claim, more evidence of Mr. Dorrit's inability
to think beyond his own self-centeredness, seems quite illegitimate—especially in a world where Little Dorrit's feeling that life has been unfair to her
father is regarded as a "taint." But the claim resonates, nonetheless—we are
forced to take it seriously.

Reasons for this resonance start to emerge when we recall that Mr.
Dorrit is explicitly seen as a child when he is first imprisoned. Asked by the
turnkey how many children he has, he answers, "Two." The turnkey says to
himself, "And you another . . . which makes three on you. And your wife another, I'll lay a crown. Which makes four on you. And another coming [. . .]
which'll make five on you. And I'll go seven and sixpence to name which is
the helplessest, the unborn baby or you!" (*LD*, 69; bk. I, ch. vi). In addition,
the reasons for Mr. Dorrit's imprisonment are opaque; his affairs had been
"perplexed by a partnership, of which he knew no more than that he had invested money in it; [. . .] nobody on the face of the earth could be more incapable of explaining any single item in the heap of confusion than the
debtor himself, [and] nothing comprehensible could be made of his case"
(*LD*, 70; bk. I, ch. vi). Mr. Dorrit is thus, in addition to being portrayed as a
child, presented as a legitimate victim of an unregulated, rapacious financial
system, and as completely ignorant of and helpless to deal with the cause of
his suffering.[31] These themes allow us to see Mr. Dorrit doubling both John
Dickens (the Marshalsea prisoner) and Charles Dickens (the suffering child
"imprisoned" in the Blacking Warehouse for incomprehensible reasons),
and, again, lend inevitable weight to the need to accommodate oneself to, or
at least become adept at survival in, the world of exchange-value.

With Doyce and Little Dorrit on one side and Gowan and Mr. Dorrit on
the other, the position of the novel on the struggle between use-value and exchange-value is equivocal. The focal point of the tension between these systems
appears after the crash, when Pancks finds Arthur alone in his counting-house:

The usual diligence and order of the Counting-house at the Works were overthrown. Unopened letters and unsorted papers lay strewn about the desk. In the midst of these tokens of prostrate energy and dismissed hope, the master of the Counting-house stood idle in his usual place, with his arms crossed on the desk, and his head bowed down upon them.

Mr. Pancks rushed in and saw him, and stood still. In another minute, Mr Pancks's arms were on the desk, and Mr. Pancks's head was bowed down upon them; and for some time they remained in these attitudes, idle and silent, with the width of the little room between them. (*LD*, 681; bk. II, ch. xxvi)

In this tableau Arthur stands in the temple of use-value, ruined by his willingness to be seduced by exchange-value. Arthur has earlier described himself as empty, citing "the void in my cowed heart everywhere" (*LD*, 33; bk. I, ch. ii), and this emptiness has allowed him to be swayed. He is both a "Fool," as Mr. F's Aunt repeatedly emphasizes, and an everyman—an empty vessel waiting to be filled up, and so a surrogate for the reader, in a sense. He is certainly good-hearted and deserving of being saved, but, in the end, the best the novel can do for him is to lower Doyce from the rafters with enough money to relieve him. The import of the ending, then, seems to be that there really are two paths, or two choices, embodied by exchange-value and use-value. But our choices as individuals are limited both by the need to have money to subsist in a capitalist system, and by the raw power and inevitability of that system. Even Arthur, whom we recognize as basically good, cannot resist the system and has to be saved somehow. Doyce, thoroughly steeped in use-value, can resist the power of financial capitalism to the extent of not letting it derail him from his chosen course, but even he is (temporarily) "ruined" by it. Only Little Dorrit, the embodiment of childlike goodness and self-effacing love for others, can pass transcendent through the "roaring streets" of a world driven by financial capitalism.

LITTLE DORRIT'S PROJECT: FROM CRITIQUE TO ANODYNE

When we consider ourselves as readers of *Little Dorrit,* the equivocal position of the novel is emphasized. In his discussion of *Bleak House* in *The Novel and the Police,* D.A. Miller explores the "interpenetration of literary and worldly interests":

No doubt, both as a system of distribution and as a text, the Victorian novel establishes a little bureaucracy of its own, generating an immense amount of paperwork and sending its readers here, there, backward and forward, like the circumlocutionary agencies that Dickens satirizes. On this basis, it could be argued that, despite or by means of its superficially hostile attitude toward bureaucracy, a novel like *Bleak House* is profoundly concerned to train us—as, at least since the eighteenth century, play usually trains us for work—in the sensibility for inhabiting the new bureaucratic, administrative structures.[32]

One could argue that in *Little Dorrit,* the novel's "training" project is to convince us of the need to practice and embrace the middle-class values embodied by Doyce—and, in his professional life, by Dickens himself. These values, William Palmer argues, are based on eighteenth–century benevolence, appearing in Dickens's work through a "chain of influence" leading from Shaftesbury to Godwin, through the eighteenth-century novels Dickens reports reading so avidly as a boy:

> [From a New Historicist perspective, the] Dickensian vision becomes a connecting link between the eighteenth-century and twentieth-century philosophical views of human existence. Defining this vision and analyzing individual novels reveals the way Dickens tended to act (and to write) based on emotion rather than practicality, on belief rather than rational analysis, on often unrewarded faith rather than empirical evidence of ugly fact. Thomas Hobbes, the author of *Leviathan,* and Lord Shaftesbury, the philosopher of perfectibility, fought this same war in the eighteenth century, the Romantics sustained a rearguard action, and Dickens, an isolated guerilla, was merely carrying on the fight a century later. Dickens's "vision" derived from an eighteenth-century philosophical view that all his life he tried to apply to an unaccommodating Victorian world. [. . .] Because of this chain of influence [. . .], the theme of the natural goodness of man as objectified in benevolence appears in all of Dickens's works, from *The Pickwick Papers* to the alleged "dark" novels, and remains essentially the same throughout.[33]

Parallel with Palmer's argument, James M. Brown in *Dickens: Novelist in the Market-Place,* applies the idea that Dickens's project is to make a case for "good" businesses as those based on "capitalism with a heart":

> In the early novels (as House has pointed out) the representative "bad businessman" tended to be the usurer, who was opposed by the ideal firm, representative of "clean" capitalism, or capitalism with a heart—the small business firm where relations between employer and workers were personal and paternalistic (e.g. the Cheeryble brothers in *Nicholas Nickleby*). In the later novels, however, the representative bad businessman is

the remotely directing capitalist or financier, and the speculator who plays the market. What is interesting is that he is still opposed by the ideal firm in the form of a small independent owner/manager concern, represented in *Little Dorrit* by the firm of Doyce and Clennam, a throwback to an earlier entrepreneurial stage of capitalism.[34]

These arguments are useful in helping us trace the roots of the emphasis on use-value in *Little Dorrit,* and in helping support the idea of a very strong opposition between "business" as practiced by Doyce and business as practiced by Merdle. But they do not help us understand why, if all of the above is true, the "good guys" in *Little Dorrit* need both a *deus ex machina* (Doyce) and the incarnation of perfect goodness (Little Dorrit) to "triumph." Rather, if we remember the Cheerybles, we are struck with the role Casby plays as the oily, ticking, parody-Cheeryble, whose "benevolence" is exposed in a very public spectacle toward the close of the novel. For readers who are reminded of the Cheerybles ("when they are not unpleasant they are tedious," says Humphry House in *The Dickens World* [51]), glee at Casby's ignominious fate prompts a look back that contaminates the remembered image of earlier benevolists, who always seemed too good to be true in any case. In this reading, we could view Casby as Dickens's admission that old-fashioned individual goodness—even the more satisfying, less stilted goodness exhibited by Mr. Pickwick, especially later in *Pickwick Papers*—is simply insufficient to deal with the world of financial capitalism as *Little Dorrit* presents it.

The fabric of the novel itself deepens this impression of the weakness of individual benevolence. Miller's comment about the Victorian novel creating a "little bureaucracy" of its own and Holway's about *Little Dorrit* recreating the Victorian economy make one ask what kind of "statement" the structure of *Little Dorrit* may be making about the question of benevolence vs. the system of financial capitalism. In fact, despite its clear criticism of the system, the novel seems unable to disentangle itself from the cycle of capitalistic enterprise it criticizes. It is embedded in the system, of course, as a money-making project, the proceeds of which were partly devoted to use-value, like groceries for the Dickens family, and partly to accumulation of capital.[35] In the novel itself, we can see this interpenetration and entanglement in the history of Doyce and Clennam, the "good" business in Little Dorrit. Doyce and Clennam *is* a business after all. Doyce makes things, to be sure, but he still exchanges them for money to make more things and thus more money. When he hires Arthur, it is as a partner "who is a man of business, and not guilty of any inventions" (*LD*, 191; bk. I, ch. xvi)—in other words to improve the efficiency and profitability of his business. Doyce's business success inevitably leads to capital accumulation, a problem the novel deals with first by ignoring it, and then by having Arthur speculate the accumulation away, thus eliminating the overhang of accumulated exchange-value in a business presented as devoted to use-value. Doyce, of course, immediately accumulates more capital through his work in Russia, thus re-starting a cycle which, the novel implies, can never finally be ended. While we are invited to view Doyce's intentions as good and his first concern the creation of use-value, even he, in the end, is caught up in a web which appears impossible to untangle. In a quiet, perhaps ironic way, this undermining of the capability of one person with good intentions to change things in any meaningful, systematic way is as powerful a criticism of benevolence as Casby's hypocrisy.

If we as readers feel this dismissal of benevolence, this admission that life can be lived uninfluenced by exchange-value only under limited circumstances, we also participate in it. As Miller points out, we as readers spend real time reading the novel—some hours on various days. And in the course of those hours we too are living within the prison-world Arthur imagines while in the Marshalsea:

> Far aslant across the city, over its jumbled roofs, and through the open
> tracery of its church towers, struck the long bright rays, bars of the
> prison of this lower world. (*LD*, 729; bk. II, ch. xxx)

This image, as many critics have noted, only sums up the innumerable prison motifs woven throughout the fabric of the novel from the jail in Marseilles to the Marshalsea, from Mrs. Clennam frozen in stasis in her house to the frozen travelers "silently assembled in a grated house" atop the Great Saint Bernard, from Mr. Merdle taking himself into custody to Mr. Dorrit imagining himself back in the Marshalsea during his last appearance in "Society." In a sense, it is natural, after all that time in prison, to desire some relief. So when Mr. Dorrit says, "I claim a return," he may also be doubling us, asserting our claim on the novel for a satisfactory ending. If we are, in fact, asserting a claim, as modern readers we are probably asking, first, for something Dickens's readers undoubtedly wanted too—a happy ending. We know, from changes he made to Walter's fate in *Dombey and Son* and from the revised ending to *Great Expectations,* that Dickens was willing and able to take his readers' desires into account when shaping his artistic vision. So he has given us—and his own readers—a "happy" ending in which the characters we care about make an accommodation with the world which seems to promise them acceptable lives going forward.

Dickens's readers probably preferred another claim, too. Humphry House, discussing Bagehot's view, from the early 1850s, of benevolence in Dickens's work, notes that, for Bagehot, the emphasis on benevolence in the novels of the first half of the nineteenth century

> was a temporary phenomenon best explained as a reaction against the harsh and narrow spirit in high places which had been typical of the period immediately succeeding the Napoleonic wars:
> "There was most adequate reason for the sentiment in its origin, and it had a great task to perform in ameliorating harsh customs and repealing dreadful penalties; but it has continued to repine at evils long after they ceased to exist. [. . .] Mr. Dickens is an example both of the proper use and abuse of the sentiment."[36]

House goes on show that Bagehot's criticism of Dickens's benevolence looks less valid "at a hundred years' distance":

> when we can see in better perspective all the complexities of the industrial revolution coming to a head, it is impossible not to find one of the chief causes of the new benevolence in fear. [. . .] Every subscription to a benevolent scheme was in part an insurance premium against a revolution or an epidemic. (49)

Thus Dickens's readers may also have been pressing an additional claim for an ending showing the ultimate triumph of the kind of middle-class values Brown and Palmer have referred to as a reassurance from the fear that individual action and benevolence were no longer possible in a world "dripping, from every pore, with blood and dirt"—in other words, as an anodyne to a psychological state engendered in them by the financial capitalism we have been discussing. And again, Dickens provides what is wanted. It was possible, perhaps, to read Doyce's rescue of Arthur as a signal that a use-value-based life is possible. In that case, Doyce's actions signal that future action to improve society and the lot of humankind is possible, and this reassurance and an exhortation toward individual benevolence become the content of Dickens's "training" project. My own view, however, is that the picture of financial capitalism in *Little Dorrit* is too savage for individual benevolism. For me, Dickens's "training" project in *Little Dorrit* is one of inculcating lower, more realistic expectations about the possibility of living free of the forces we have been discussing, and of urging us to embrace love if we are lucky enough, like Arthur Clennam, to find it.

Chapter Four

"Among the dying and the dead": Metonymy and Finance Capitalism in *Our Mutual Friend*

While several of Dickens's earlier works offer critiques of capitalism, *Our Mutual Friend* (1864–65) plunges beneath the obvious outward representations of the capitalist system to grapple with the process (and the figure) at its heart: metonymy. *Our Mutual Friend*'s foundational figure of speech is metonymy, and its fundamental project is metonymic. That is, the novel seeks to understand and arrest the process by which "value" moves from commodity to commodity, a process which seems, in capitalist society, to operate more or less autonomously. Then, given this understanding, the novel attempts to discover alternatives, ways for humans to choose their destinies in such a society, rather than simply succumbing to capitalism's powerful shape-shifting process.

To explore the novel's highly molecular, fundamental critique of capitalism, I will look first at the figure of metonymy itself. I will argue a connection between metonymy's status as an "accidental" trope based on "contiguity" and the shape-shifting, opportunistic nature of the movement of value between commodities and money in a capitalist economy. With this in mind, I will then attempt to show that the novel's insistent focus on deconstructing capitalism at this elemental level is an outgrowth of its portrayal of a world in which less radical critiques are useless—a world fully and hopelessly commodified, in which even human biology is compromised by the capitalistic process. Finally, I will examine the several responses to the problem of capitalism offered by the novel. I will argue that, despite the endings to the stories of Bella and Eugene, true "redemption" or "conversion" from the toils of capitalism is impossible. However, I will also argue that, finally, the text contains at least a possibility for understanding and conducting life differently. In the end, the text inscribes this possibility on the reader as a legacy or lasting store of potential value, potential meaning, standing outside of and in opposition to the ubiquitous metonymic processes of capitalism.

METONYMY, CONTIGUITY AND MEANING

Modern theoretical discussions of metonymy have stressed its nature as a figure based on contiguity—an "accidental" trope that is more opportunistic and less thoughtful than metaphor. Roman Jakobson provided the foundation for this thinking when he described the "two semantic lines" along which "the development of a discourse may take place":

> one topic may lead to another either through their similarity or through their contiguity. The metaphoric way would be the most appropriate term for the first case and the metonymic way for the second, since they find their most condensed expression in metaphor and metonymy respectively. [. . .] In normal verbal behavior both processes are continually operative, but careful observation will reveal that under the influence of a cultural pattern, personality, and verbal style, preference is given to one of the two processes over the other.[1]

Jakobson does not specifically present metonymy as an inferior figure, but links it with the "preference" of realistic writers:

> Following the path of contiguous relationships, the realist author metonymically digresses from the plot to the atmosphere and from the characters to the setting in space and time. He is fond of synecdochic details. (58)

Thus factors like the "cultural pattern" of the society and the "personality and verbal style" of the author can dictate a preference for contiguity rather than similarity as the motivating force behind the construction of figures in a text.

Paul de Man approaches the topic of metonymy in the context of the relationship between sign and meaning; he notes the influence of semiology in decoupling the meaning of language within a text and the "authority of reference" from outside the text.[2]

With this proposition in mind, de Man goes on to discuss metonymy and metaphor in a passage from Proust's *Swann's Way*. De Man builds on Jakobson's distinction between similarity and contiguity by linking metaphor with "necessity" and metonymy with "chance":

The passage contrasts two ways of evoking the natural experience of summer and unambiguously states its preference for one of these ways over the other: the "necessary link" that unites the buzzing of the flies to the summer makes it a much more effective symbol than the tune heard "perchance" during the summer. The preference is expressed by means of a distinction that corresponds to the difference between metaphor and metonymy, necessity and chance being a legitimate way to distinguish between analogy and contiguity. The inference of identity and totality that is constitutive of metaphor is lacking in the purely relational metonymic contact: an element of truth is involved in taking Achilles for a lion but none in taking Mr. Ford for a motor car. (14)

In his reading of Proust, de Man seems to go beyond Jakobson by emphasizing not only metaphor's difference from metonymy, but also its alleged superiority—its status as a more capable and more stable figure. He notes: "If metonymy is distinguished from metaphor in terms of necessity and contingency (an interpretation of the term that is not illegitimate), then metonymy is per definition unable to create genuine links" (63).

Given these arguments, we can see metonymy as a relational, unstable figure—an opportunistic trope lacking in "identity and totality" and a generator of links based solely on the accident of proximity. One implication of this view is that metonymy is a less reliable figure than metaphor because it is less a product of authorial will than of the pressures of environmental and textual contiguity. Another implication is that metonymy itself, by virtue of its opportunism, possesses a kind of agency within a text—a hungry desire (or perhaps simply what de Man calls "the habit of contiguity") to continue to link random items ad infinitum, regardless of any "transcendental meaning" (66–67). De Man's reading of Proust's passage underlines both the unreliability of metonymy and its "agency" within Proust's text:

The structure is typical of Proust's language throughout the novel. In a passage that abounds in successful and seductive metaphors and which, moreover, explicitly asserts the superior efficacy of metaphor over that of metonymy, persuasion is achieved by a figural play in which the contingent figures of chance masquerade deceptively as figures of necessity. A literal and thematic reading that takes the value assertions of the text at their word would have to favor metaphor over metonymy as a means to satisfy a desire all the more tempting since it is paradoxical: the desire for a secluded reading that satisfies the ethical demands of action more effectively than actual deeds. Such a reading is put into question if one takes the rhetorical structure of the text into account. (67)

The ability of metonymy to "masquerade deceptively" as the more "necessary" figure of metaphor recalls de Man's division between "the technique of form and the substance of meaning." Metonymy, by implication, powerfully and constantly threatens to seep into a text and alter its meaning. Thus de Man's analysis positions metaphor as "an error" in that it "overlooks the fictional, textual element in the nature of the reality it connotes. It assumes a world in which intra- and extra-textual events, literal and figural forms of language, can be distinguished, a world in which the literal and the figural are properties that can be isolated and, consequently, exchanged and substituted for each other. This is an error, although it can be said that no language would be possible without the error" (152). Such a characterization of metaphor, as a figure incapable of grappling with "the fictional, textual element in the nature of [. . .] reality," implies that metonymy, which has no need to distinguish elements as long as they are contiguous, is a figure uniquely fitted to thrive in the modern urban environment—a landscape of densely packed, undifferentiated objects, texts and signs, where the possibilities of making contiguous links are infinite.[3]

Finally, de Man's analysis returns us to the form/meaning polarization with which he began, and highlights the role of metonymy (among other "mechanical" forms) in creating meaning within a text:

> By passing from a paradigmatic structure based on substitution, such as metaphor, to a syntagmatic structure based on contingent association such as metonymy, the mechanical, repetitive aspect of grammatical forms is shown to be operative in a passage that seemed at first sight to be the self-willed and autonomous inventiveness of a subject. Figures are assumed to be inventions, the products of a highly particularized individual talent, whereas no one can claim credit for the programmed pattern of grammar. Yet, our reading of the Proust passage shows that precisely when the highest claims are being made for the unifying power of metaphor, these very images rely in fact on the deceptive use of semi-automatic grammatical patterns. The deconstruction of metaphor and of all rhetorical patterns such as mimesis, paronomasia, or personification that use resemblance as a way to disguise differences, takes us back to the impersonal precision of grammar and of a semiology derived from grammatical patterns. Such a reading puts into question a whole series of concepts that underlie the value judgements of our critical discourse: the metaphors of primacy, of genetic history, and, most notably, of the autonomous power to will of the self. (15–16)

De Man's argument here reinforces the idea of the power of metonymy—a "semi-automatic" grammatical pattern that occurs with "impersonal precision"—especially in a world made up of infinite numbers of contiguous, undifferentiated objects. The implication of metonymy's power to inject meaning (to override the author's "autonomous power to will") is that the critical reader becomes an important arbiter of the text's meaning.

Thus rhetorical theory positions metonymy as an accidental figure based on contiguity; a figure that, by virtue of its reliance on contiguity, possess a form of agency that allows it to shape texts by slipping meaning into them on its own account; and a figure whose action "suspends" meaning and therefore requires the extraction of meaning (at least his or her own) by a critical reader. Such a view of the figure renders the metonymic text, perhaps, a highly likely site for the decoupling of "author" and "meaning" described by Roland Barthes in his essay, "The Death of the Author," where "author" has become "scriptor":

> Linguistically, the author is never more than the instance writing, just as I is nothing other than the instance saying I; language knows a 'subject' not a 'person,' and this subject, empty outside the very enunciation which defines it, suffices to make language 'hold together,' suffices, that is to say, to exhaust it.[4]

Barthes goes on to find the "voice" or meaning in the scriptor's words in the autonomous power of language itself:

> Having buried the Author, the modern scriptor can thus no longer believe, as according to the pathetic view of his predecessors, that this hand is too slow for his thought or passion and that consequently, making a law of necessity, he must emphasize this delay and indefinitely 'polish' his form. For him, on the contrary, the hand, cut off from any voice, borne by a pure gesture of inscription (and not of expression), traces a field without origin—or which, at least, has no other origin than language itself, language which ceaselessly questions all origins. (146)

The power of language may be indisputable, but I would connect it, at this point, with Jakobson's notion of "cultural pattern" and de Man's of "the impersonal precision of grammar"; if language, and not "Dickens the author" is writing *Our Mutual Friend,* we must examine the forces driving language. Without disputing de Man's view of the power of "the programmed pattern of grammar," I would argue that the "patterns" in *Our Mutual Friend* are largely those of capitalism itself—linguistic and cultural patterns and repeating grammatical constructs which mirror and relentlessly enforce capitalism's agenda within the novel and within its author, giving capitalism itself a share in the "authorship" of the novel.

METONYMY AND THE MYSTERY AT THE HEART OF CAPITALISM

Capitalism's power to "author" texts can be seen if we compare the characteristics of metonymy highlighted by de Man and Jakobson with the characteristics of the "metonymy" (the shape-shifting nature of the commodity) at the heart of capitalism—the metonymic elision, concealment and revelation of value we find stressed in Marx's discussion of the commodity. One basis of the constant tendency toward elision in a society based on capitalism, Marx notes, is in the nature of exchange-value itself, as a factor which makes any two things (here a quarter of corn and some hundredweights of iron) reducible to a third (exchange-value) and hence reduces or eliminates the distinctions between things:

> Let us [. . .] take two commodities, for example, corn and iron. Whatever their exchange relation may be, it can always be represented by an equation in which a given quantity of corn is equated to some quantity of iron, for instance, 1 quarter of corn = x cwt. of iron. What does this equation signify? It signifies that a common element of identical magnitude exists in two different things, in 1 quarter of corn and similarly in x cwt. of iron. Both are therefore equal to a third thing, which in itself is neither the one nor the other. Each of them, so far as it is exchange-value, must therefore be reducible to this third thing. [. . .] This common element cannot be a geometrical, physical, chemical, or other natural property of commodities. Such properties come into consideration only to the extent that they make the commodities useful, i.e. turn them into use-values. But, clearly, the exchange relation of commodities is characterized precisely by its abstraction from their use-values. Within the exchange relation, one use-value is worth just as much as another, provided only that it is present in the appropriate quantity. [. . .] As use-values, commodities differ above all in quality, while as exchange-values they can only differ in quantity, and therefore do not contain an atom of use-value. (*Capital*, vol. I, 127–28)

Thus one use-value is "worth just as much as another" in a system where objects are measured or valued only by their exchange-value. Such a system, then, installs a metonymic process based on more or less "accidental" equivalents at the heart of many, if not most, of the transactions between people. Then, when money is introduced, the power of this metonymic system to erase distinctions between objects is multiplied. As I have noted in earlier chapters, the effect of this metonymic process is to turn everything, even people, into objects subject to bargain and sale; moreover, the process is powerful, and seemingly ubiquitous: "Nothing is immune from this alchemy, the bones of the saints cannot withstand it" (*Capital*, vol. 1, 229).

Thus capitalism mirrors the figure metonymy because there is a kind of "opportunistic," "accidental" elision based on exchange-value at its heart; in this sense the figure and the economic system use the same mechanism to produce their outcomes and, by extension, may even be seen as two branches of the same tree—metonymy as rhetorical "capitalism." But this analogy can be extended when we look at Marx's attribution of agency first to commodities then, more significantly, to capital. Marx's comments on the "mystery" of the commodity in his discussion of commodity fetishism set the stage for the proposition that, within the commodity, there is a form of life or agency, where "the products of the human brain appear as autonomous figures endowed with a life of their own, which enter into relations both with each other and with the human race" (*Capital*, vol. 1, 165).[5] This passage casts "the products of the human brain" as "autonomous figures," implying a world in which "authorial will" could easily be thwarted or usurped by meaning created as imaginative products combine of their own accord, just as de Man sees them doing in Proust. This sense of agency grows stronger when Marx extends it to capital which "steps onto the stage—i.e. the market, whether it is the commodity-market, the labour-market, or the money-market—in the shape of money" (*Capital*, vol. 1, 247). What is "alive" within capital, we find, is value:

> In truth, however, value is here the subject of a process in which, while constantly assuming the form in turn of money and commodities, it changes its own magnitude, throws off surplus-value from itself considered as original value, and thus valorizes itself independently. For the movement in the course of which it adds surplus-value is its own movement, its valorization is therefore self-valorization [*Selbstverwertung*]. By virtue of being value, it has acquired the occult ability to add value to itself. It brings forth living offspring, or at least lays golden eggs. (*Capital*, vol. 1, 55)

Here the agency involved in the metonymic process of capitalism takes on the characteristics of an organism "constantly" replicating itself, and doing so quite independently of any human will or intervention. Later, as Marx discusses capital in more detail, this "organism" appears both superhumanly powerful (value as "God the Father" creating "God the Son" in its own image [256]) and cruelly voracious ("ready to trample on all human law" [926]) in pursuit of its aims.

Thus "agency" and "voraciousness" can be added to the "contiguity" of "accidental" elision as characteristics of the capitalist system that mirror the rhetorical system based on metonymy as de Man describes it in Proust. Metonymy, in certain texts appears to function rhetorically the way the "metonymic" process of capitalism functions economically, invading its surroundings and creating combinations of meaning without human intent. This is apparent, as Thomas Richards points out, even in Marx's own text, where the various metaphors used to describe the commodity appear to "go haywire":

> Throughout [*Capital*], Marx develops a number of different metaphors, each of which appears to contradict the others, but all of which turn out to be quite complementary when seen as the constitutive elements of a new semiotics of commodity spectacle. Marx uses three distinct kinds of metaphors to evoke the complexity of commodity relations: metaphors of transcendence, of community, and of sensory experience. [. . .] Taken together, all three kinds of metaphor approach the commodity not simply as a form of exchange but as a powerful and essentially unstable form of representation. (Richards, 68)

Without contradicting Richards's important point on the development of the commodity spectacle, I would note that the variety of Marx's metaphors in the commodity fetishism and other portions of *Capital* is similar in effect to those noted by de Man in Proust: they suggest more than the "complexity of commodity relations." As Richards implies, they are themselves influenced by the power and instability of the commodity itself (the results of the essentially metonymic—"accidental," "contiguous," "voracious"—process inherent in capitalism). Thus even in a text analyzing the metonymic process at the heart of capitalism, the commodity's shape-shifting appears to force recourse to a series of changing metaphors—perhaps accidental, certainly not unified under a single rhetorical conception: capital is an actor on "the stage" (*Capital,* vol I, 247); value is "God the Father" (256); capital will allow its owner to be hanged for "300 percent"(68).

What all this shows, in my view, is that metonymy must be seen as more than a figure when examining texts implicated in capitalist society. As Jakobson suggests, the "cultural pattern" of such a society may allow metonymy to influence the creation of meaning (even the selection of metaphors them-selves) within such a text. In my view, *Our Mutual Friend* is such a text, influenced by such a pattern. The novel overtly attempts to explore and transcend the "metonymic" world created by capitalism, and uses metonymy constantly in its explorations; but the novel and the figures within it are also "independent beings endowed with life," commodities in their own right, with a kind of agency and the ability to create their own meaning. Thus the central position of metonymy within capitalism is matched by its position in this text; it becomes both focus and tool as the novel is "authored" by language which is in turn "authored" by a capitalistic cultural pattern and by tropes that mirror the action of capital itself. If this is true, it removes the kinds of options afforded to "authors" (like Doyce or even Dickens himself) who struggle to find ways to remove their art (and themselves) from the processes of commodification. Instead, the ability of capitalism, via metonymy, to "author" the text forces an author like Dickens to find new ways to separate out and preserve his own value within the text, as I will argue in the conclusion to this chapter.

THE FINANCIAL CONTEXT: AN IRRETRIEVABLY COMMODIFIED WORLD

Our Mutual Friend's critique of capitalism takes place on a more "molecular" and fundamental level than the more "molar" critiques in Dickens's earlier works. At the same time, this novel seems to me to offer the fewest and narrowest "solutions" to the problem of living in a capitalist society. Before considering *Our Mutual Friend*'s critique and solutions, it is worth asking why this novel adopts its more pessimistic stance towards capitalism's power, and towards ways of transcending it. One reason for the novel's stance is reflected in its accurate and acerbic portrayal of the financial world of the 1860s.

"In these times of ours" (13; bk. I, ch. 1), *Our Mutual Friend* presents the Marxian nightmare of a irretrievably commodified world where capital is autonomous, self-referential and self-replicating, and where humans have been all but completely absorbed into an all-encompassing circulation turning everything into money. In earlier works commodification (of children, or women, for example) is presented with an invitation to outrage—as in the near-pornographic fantasies Dickens gives to Arthur Gride, or the sermonizing on Ignorance and Want the Ghost of Christmas Present delivers in *A Christmas Carol*, or the refusal of Daniel Doyce to participate in speculation in *Little Dorrit*. In these works, we are invited, by direct exhortation or by example, to resist the commodification of things, emotionally, and even actively. In *Our Mutual Friend*, however, the "bargain and sale" mentality is pervasive, and, aside from offering constant blasts of irony, the novel appears to have given up on forcing any kind of societal change: dead humans are mere occasions for profit of various kinds; the "market" in orphans is "rigged" when it is discovered the Boffins want one; the only relationship Eugene can conceive of with Lizzie is as a commodity, and her response, like that of a too-often-shocked lab rat, is to "leave the field"—to retreat into the country.

Behind this Marxian nightmare and the novel's reaction to it is the specific financial context within which *Our Mutual Friend* was written, a context in which any hope for a benign or "moral" capitalism, is, at best, remote. As Mary Poovey notes, the 1860s had become a time of dramatically increased, and widely recognized, looseness and opportunism in London financial markets:

> The speculative boom of which these [joint-stock] company flotations [of the late 1850s and early '60s] were a part was fueled by a number of factors in addition to limited liability. Among these were the abandonment of trade restrictions between 1842 and 1860, improved and expanded transport systems both at home and abroad, the increase in "invisible exports" [e.g., services, like shipping, banking, etc.] facilitated by Britain's transportation superiority, and the influx of gold from California and Australia in the 1850s. As confidence grew and knowledge about the financial possibilities available in various parts of the world became more sophisticated, both individuals and banks aggressively sought investment opportunities that could return quick profits and high yields. In London, it even became common practice for some businessmen to borrow money for their regular transactions in order to be able to invest their own resources in potentially lucrative joint-stock companies or foreign loans. A general reluctance developed to keep even small amounts of capital idle. In the words of one modern economic historian, "everybody wanted [capital] to circulate and fructify the ground."[6]

This looseness, the mania for capital growth at any price, and the aggressive disconnection of investment from any purpose other than accumulation, is echoed clearly in Dickens's own *All the Year Round* in the 1860s, particularly in the work of M. L. Meason, a frequent contributor and writer on financial matters.[7] For example, in his 1864 article "Starting the Rio Grande Railway," Meason's narrator explains the attitude toward investing typical of the time:

> In England—on the Stock Exchange and in the open market for shares—speculation has got to such a pace, that it does not care one iota whether an undertaking will eventually pay or not. Who now applies

for shares as an investment? Provided the concern will rise to a premium, who cares what is its eventual fate?[8]

And more troubling than this, perhaps, is another notion repeated in several of Meason's 1864–65 articles: the idea that no capital, or even expertise, is required to set oneself up in the financial business:

> "Capital!" exclaimed the Greek [merchant with whom the narrator is discussing business], "that is what you Englishmen are always talking about, and the craving after it puts you always behind the rest of the world. Give me pen, ink, paper, combined with commercial credit, *and I will never ask for capital.* Capital, my dear sir, *is merely nominal and can be increased to any extent you like, in five minutes.*"[9]

Meason's articles, written as explicit cautionary tales for Dickens's middle-class audience, make the crucial point that the capitalist process Marx describes rested, in fact, on nothing—there was no real capital required, no "barriers to entry," so that anyone could—and did—set himself up in businesses (like the slick new finance companies) which served in the end to enrich their promoters and impoverish everybody else. This is a depiction of the metonymy of capitalism (one value becoming another) dangerously out of control—where contiguity, accident and opportunism allow the unscrupulous to profit, while those who believe profit is linked with investment logic or productive effort receive "nothing."

These ventures, in addition, remind Meason's narrators of nothing so much as the predatory self-interest of carrion-eaters, who survive by finding "value" in the dead. Contemplating the demise of yet another public company, a Meason narrator addresses his readers:

> Who that has been in the East has not often seen high up in the air numerous vultures [. .] hovering round and round in slow circles [. . .] biding their time until [some] creature be really dead to pounce down upon the carcase, and feed and quarrel over all of it that is worth eating. [. . .] As with the vultures, so with the legal advisers. It is the very fighting, which they join and promote amongst themselves, that causes the delay of final settlement, but that very delay brings to the claws of the stronger vulture those tit-bits which, in the case of the dead animal, we should call fat flesh, but to which, in that of the dying company, we give the sweet name of "costs."[10]

Value built on "nothing" can easily turn back into "nothing" for the investors, who have no ability to control the metonymy inherent in capitalism. More significantly, investors' assets are seen as "fat flesh" on which feast the very vultures (solicitors and accountants) who had brought the company to life in the first place; this comparison links biology and paternity with the processes of creating and destroying capital, pessimistically suggesting both a ruthless system and one which is ingrained in the very biology by which we live.[11]

Meason's cynical sentiments on contemporary finance foreshadow the collapse of Overend, Gurney in 1866 (which, though widely expected, created a panic that nearly took the entire City down with it),[12] and parallel the attitude toward "Shares" expressed in the often-quoted passage from *Our Mutual Friend*:

> Have no antecedents, no established character, no cultivation, no ideas, no manners; have Shares. Have Shares enough to be on Boards of Direction in capital letters, oscillate on mysterious business between London and Paris, and be great. (*OMF*, 118; bk. I, ch. x)

Resting on "nothing," such concerns were dangerous enough. But they become more dangerous in a context where their victims understand that they are based on nothing, and still beg to be ruined by them, as the passage below emphasizes:

> O mighty Shares! To set those blaring images so high, and to cause us smaller vermin, as under the influence of henbane or opium, to cry out, night and day, "relieve us of our money, scatter it for us, buy us and sell us, ruin us, only we beseech ye take rank among the powers of the earth, and fatten on us! (118)

Here is finance capitalism in its most fully-developed state. The "henbane or opium" may be thirst for gain, or it may simply be the irrationality of the herd. It really does not matter; capital continues to take its own course, and we are consumed—willingly, the novel says—by a process in which our own biology is suddenly implicated, as "ruin us" turns to "fatten on us!" The sense of inevitability on view in this passage is what differentiates Veneering's putative smash from Merdle's in Little Dorrit: Merdle's smash matters to almost everyone in the novel; he dies as a result and his dead body becomes a cautionary spectacle, a death's head that typifies the inevitable link between capital and death. But *Our Mutual Friend* makes no such effort: Veneering's smash is so inconsequential we are told about it as an aside as his dinner party continues (*OMF*, bk. IV, Chapter The Last), and we cannot imagine him committing suicide over it. We are inured to such things now, the novel seems to say, as we become to casualties in a long-continuing war.

CAPITALISM AND BIOLOGY

Others of Dickens's works, as I have shown in earlier chapters, had covered the teleology of capital in detail. But *Our Mutual Friend* goes further, and in so doing provides another explanation for the pessimistic and limited stance I ascribe to it above. A new factor shaping the novel's nightmarishly pervasive capitalism is its insistence on locating capitalism and capitalistic processes within and around the human body: not only does capital lead to death, the novel tells us, its metonymic processes are inside us as well, truly inescapable. Thus the "meat and drink" the Thames provides Lizzie, according to Gaffer, is derived from the exchange-value of the dead bodies Gaffer fishes out of the river. The same river, as Lizzie grew up around it, would have been an open sewer, and she would have been surrounded by waste which Chadwick and others saw as the bearer of exchange-value in its own right.[13] The dust of the Harmon mounds may or may not have contained human waste, but it certainly contained "ordure" in the form of rotting animal carcasses, animal waste, vegetable matter, and so on—all of which bore exchange-value.

As Catherine Gallagher has noted in "The Bio Economics of *Our Mutual Friend*," the novel is really engaged in an examination of "value" as it uncovers the links between capitalism and human biology. Building on Ruskin's point that "There Is No Wealth But Life,"[14] Gallagher examines the assertion of Malthus, Ruskin and others that true "value" is based on biological usefulness, the biological equivalent of the "toil of the body":

> [C]ritics [of political economy] often accord a privileged position to the commodities that are most easily turned back into flesh. Malthus and Ruskin alike, then, wanted economic exchange to proceed from flesh back to flesh by the least circuitous route: life expended immediately converted into life replenished. [. . . T]he humane critics of political economy imagine the commodity, the bearer of value, as freighted with mortality, as a sign of spent vitality, in order to demand all the more strenuously that it have a vitality-replenishing potential. (Gallagher, "Bio Economics," 351)

However, as Gallagher points out, such "equivalence" opens the door to the shape-shifting Marx describes, and to the ultimate probability of confusion between "biological equivalents," other objects, and the human body itself:

> [I]t is precisely because the "toil of the body" is a universal equivalent determining exchange-value that commodities can acquire abstract value independent of their biological usefulness. The very ability to calculate, through the common measure of labor, the relative values of

commodities led away from a hierarchy of commodities based on ultimate biological usefulness. The labor theory of value could "equate" a
bushel of corn, for example, with a bit of lace, even though, from another physiological point of view, the corn would seem intrinsically
more valuable. (Gallagher, "Bio Economics," 349–51)

This is the problem, this need to locate the true value of the human
being and his or her body amid the constant shape-shifting of capitalistic economic activity, that focuses *Our Mutual Friend*'s investigation of the
metonymy of biology. In her essay, Gallagher goes on to point out the importance of what she calls "life in abeyance [. . .] the condition underlying the
narrative itself. Moreover, especially for those who insist most strenuously on
the flesh and blood origins of economic value, 'life in abeyance' is the definitive condition of commodities and their representation, money" (Gallagher,
"Bio Economics," 357). If this is true, it complicates *Our Mutual Friend*'s critique of capitalism; if in other works it was enough to protest the commodification and sale of human beings, or to offer alternative models for economic
relations, here the novel anatomizes the value that is being shifted, and suggests that true value (life itself) does not inhere only in living beings (like humans), but can be "stored" in commodities themselves. In other words,
commodification itself assumes new moral value, and may be more than simply an evil; such a view places new importance on understanding and gaining
control of the metonymic process by which one value becomes another.
    We can see the intersection of capitalism and biology in microcosm in
the results of Boffin's research into the lives of misers (those personal capitalists whose obsessions receive far more of the novel's attention than those of
the corporate money-men like Veneering do). Boffin's readings, many drawn
from *Merryweather's Lives and Anecdotes of Misers,* yield seemingly endless
equations between money and filth, between people and filth, and people
and money. A common effect of the overlap of biological and economic
processes, we see, is simply the kind of confusion Gallagher's comment identifies: one thing or value becomes another, and can hide itself or be hidden in
another. Thus Merryweather describes Daniel Dancer's "coat of many
colours [. . .] made of pieces of every hue, and fragments of every texture,
collected from the streets or raked out from the dust heaps."[15] Dancer's
wealth itself was immersed in ashes and dung—"stored" there to safeguard it
from theft. Upon Dancer's death, Merryweather reports that the miser's
property went to a Captain Holmes, who was distantly related:

    It took many weeks to explore [Dancer's house's] whole contents; and
    Captain Holmes found it a very agreeable task to dive into the miser's

secret hoards. One of Mr. Dancer's richest escritoires was found to be a
dung heap in the cowhouse; a sum but little short of two thousand five
hundred pound was contained in this rich piece of manure. (Merryweather, 127)

At one level, the prize in the cowhouse is perfectly appropriate as an emblem of a capitalist financial system based on chrematistic accumulation,
the hoarding of exchange-value for its own sake—a situation in which
money is truly no more valuable than dung. But the image is also interesting because it literally mixes money and biological matter, providing an elemental example of a metonymy based on contiguity and challenging us to
identify and separate out the true value—something that the miser (or
Marx's "rational miser," the capitalist) is unable to do.

This overlap of biology and economics in Merryweather becomes more
pointed in situations where we are implicated through our own biology in
the metonymy confronting us. For example, Dancer would usually buy
spoiled meat or even pick up dead animals with which to supplement his
diet. Merryweather comments:

Daniel used to observe [when hot weather further damaged the "coarse
beef" he and his sister ate every week] that those who were devoted to
saving, should feel satisfaction at these circumstances; for if [decomposi-
tion] did not improve the flavour of the meat, it rendered it more eco-
nomical, because a less quantity proved sufficient; and, as none could be
wasted, it lasted all the longer. (Merryweather, 115)

Dancer, who cannot tell the difference between money and filth, here cannot
tell the difference between filth and food—money, the great leveller, obliter-
ates even these elemental distinctions within a presumably hungry man.
Later, when his sister is dying, we see that Dancer can no longer tell the difference between life itself and the money/filth he has been accumulating:

It was during the last illness which terminated his sister's life, that he
was importuned to afford her some medical advice and assistance; to
which he shrewdly replied, "It would cost him money, and besides,"
continued he, "why should I waste my money in wickedly and wan-
tonly trying to oppose the will of God! If a girl has come to her latter
end, nothing can save her, and all I may do will only tend to make me
lose my money; and she may as well die now as at any other time. If I
thought bleeding would recover her, I would open a vein myself; but I
cannot think of paying for physic for dying people." The dread of incur-
ring expence, and parting with his darling coin, was insurmountable.

> Mr. Dancer's reasoning on the conduct of Providence, ever tended to-
> ward his favourite penchant—"Save money." (Merryweather, 118)

Here Dancer confronts the problem of finding the true value in a capitalistic
metonymy where "value" has changed form; he addresses this problem
thoughtlessly—as a single-minded accumulator of exchange-value. Ironically,
he cannot see that his own biological substance is part of the value-chain he is
examining, and that his own life itself is the very value he is denying.

Dancer's story drives home the point that we are, biologically, implicated in the capitalist system. This implication puts us in jeopardy of being
fish who must define water as we try to find alternatives to the forces of
money, accumulation and exchange-value, but it also makes it more essential for us to do so, since we no longer stand outside the system.[16] In *Our
Mutual Friend*, the only way John Harmon can discover and liberate the
real value (in Ruskin's terms) of the Harmon fortune is to immerse himself
in the biological medium of the filthy river;[17] this immersion figures a need
to come to terms with his own position as a commodity within the
metonymic processes swirling around him before he can discover true
"value" for (and in) himself. To define value successfully, therefore, Harmon and we as readers need to understand the metonymic processes we are
surrounded with and subject to.

THE USES OF METONYMY IN *OUR MUTUAL FRIEND*

As an "opportunistic" trope, metonymy needs contiguity—things densely
packed together, touching and overlapping each other—to create meaning.
Any Dickens novel is filled with such contiguity, but *Our Mutual Friend*,
with the dust heaps—vast masses of contiguous objects in the process of elid-
ing from one form to another—as one of its central images, is even more
densely packed. J. Hillis Miller notes

> [In *Our Mutual Friend*, t]he environments of [the] characters have a
> crowded, built-up quality. The characters are slowly fabricating a thick
> texture of humanized things around themselves, as, for example, Mr.
> Venus is surrounded by the products of his craft, the bones which he has
> been articulating piece by piece with the care of a jeweler. But his shop
> is not static and complete. It is in process[.][18]

In Miller's view, this extremely packed world functions both as a means of
communication and as a metaphor for the "intersubjectivity" of the world
(288); he characterizes the world of the novel as "a non-Euclidean space in

that it is a plurality of worlds rather than a single world" (291), and he emphasizes the essentially formless nature of this world:

> Whereas *Bleak House* in the end put an apparently dispersed world back together, *Our Mutual Friend* remains true to its rejection of the idea that there is an ideal unity of the world transcending the differences between individual lives, and perceptible from the outside by Providence or by the omniscient eye of the narrator. (291)

In his argument, Miller sees this formless, "humanized" world of objects as the milieu one must transcend to achieve true value, and discusses various forms of "death" (Riah's rooftop, Eugene's baptismal plunge into the river, etc.) as means of transformation:

> [The characters'] near-death permits a transformation of [their] situation, not an escape from it, or a total rejection of it. It is a liberation from the absurdity, the coerciveness of that situation, a liberation which allows their former lives to begin again. But now, rather than being made by their situations, such characters make their places in the world and give them value. (325)

Miller's description of the world of *Our Mutual Friend* and its moral emptiness is helpful, but in my view his ultimate argument for "transformation" ignores some important implications of the landscape he has described. First, the "objects" in the world Miller describes are not merely lifeless extensions or creations of the novel's characters, but commodities with the life and "mystery" Marx describes inherent in their natures. Also, this is a world whose mainspring is metonymy, a figure with agency and a voracious appetite for imposing its own meaning. In such a world, the kind of "transcendence" any character can achieve must either take these complexities into account, or somehow overcome them. As I will argue later in this chapter, neither the characters nor the various "authors" who attempt to enact or depict forms of salvation from or transcendence of this world are able to do so with complete effectiveness: totalizing "transformational" change cannot occur in the novel (although, in my view, it does not leave the reader in complete despair either).

Analysis of one set-piece, the description of Mr. Venus's shop in book I, chapter vii, will enable us to see the constant reliance on metonymy as a way of presenting reality in *Our Mutual Friend*, and the uses to which the figure is put. It is true that commodification of the living body—the ultimate reduction of life to salable objects and a Marxian nightmare identical with "the capitalized blood of children" (*Capital*, vol. I, 920)—appears universal and inescapable in Venus's world. "How have I been going on, this long time?" Wegg asks Venus matter-of-factly as if *he* were stored in the shop rather than his leg, and as if there were nothing out of the ordinary in this. And Venus's inventory of his stock includes enough formerly living things to stock a natural history museum:

> "Bones, various. Skulls, various. Preserved Indian baby. African, ditto. [. . .] Everything within reach of our hand, in good preservation.
>
> [. . .] What's in those hampers over them again, I don't remember. Say, human warious. Cats. Articulated English baby. Dogs. Ducks. Glass eyes, various. Mummified bird. Dried cuticle, various. Oh, dear me! That's the general panoramic view." (*OMF*, 86–88; bk. I, ch. vii)

But commodification here is balanced between life and death, as if the novel has suspended the metonymy in mid-process, isolated the living value that is being transferred, and frozen that value in time. We can see this clearly when Wegg leaves the shop:

> As he pulls the door open by the strap, [he] notices that the movement so shakes the crazy shop, and so shakes a momentary flare out of the candle, as that the babies—Hindoo, African, and British—the "human warious," the French gentleman, the green glass-eyed cats, the dogs, the ducks, and all the rest of the collection, show for an instant as if para-lytically animated; while even poor little Cock Robin at Mr. Venus's elbow turns over on his innocent side. (*OMF*, 91; bk. I, ch. vii)

Thus stored-up life bursts out. We see that in Venus's shop the figure of metonymy is recognized as the central process of a commodified world and is made the practice ("my art") of the shop and the practitioners within it. Venus and his assistant arrest and shape metonymy; their practice involves both isolating the "value" inherent in things and shaping or directing the process by which one object changes into something else. In the shop, for ex-ample, a pile of "warious" bones, rather than decomposing, becomes a skele-ton, which has value both in money terms and as a teaching tool. If, as Catherine Gallagher has said, the commodity is "life in abeyance,"[19] in Venus's shop the mechanism of the commodity—metonymy—is disassem-bled, experimented with and, in a sense, subverted.

We can see this deconstruction of the nature of the commodity before Wegg even arrives at Venus's shop. In the street, the stage is set with a brief exposition of the dynamics of economic value:

Not, however, towards the [jewelers'] "shops" where cunning artificers
work in pearls and diamonds and gold and silver, making their hands so
rich, that the enriched water in which they wash them is bought for the
refiners;—not towards these does Mr. Wegg stump, but towards the
poorer shops of small retail trades in commodities to eat and drink and
keep folks warm. (*OMF,* 83; bk. I: ch. vii)

As an introduction to Venus's world, this brief passage sounds a complex
keynote: there is the expected duality of exchange-value ("gold and silver")
vs. use-value ("commodities to eat and drink and keep folks warm"), but the
exchange-value here is ground into human hands, and suspended in water—
visible, identifiable, and blended, as it were, with human biology.

Then, in Venus's shop window Wegg is confronted by a bizarre version
of the shop-window spectacle, a parodic version of spectacles like that in
"Meditations in Monmouth Street," where clothes metonymically assume
the attributes of former owners.[20] But here, the objects on view engage in a
more elemental metonymy:

a tallow-candle dimly burning [. . .] surrounded by a muddle of objects
vaguely resembling pieces of old leather and dry stick, but among which
nothing is resolvable into anything distinct, save the candle itself in its
old tin candle-stick, and two preserved frogs fighting a small-sword
duel. (*OMF,* 83; bk. I, ch. vii)

The spectacle interpellates us, but what we are being called upon to desire is
not immediately clear. Inside, we get a clue, as the contents of the shop begin
to emerge from the shadows:

Mr. Wegg gradually acquires an imperfect notion that over against him
on the chimney piece is a Hindoo baby in a bottle, curved up with his
big head tucked under him, as though he would instantly throw a sum-
mersault if the bottle were large enough. (84)

Perhaps at this point the shop window's interpellation becomes clearer: we
are being shown that, even in "old leather and dry stick" life may inhere, just
as death may inhere in the lifelike frogs or in "pretty" and "innocent" Cock
Robin, and we are being called upon to recognize and deal with the slipperiness of life itself—to accept that metonymy is the foundation of the situation
we find ourselves in, and to examine our options.

Clearly, some of these options revolve around the hopefulness inherent
in the emergence of life from the dead "old leather and dry stick" world of

the commodity. As the scene continues, this metonymic emergence of life from death is explored, and even parodied. The "French gentleman" is represented only by his ribs, but is referred to as if he were really present. Although "Cock Robin," the "pretty little dead bird" on the counter is actually dead, it moves. Later, Venus presents the boy's "stuffed canary" as if there were really no gap between its "dead" state and true life:" There [. . .] There's animation! On a twig, making up his mind to hop!" (*OMF,* 86; bk. I, ch. vii). But the scene is also careful to emphasize that the metonymic process can work in reverse as well: the boy himself is reminded of the fungibility of his own position when Venus informs him how easily his own "value" could be removed and "stored": "You have no idea how small you'd come out, if I had the articulating of you" (86).

Finally, while the passage literally deals with life and death, its tone is comic, even parodic, with Venus as a near-sighted, dusty "god" (of life and love) who provides "paralytic" animation which itself is a mere parody of real life, just as his thwarted love for Pleasant Riderhood parodies the "real" love of Rokesmith and Bella. Here the novel turns on us, the subjects it has interpellated, to remind us again of our situation: we are surrounded by the elision, the slipperiness inherent in a commodified world, but do not understand it. We are unable to penetrate the mystery of the commodity and therefore we are deluded even when we want to do what is morally right; our situation is both tragic and ridiculous. Thus the novel's central question is whether we human beings—or some of us at least—have the potential to find our way out of the mess we are in: to take control of the metonymy that surrounds us, so to speak, to discern true value and choose it, instead of the death inherent in a society dominated by capital.

"SOLUTIONS" TO THE PROBLEM OF FINANCE CAPITALISM: BELLA'S REDEMPTION

Our Mutual Friend posits a state of liberation from the capitalistic world of the commodity, as we see when Jenny Wren describes the sense of being "dead" on Riah's rooftop:

> "Oh, so tranquil!," cried the little creature, smiling. "Oh, so peaceful and so thankful! And you hear the people who are alive, crying, and working, and calling to one another down in those dark streets, and you seem to pity them so! And such a chain has fallen from you." (*OMF,* 279; bk. II, ch. v)

This state implies a distance from the metonymic world of the commodity, and Jenny's description of the clouds demonstrates the ability to see beyond what Hillis Miller calls the "human" to something more transcendent. Yet even for Jenny this "dead" state is transitory. While admitting a state of liberation from capitalistic processes is possible, at least for some, the novel still faces the problem, given its intensive and uncompromising portrayal of a fully-commodified society, of getting certain characters into that state and keeping them there—of "saving" them. *Our Mutual Friend* overtly offers two variants on this theme, both driven by different responses to the need for "redemption," and neither fully able to counter the strength of the portrayal of the moral and social impact of capitalism the novel presents.

The first variant is Bella's redemption, brought about by the machinations of Rokesmith and the Boffins. Rokesmith's "story" or script involves "proving" Bella, who at first appears to him as likely to "love me for my own sake, as she would love the beggar at the corner" (*OMF*, 366–67; bk. II, ch. xiii). As the plot develops, Bella is subject to substantial "reeducation" via the misers and Boffin's re-enactment of their accumulative obsessions, allowing her to look inside the metonymy and observe the change taking place. For example, in book III Bella is made to witness, in real time, the metonymy which turns a man into a commodity, as Boffin humiliatingly "values" Rokesmith: "A sheep is worth so much in the market, and I ought to give it and no more. A secretary is worth so much in the market and I ought to give it and no more" (*OMF*, 457; bk. III, ch. v). Afterwards, Boffin tries to draw Bella herself into the metonymy: "[Y]ou have no call to be told how to value yourself. [. . .] You are right. Go in for money, my love. Money's the article. You'll make money of your good looks, and of the money Mrs. Boffin and me will have the pleasure of settling upon you, and you'll live and die rich" (*OMF*, 459–60; bk. III, ch. 5).

The lessons work. Bella passes part of her "test" when she renounces Boffin's money. When she says, "I must go home for good," Boffin warns:

"Don't do what you cannot undo; don't do what you're sure to be sorry for. [. . .] You mustn't expect [. . .] that I'm a-going to settle money on you, if you leave us like this, because I am not. No, Bella! Be careful! Not one brass farthing."

"Expect!" said Bella, haughtily. "Do you think that any power on earth could make me take it if you did, sir?" (*OMF*, 587; bk. III, ch. xv)

The lessons work, in part, because Bella is made to see and feel the difference between a "patient, sympathetic, genial, fresh young heart" like her father's

(*OMF,* 454; bk. III, ch. iv), and the combination of obsessive accumulation and paranoia enacted by Boffin in his feigned transformation. But Bella, as we see through her relationship with her father, and her instant rapport with Lizzie, also possesses a core of innate goodness.

Bella's goodness blossoms when she is married to Rokesmith, and she seems quite content with the hundred pounds a year he tells her he's earning. But at this point, Rokesmith's project seems to mutate—to go beyond converting Bella from the ethic of exchange-value to something else: the perfect wife. Rokesmith tells her, "[Y]ou will undergo a trial through which you will never pass quite triumphantly for me, unless you can put perfect faith in me" (*OMF,* 726; bk. IV, ch. xi), and he postpones telling Bella the truth even after she has turned from chrematistics to the "economics" of *The Complete British Family Housewife* in order "to triumph beyond what we ever thought possible" (*OMF,* 753; bk. IV, ch. xiii). Part of this "triumph" is to turn Bella into "the bright light of the house"—to drive the marketplace out of the house, and replace it with a Patmorian "angel."[21] But Rokesmith's real "triumph" is the assertion of control over Bella, the female, by Rokesmith and Boffin, the males, and their supporter, Mrs. Boffin: as a female interested in money, Bella must be brought into line; as a sexual being, she must be regulated as well ("And if I had been inclined to be jealous, I don't know what I mightn't have done to you," Mrs. Boffin tells her [*OMF,* 752–53; bk. IV, ch. xiii]). In effect, Bella herself becomes the commodity Boffin's multiple references to her as "true golden gold" imply, and though Rokesmith's stated goal is to liberate himself and her from the power of old Harmon's money "to spoil people" (754), he is really engaged, in this struggle for her soul, in a struggle to reshape and possess her as a piece of ("economic," in terms of the orderly use of wealth in the home) property.

Bella's redemption is further undercut because it is "panoptic"—both untrusting and coercive, much more obsessively capitalistic than loving in its underpinnings.[22] Although his project is couched as a "pious fraud," Rokesmith insistently requires proof that Bella is indeed the "true golden gold," and he and the Boffins observe Bella continually, meeting each night to "debrief" her progress: "But every night he says to me, 'Better and better, old lady. What did we say of her? She'll come though it, the true golden gold'" (*OMF,* 753; bk. IV, ch. xiii). But the redemption here may also be undercut by Dickens's own struggles to deal with the questions Jeff Nunokawa raises about the vulnerability of home and hearth to capitalistic forces, and the struggle of the Victorian male to "own" the female without putting her "on the market" as another commodity. It is tempting, certainly, to try to link the novel's "management" of Bella with Dickens's own position as "manager" of his complicated life—especially of his relationship with Ellen Ternan. In *The Invisible Woman,* Claire Tomalin describes a Dickens clearly exhibiting the kind of obsessional nature we have found in capitalistic accumulation, and beset by the need to "manage" his relationship with Ellen—to avoid scandal and any possible damage to what he sometimes referred to as "the property," his earning power:

> What [Dickens's pocket-diary of 1867] reveals with perfect clarity is a
> man intent on a split life; a man almost demented in his determined
> pursuit of it, despite the exhaustion and illness we know of from his let-
> ters and the reports of friends. [. . .] The difficulty for Dickens was
> [. . .] that he had picked the wrong sort of woman to be his second
> 'wife.' [Unlike the mistresses of Wilkie Collins or W. P. Frith], s]he was
> neither a modest girl of the people nor a grateful widow. If she had
> given up her professional ambitions, she still had social ones, and she
> was backed by an intelligent, aspiring and watchful family.[23]

In this context, certainly, Bella's redemption (and with it Rokesmith's "escape" from the capitalistic matrix in which he is trapped as the novel begins) may be the last in a line of wished-for resolutions to the problems posed by financial capitalism: in fact, Boffin's "trotting" and benevolence may remind us of the Cheerybles, and Bella's "doll's house" of the walled garden within which Nicholas and Kate Nickleby retire. But the waters here, as in *Our Mutual Friend* in general, are too turbulent. The society the novel depicts, seemingly hopelessly implicated in capitalism, is unlikely to leave Rokesmith and Bella undisturbed, and the deeply conflictive pressure Dickens/Rokesmith is under in the relationship with Ellen/Bella (how to possess a woman while still shutting commodification and the marketplace out of the relationship), is too powerful for this "escape" to be fully convincing.

"SOLUTIONS" TO THE PROBLEMS OF FINANCE CAPITALISM: EUGENE'S REDEMPTION

Eugene's redemption, while also undercut, is more powerful because it is grounded in the imagery and biological themes which mark the novel. Like Rokesmith's, Eugene's "plunge" out of the commodified world is a physical one, into the financial and biological medium of the river. Lizzie recovers him for his true value—his life and his potential as a lover and husband—in a reverse parody that sets right Gaffer's recoveries of (exchange) value from the river. In addition, Eugene's redemption is a *literal* metonymy—a synecdochic change from vibrant young man to near corpse. First, Bradley's vicious attack literally changes Eugene's body:

> He turned under the blows that were blinding him and mashing his life
> [. . .] Eugene was light, active, and expert; but his arms were broken, or
> he was paralyzed, and he could do nothing more than hang on to the
> man.

When Lizzie finally examines Eugene's body, it is "insensible, if not virtually dead; it [is] mutilated, and streak[s] the water all about it with dark red streaks" (*OMF,* 682, 683–84; bk. IV, ch. vi). Here we see Eugene's body resolving itself back into the biological matter ("mashed [. . .] broken [. . .] red streaks") from which it was made. Eugene's vision changes, too:

> In an instant, with a dreadful crash, the reflected night turned crooked,
> flames shot jaggedly across the air, and the moon and stars came bursting from the sky [. . .] he caught [the attacker] by a red handkerchief—
> unless the raining down of his own blood gave it that hue (682).

And even Eugene's language—delivery system for his ready wit—is "mashed" and his utterances reduced to elemental, obsessive repetition during this metonymy, as the word "Lizzie" seems to contain all his hopes and fears.

The attack renders Eugene another person: his face is "so much disfigured that his mother might have covered it" (684). And it places him firmly in the borderland between life and death as the doctor pronounces, "it is much to be feared that [Lizzie] has set her heart upon the dead" (685). Eugene stays in this borderland for days, suspended in the metonymy he is undergoing, and, like Rokesmith, dissolving his worldly identity ("no spirit of Eugene was in Eugene's outer form"; his expression is "so evanescent that it was like a shape made in water" [*OMF,* 717; bk. IV, ch. x]). That in so doing he seems to gain some perspective on what true value means is evident when he calls for Jenny, disfigured herself and possessor of changed vision, who acts as "an interpreter between this sentient world and the insensible man" (*OMF,* 720). This "drowning man" is brought back, reborn with Jenny's help, to marry Lizzie, "that [his] reparation may be complete," and to carry out "the right course of the true man," as Mortimer tells him *OMF,* 722–23; bk. IV, ch. x). Thus Eugene's conversion figures both Christian baptism and the expiation of sins through penance or Purgatory. It compensates for the perverted "baptism" of the dead Gaffer ("Was it you, thus baptized unto Death, with these flying impurities now flung upon your face?"; 175; bk. I, ch. xiv)[24]; it also enacts a "transaction" in which true value is received at great personal cost, thus providing a corrective reverse parody of the financial transactions based on nothing typified by Veneering, by Riderhood's hypocritical "sweat of an honest man's brow," and by Fledgeby's friends, "always coming and going across the Channel, on errands about the Bourse, and Greek and Spanish and Indian and Mexican, and par and premium and discount and three quarters and seven eighths" (*OMF,* 260; bk. II, ch. iv).

But the value of Eugene's conversion as a "solution" or alternative to capitalism is limited, too, in ways that mirror Dickens's life-long struggle with this question. At one level, Eugene's conversion is as suspect as any death-bed turn toward morality, especially in light of his inability to do the right thing (i.e., abandon his attempt to possess Lizzie) in the very instant before the attack. Further, Eugene's conversion, mirroring the resolution of *Little Dorrit*, is purely private, and thus limited in its effects; aside from the momentary surprise at Veneering's table, society, the novel says somewhat wearily, will continue on its own entropic way no matter what Eugene and Lizzie do.

More significantly, perhaps, Eugene's conversion is undercut because it is, in a sense, as coercive as Bella's—as unable to disengage from the processes inherent in capitalism as hers is. Eugene, at the start of the novel, is a footloose, unmarried wastrel with one deep relationship—a homosocial one with Mortimer, his lifelong friend and "double"; thus, Eugene is a dangerously loose cannon in a society where social control over money and sexual matters is paramount. Sedgwick notes:

> In the violence at the end of the novel, we see the implacability with which [. . .] heterosexual, homophobic meaning is impressed on Eugene's narrative: Bradley, his rival, nearly kills him by drowning; Lizzie saves him; while he seems to be dying, Mortimer interprets his last wishes as being that he might marry Lizzie; and when he comes back to life, he is already a married man. (Sedgwick, p. 177)

Thus the true conversion here might be back to mainstream middle-class values, to the middle-class morality. In that sphere, Eugene's unmarried, homosocial existence, along with Lizzie's "masculine" skill and control in the reservoir of value (the "marketplace") that is the river, might together embody an urgent threat that can only be mitigated by requiring Eugene to marry Lizzie—to heterosexualize him and "femininize" her (Sedgwick, 177). This societal coercion mirrors Rokesmith's control over Bella, and signals the difficulty of any moral change when the subject is embedded in a developed, complex and powerful society; in this sense, the coercion here lowers but does not eliminate the value of the change in Eugene, who, after all, has paid in real currency (even if his financial situation is mitigated later on by MRF) for his capitalist sins.

The final, and probably most meaningful, undercutting of Eugene's conversion as a solution to the problems of living in a capitalist society is related to Dickens himself—his practice as a producer of commodity products, his view of the question of "value" in the real world he inhabited, and his own body and biology. Although Dickens was long out of the financial distress that had plagued him in his early career,[25] the obsession with earning had never left him; obsessive concern with money drove him to begin reading for money, and was at least a partial factor behind the self-destructive reading tours he undertook in his last years. And *Our Mutual Friend,* the project of which was a deep questioning of the core of capitalism, was also a deeply commercial venture brought into being by a businessman who knew he was at the height of his considerable powers, as we can see in his letter of 8 September 1863, proposing the novel to Chapman & Hall:

> In reference to a new work in 20 monthly Nos. as of old, I have carefully considered past figures and future reasonable probabilities. You have the means of doing the like in the main, and no doubt will do so before replying to this letter. I propose to you to pay me £ 6000 for the half copyright throughout and outright, at the times mentioned in your last letter to me on the subject. For that consideration I am ready to enter into articles of agreement with you securing to you the publication of the work when I shall be ready to begin publishing, and the half share. [. . .] Of course you will understand that I do not press you to give the sum I have here mentioned, and that you will not in the least inconvenience or offend me by preferring to leave me to make other arrangements. If you should have any misgiving on this head, let my assurance that you need have none, set it at rest.[26]

This understated ultimatum is about power and who "owns" the business venture between Dickens and Chapman & Hall. Dickens's terms were accepted by the firm, which never lost by its association with him, and certainly we do not see in Dickens the businessman the gouging of a Ralph or a Fledgeby, nor the "accumulate at any cost" mentality of a Daniel Dancer or a "Vulture" Hopkins. But what we do see is an unsentimental entrepreneur with an undeviating, watchful eye on, and an obsessive concern for, his own interests—someone pretty far from the "patient, sympathetic, genial, fresh young heart" that had such an influence on Bella.

Such a businessman, also an artist with strong moral objections to capitalism's excesses, was bound to feel the pressure, the cognitive dissonance, of holding two perhaps irreconcilable positions. This would have been especially true of a man like Dickens who could put such pressure on himself in any case. Such radical duality undercuts, or at least tempers, the solidity of Eugene's conversion as Dickens's "solution" to the problems of capitalism.

Again, the conversion probably is most effective as an embodied wish that, given sufficient payment in suffering, one could be rewarded with true value, and in the process "pay for" one's own errors—a sincere and highly personal wish to be saved from the hell of a world dominated by commodification and accumulation. But the dualism embodied in Dickens and in society makes this wish impossible. Even within the wish for salvation, the capitalistic sense of "bargain and sale" creeps into the formulation: If I suffer enough, I can "pay for" my sins, or "win" salvation. "You ask her to kneel at this bedside and be married to you, that your reparation may be complete," Mortimer says to Eugene, proposing the bargain; "Yes. God bless you! Yes," replies Eugene, confirming the sale (*OMF,* 722; bk. IV, ch. x). Capital, the "author," continues to write on despite Dickens's best efforts, and capitalism's influence is found even inside the moment of salvation.

INTO THE TEXT

Thus the novel presents a world where "conversion" or wholesale "redemption" seems impossible, and where even the success of the kind of limited "escape" made by Clennam and Little Dorrit appears doubtful at best. Moreover, the novel's almost obsessive doubling of Dickens and various characters functioning as "authors"[27] problematizes his own position with regard to transcending capitalism. Dickens the artist-businessman, in fact, faced a seemingly irreconcilable internal divide. In the novel such split natures (Rokesmith's, Eugene's, Bella's) are healed by immersion and reemergence: Rokesmith submerges himself in his own fiction; Eugene nearly dies in the Thames; Bella is submerged in uncertainty.[28] But such redemption is imperfect, as we have seen, implicated in the processes and repetitive constructs of capitalism and its language. It would seem there is no escape from the dilemma of the artist who would attempt to find alternatives to capitalism while living in a capitalist world—no opportunity for such an artist to arrest the metonymy singlemindedly turning his or her works into commodities equal to such and such an amount of money, such a number of shoes or iron bars, and no more. *Our Mutual Friend,* in my view, never discovers such an escape. But the novel does not end in complete despair, either. Instead, it considers art's role in creating and preserving the possibility of a different kind of life, a possibility capable of standing outside of and in opposition to the metonymic processes of capitalism.

To understand this, we need to look at the novel's "Postscript," in which Dickens describes part of his experience in the railway disaster at Staplehurst:

On Friday the Ninth of June in the present year [1865], Mr. and Mrs. Boffin (in their manuscript dress of receiving Mr. and Mrs. Lammle at

breakfast) were on the South Eastern Railway with me, in a terribly destructive accident. When I had done what I could to help others, I
climbed back into my carriage—nearly turned over a viaduct, and
caught aslant upon the turn—to extricate the worthy couple. They were
much soiled but otherwise unhurt. [. . .] I remember with devout
thankfulness that I can never be much nearer parting company with my
readers for ever, than I was then, until there shall be written against my
life, the two words with which I have this day closed this book:—THE
END. (*OMF,* 799–800)

Of this passage, Catherine Gallagher comments, "The author heroically risks
his life to deliver his manuscript in this passage and then apparently dies into
that commodity, where he remains immortally suspended" (Gallagher, "Bio
Economics," 364). Gallagher's ironic reference to heroism points up the notion that there is more than art at stake in this situation. Is this the artist risking his life for his art, or the producer of a lucrative commodity text risking
his life to rescue an important quantity of exchange-value?[29] Undoubtedly
both, in a divided Dickens. The presence of both the "artist" and the "author" at this particular scene, in fact, allows us to see Dickens observing and
analyzing at first hand the metonymic process his novel has been so concerned with—thus Staplehurst provides a kind of "thought experiment"
(what does the creator of metonymy do when taken by the throat by
metonymy?) that may define Dickens's view of the true path to whatever
transcendence of capitalism is possible. To test this hypothesis, we should examine Staplehurst and its impact on Dickens in more detail.

First of all, Staplehurst was a horrific railway accident. Dickens was
travelling with Ellen Ternan and had in his possession the manuscript for the
August 1865 number (xvi) of *Our Mutual Friend.* The accident affected
Dickens strongly—it was a trauma from which he never fully recovered. On
13 June 1865, Dickens wrote an account of his experience to Thomas Mitton, his solicitor:

I got into the carriage again for my brandy flask, took off my traveling
hat for a basin, climbed down the brickwork and filled my hat with
water. Suddenly I came upon a staggering man covered with blood (I
think he must have been flung clean out of his carriage) with such a
frightful cut across the skull that I couldn't bear to look at him. I poured
some water over his face, and gave him some to drink, and gave him
some brandy, and laid him on the grass, and he said "I am gone" and
died afterwards. Then I stumbled over a lady lying on her back against a
little pollard tree, with the blood streaming from her face (which was
lead color) in a number of distinct little streams from her head. I asked

her if she could swallow a little brandy, and she just nodded, and I gave
her some and left her for somebody else. The next time I passed her, she
was dead.[30]

The sense of being among the dying as they become the dead is repeated in other letters, like that of 18 June 1865, to Mrs. Hulkes:

As I ran back to the carriage for [additional brandy he had in is lug-
gage], I saw the first two people I had helped, lying dead. A bit of shade
from the hot sun, into which we got the unhurt ladies, soon had as
many dead in it as living. (Pilgrim *Letters,* vol. XI: 62)

Dickens the exemplar of active, even heroic, humanitarianism is comple-
mented here by Dickens the acute observer—the novelist pressed into service
in an emergency. But the letter also reveals a preoccupation with the change
from life to death ("I am gone") and with the interval during which this
metonymy occurs ("The next time I passed her, she was dead"; "soon [. . .]
as many dead [. . .] as living"). This preoccupation with being *among* the
dying as they become the dead is the primary burden of the many letters and
notes Dickens sent following the accident. He worked "for hours among the
dying and the dead," as he wrote to Forster the day after the accident (Pilgrim *Letters,* vol. XI: 50); to Miss Burdett Coutts and Mrs. Brown he writes,
"I worked hard afterwards among the dead and the dying, and it is that
shock—not the shock of the stumbling carriage, which was nothing—that I
feel a little. I could not have imagined so appalling a scene" (11 June 1865;
Pilgrim *Letters,* vol. XI: 51).

In fact, the mental and emotional trauma of this work among the
dead and dying appears to have been severe: the same point—the impact of
the "terrible" experience of the aftermath of the accident, versus the effects
of the accident itself, recurs in almost every letter he wrote (and those taken
down for him by Georgina Hogarth, in which letters there truly is no "I,"
as Barthes might have pointed out) on the subject of Staplehurst.[31] These
texts render the metonymy at the heart of *Our Mutual Friend* a figuration
of a directly-observed fundamental life-process, rather than simply a
rhetorical device. Here, the author describes metonymy in action: Dickens's
hat becomes a basin; he retrieves water which happens to be nearby; he encounters people at random; living people suddenly become dead bodies.
These observations figure the figure of metonymy itself. This figuration becomes a warning that the potential for the "accidental," "contiguous" nature of the modern world obscures and ultimately destroys true value. But
it also suggests that metonymy as a process can be observed, understood

and, momentarily, halted—implying the possibility, at least, that value may somehow be isolated and preserved despite the metonymic processes inherent in the capitalist world.

The impact of the accident on Dickens appeared in an additional way as well, and one that also relates to his role as author of (and "author" within) *Our Mutual Friend.* Late in June 1865 Dickens wrote to Forster,

> I am getting right, though still low in pulse and very nervous. Driving into Rochester yesterday I felt more shaken than I have since the accident. I cannot bear railway travelling yet. A perfect conviction, against the senses, that the carriage is down on one side (and generally that is the left, and not the side on which the carriage really went over), comes upon me with anything like speed, and is inexpressibly distressing. (Pilgrim *Letters,* vol. XI: 65)

Here we see Dickens's own body drawn into the matrix of emotions and imagination surrounding the accident. Again, we see this text reflecting in personal terms the preoccupation of *Our Mutual Friend* with metonymy and the physical body—the accident was writing on Dickens's physical body the way Dickens the author was inscribing, for example, the weight of the stress and guilt of Bradley Headstone's life upon the character's body:[32] the imaginative metonymy is brought home forcefully in the world of the real Dickens.[33] Thus, Staplehurst is an emblem—a concentrated presentation and reiteration—of the themes and preoccupations that inform the novel. The real events the author was living and writing about, after Staplehurst, mix strangely with the imaginative events of *Our Mutual Friend,* operating in parallel, serving to confirm and even deepen the view of the world and of society the novel promulgates, and at the same time to suggest a more substantial "solution" than any in the novel itself.

*   *   *   *

A curious intertwining of the fiction's thematic content with real and desperate events in the life of the author, Staplehurst is the context within which Dickens makes his "plunge" into the text of *Our Mutual Friend* in his "Postscript." As Dickens relives the "metonymic" moments when accident victims were passing from life to death, and as he returns to these moments in letter after letter, as if to say "There is some value here," he places himself metaphorically in the very same position—between life and death—in terms of his text. This move parallels the "deaths" of Rokesmith and Eugene Wrayburn, and suddenly places Dickens in their company—no longer an author per se, but now part of the story—more data in the analysis of capitalism and the search for alternatives to it.

Of course, one doubts Dickens would see himself as a Barthian "scriptor," but the effect on us as readers (especially in light of the catalogue of doubles Dickens has placed within the text) is to install the author Dickens, and his struggle with the question of capitalism, inside his own text "for ever." This "dying into the text," a giving up of the role of "author" and all the expectations, control and constrictions that go with it, parallels Rokesmith's "giving up" of his role and fortune as John Harmon. But Rokesmith must return to the capitalistic world and its pressures, where he is almost certain to be compromised. In the text of the "Postscript," however, the author Dickens faces no such necessity. In the "Postscript," his "dying" makes Dickens and his struggle part of the text of *Our Mutual Friend*, infusing his own value into something which thus becomes more than a "product" of his, more than a commodity, and no longer reducible to money terms.[34]

In this sense, the "Postscript" describes a way Dickens the author can transcend what has up until now seemed the inescapable control of the forces of financial capitalism on his society, his body, his life and his work. Barthes's comments from "The Death of the Author" describe this kind of transcendence:

Once the Author is removed, the claim to decipher the text becomes quite futile. To give a text an Author is to impose a limit on that text, to furnish it with a final signified, to close the writing. [. . . C]riticism [. . .] is today totally undermined, along with the Author. In the multiplicity of writing, everything is to be *disentangled*, nothing *deciphered*; the structure can be followed, 'run' (like the thread of a stocking) at every point and at every level, but there is nothing beneath: the space of writing is to be ranged over, not pierced; writing ceaselessly posts meaning ceaselessly to evaporate it, carrying out a systematic exemption of meaning. In precisely this way literature (it would be better from now on to say *writing*), by refusing to assign a 'secret,' an ultimate meaning, to the text (and to the world as text), liberates what may be called an anti-theological activity, an activity that is truly revolutionary since to refuse to fix meaning is, in the end, to refuse God and his hypostases—reason, science, law. (Barthes, 147; Barthes's emphasis)

While "revolutionary" may be too strong a description, given Dickens's equivocal position as artist-capitalist, *Our Mutual Friend* is at least an "anti-theological" attempt to respond to capitalism in a way that breaks the stranglehold of the capitalist system on society and of the "author" capital on the novel, its author and its readers. First, it is perhaps a conscious attempt to "refuse" if not God, at least his hypostases that concern economics, finance, value and humanity. Second, the novel, read in this way, is radical in the way it tries to transcend its own status as a commodity: as a meditation on commodities and their metonymic properties, the novel is at once a commodity and an anti-commodity—a commodity bent on destabilizing the idea of the commodity. Finally, as a text into which Dickens "dies," the novel ceases to be about Dickens's authorial agenda or about his capitalist agenda and becomes something larger and separate from these; here, the author gives up his own purpose and, in so doing, is finally free (in a way Bella and even Eugene are not) from the ubiquitous processes of capitalism, which depend, after all, on desire for something other than what one has at any given moment. Barthes says such a text is an "immense dictionary from which [the scriptor] draws a writing that can know no halt," ready for the "birth of the reader" as the "space on which all the quotations that make up a writing are inscribed" (Barthes, 147, 148)—a text in which the "author" capital is as powerless to dictate meaning as the "scriptor" Dickens.

In this last sense, *Our Mutual Friend* may complete the project undertaken by, for example, *A Christmas Carol*—which tried to "convert" readers to a different approach to capitalism. But now, at the end of Dickens's career, the project becomes one of inscribing a "tissue of signs" on and for the reader—arresting the metonymic processes of capitalism, stilling the voice of the "author" capital, and creating within the reader the possibility, at least, for understanding and conducting life differently. Such an "anti-theological" strategy must not allow the voice of the "author" capital to "sell" this possible different way of living to us, or to make it a "choice" as if it were a commodified product. Rather, the possibility is simply inscribed—in the text and on us as readers—so that meaning *can* be made of it. Such an inscription, juxtaposed within the "Postscipt" with the ideas of Dickens's long-term relationship with his audience and with his own death, constitutes a legacy, a lasting store of value, not subject, perhaps, to the intense, ubiquitous and constant metonymic pressures of capitalism.

Conclusion

To conclude this book I will put what I have said about Dickens's work in perspective by examining the ways two other Victorian authors approach the issue of financial capitalism. I will focus here on two motifs—the "Jewishness" of finance, and the solution of "economy" as a viable alternative to the "chrematistics" of capitalism. Both of these motifs, as I have shown, are present in Dickens's works: the problem of the Jewishness, or the "otherness" of the financier is reflected in Ralph Nickleby and in Scrooge, and is turned inside-out in the Riah/Fledgeby pairing; "economy" as a household-oriented, productive use of money is part of every alternative Dickens offers to capitalism—and is even imposed by force on Bella at the conclusion of *Our Mutual Friend*. In this conclusion, I will examine these motifs in two other important critiques of finance capitalism—Trollope's *The Way We Live Now* (1875) and Eliot's *Daniel Deronda* (1876); in this examination I hope to show, amid significant differences of purpose, tone and rhetoric, fundamental similarities in how finance itself is viewed. In addition, although these later novels reflect contemporary changes in the financial world after Dickens's death, their authors share Dickens's inability to imagine a "solution" to the problems of capitalism unimplicated in and untainted by the pervasive power of capitalism itself.

FINANCE AND JEWISHNESS

While the familiar role of the Jew as usurer and moneylender dominates earlier fiction, the novels I am considering here, both written in the 1870s, emphasize the role of Jews in more sophisticated and socially influential forms of finance. Melmotte in *The Way We Live Now* clearly enacts this broader role; he initiates stock-market operations involving millions of pounds, loan operations "bankrolling" the military and political ventures of nations, and so on. But the same linkage of Jews and high finance is also explored in *Daniel Deronda*, which offers a mirror-image of Melmotte's operations in which Jewishness and high finance are decoupled, and the Jew (a certain kind of Jew, at least) is freed to go about the business of statecraft which he had previously only been allowed to finance. Before examining the novels themselves, I would like, briefly, to raise the question of why this linkage should, in these novels of the 1870s, suddenly become so visible, and offer two hypotheses—one relating to the growth of middle-class investment in the latter part of the nineteenth century, the other to the growth of British imperial power—about why this might be so.

My first hypothesis revolves around the increased participation of middle-class Britons, primary consumers of the novel, in financial markets. As Wilfred P. Dvorak notes, the connections between such readers (represented by those of *All The Year Round*) and finance were undergoing a sea-change by the 1860s:

> The main argument in *All The Year Round* in the 1860s is that something new is happening both in the way in which Englishmen accumulate wealth, and in the way in which they distribute its blessings: thus the rash of articles on speculation and investment, especially between 1864 and 1865, at the same time that Dickens is writing *Our Mutual Friend*. Of course we know historically that something new *was* happening: extensions of limited liability, the French *Crédit Mobilier* system, and an increasing publi: confidence in dealing by check and in speculating on the stock-market. ("Dickens's Ambivalence as a Social Critic in the 1860s," 90; Dvorak's emphases)

Such increased participation in financial markets meant that more small investors were hurt when markets inevitably collapsed, as they did in 1866. It is reasonable, then, to hypothesize that the "victims" of the markets at that point would look for a scapegoat. While both Jewish and Gentile scapegoats abounded (the Jews included the infamous Albert Grant, actually Gottheimer, a "former wine-merchant, who had also found it convenient to change his name" and founder of several notorious financial companies; the Gentiles, the officers and directors who took Overend, Gurney public in 1865, knowing the firm was insolvent),[1] the link between Jewishness and financial victimization was an easy one to make, and perhaps, as a means of denying that anything was wrong with the "British" financial system, a necessary one. Certainly, the financial writing of the time persistently links speculation with fraud, and fraud with Jews, as the following passage from an 1876 article in *Fraser's Magazine* illustrates:

> [Speculation in stock] is indeed a dangerous game for all concerned, and unless a man plays it with loaded dice he generally loses in the end [. . .]

the German Jew jobber, with his agents and colleagues all over the Conti-
nent, sharp as detectives, to pick up news and send it in advance—these,
and such like people, may make huge fortunes, but not so the mere outsider who dabbles in Stock Exchange gambling, and knows nothing. [2]

Here the writer focuses ostensibly on the Jews' astuteness, but is really inviting the reader to view the Jews, "sharp as detectives," as possessors of inside
knowledge unavailable to the "mere outsider"—to position the Jews at the
heart of the market's fraudulent nature, in fact. Such willful blurring of cause
and effect enabled commentators and investors to register their outrage while
avoiding the question of whether there was anything intrinsically rotten in
the financial system that had just victimized them—by blaming their financial woes on the financial Jew, a "non-British" outsider.

My second hypothesis accounting for the increased visibility of the financial Jew in novels of the 1870s is based on the position of Jews at the center of
what might be termed "high finance"—that is, "wholesale" finance involving
companies and, most importantly, nations. In the world of the City, this involvement of Jews in high finance was not new, as Niall Ferguson points out:

By the summer of 1825 [. . .] the Rothschilds had succeeded triumphantly in establishing themselves as the leading specialists in European public finance—and not only European. One by one, the powers of
the Holy Alliance had followed the British lead, entrusting their loans to
Rothschilds; first Prussia then Austria, then Russia. Finally, France, too
had to abandon her preference for more established Parisian houses. [3]

In fact, a cornerstone of Britain's financial preeminence, the National Debt
itself—the foundation of the London Money Market and the means used to
finance British military power—was seen by a not untypical mid-century financial writer as nothing more than a Jewish money-making scheme:

The principal negotiators of the first British loan were Jews. They as-
sisted the Stadt-holder with their counsel, and a Mephistopheles of the
money-making race attached himself even to the side of Marlborough.
[. . .] It has been estimated, upon good authority, that from fifteen to
twenty per cent of every loan raised in England, has, directly or indirectly, found its way to the coffers of those unconscionable Shylocks; so
that it is small wonder if we hear of colossal fortunes coexisting with extreme national depreciation and distress. [4]

The creation of the National Debt in the form of tradable bonds (referred to
as "stocks") in turn created a market for these—the Stock Exchange. By the

1870s the Stock Exchange, on which, by then, many different kinds of securities could be traded, was the capital-creating engine powering imperial economic expansion, but it, too, was seen by many as a decidedly Jewish milieu:

> The trade of a stockbroker is a modern one—hardly two hundred years old. It may be said to have begun in this country with the beginning of our funded debt, and with the incorporation of the Bank of England. Before that time the peculiar documents called stocks and shares did not exist in sufficient quantity, if at all, to make dealing in them a profitable business. But with the creation of this new form of representative wealth came a new occupation, which was early taken advantage of by the Jews, who have ever since been conspicuous as dealers of the Stock Exchanges of the world. ("Stockbroking and the Stock Exchange," 149)

This linkage between Jewishness and the core elements of the British financial system assumed a new importance in the last third of the century, as Britain's political and economic power, enabled by this financial system, was projected to cover the globe. As Mary Poovey points out, the representation of this growing power was increasingly bound up with both economic potency and British masculinity as the century went on:

> The power of English men (hence the "proof" of their "natural" superiority) rested upon their ability to make the world over in their own image. In the 1840s and early 1850s, this quest primarily took the form of religious conversion, as missionaries set about transforming "heathens" in India, South and Central America, and Africa into Christians with the carrot of philanthropy and the stick of brute force. Economic investment in these areas accelerated throughout this period often [. . .] by piggybacking on the missionary and philanthropic rhetorics that already defined relations with those countries.("Speculation and Virtue in *Our Mutual Friend,*" 178)

But this "superiority" (making the world over in one's own image) required money to project; the role of the Jewish financier as the provider of the motive power for economic and political imperialism must have produced cognitive dissonance as this power grew and Empire became more and more a part of British identity. Such dissonance is apparent in a mid-century description of Nathan Rothschild, which could serve as Melmotte's prototype:

> Rothschild was, in fact a usurer to the state, as greedy and unconscionable as the humbler Hebrew who discounts the bill of the spendthrift at forty per cent. and, instead of handing over the balance in cash

to his victim, forces him to accept the moiety in coals, pictures, or cigars. His information was minute, exclusive, and ramified. All the arts which had been employed on the stock exchange in earlier times were revived by him, and new "dodges" introduced to depress or raise the market. (Aytoun, "The National Debt and the Stock Exchange," 144–45)

Here the Jewish financier is portrayed as usurer once more, and the whole transaction (the creation and sale of bonds to finance an addition to the National Debt) is lowered to the level of a spendthrift being cheated by a (non-British, "Hebrew") moneylender. The clever, cosmopolitan financial Jew is seen to undermine British masculine power as expressed in economic terms: Britain itself becomes the passive "victim," a dupe humiliatingly forced to accept the "moiety" of the loan in unwanted junk. And this Jewishness at the center of the financial system enabling British power, this Jewishness at the core of Empire, must have threatened confidence in the superiority of British power, even of British masculinity—which could be seen, from a certain point of view, as fictions propped up by Jewish money. As Ferguson notes:

[a]t the time of the wars of Italian unification—which it was believed [the Rothschilds] were anxious to avert—the Earl of Shaftesbury found it "strange, fearful, humiliating" that "the destinies of this nation are the sport of an infidel Jew!" (*The House of Rothschild*, 20) [5]

Shaftesbury seems almost unmanned here, and does not sound like a representative of an imperial power. The sentiments prompting his comments were widely held, suggesting profound "dis-ease" about the role of the financial Jew in underpinning Britain's power, a hallmark of Britishness itself.[6] Such sentiments could easily be voiced by Roger Carbury in *The Way We Live Now;* and it was the mirror-image of these sentiments (the view of the Jewish nationality itself in danger of being destroyed by "Jewish" financial activity) that prompted Eliot's project of decoupling Jewishness and the cosmopolitanism of finance in *Daniel Deronda.*

THE WAY WE LIVE NOW: MELMOTTE AS THE FINANCIAL JEW

All of the themes suggested above are present in the portrayal of Melmotte in *The Way We Live Now.* Melmotte is widely believed to be a Jew, though the vagueness of his background makes him less overtly Jewish than Breghert or Cohenlupe—and thus potentially more acceptable in a hypocritical society.

His financial career is vague as well, but is "said" to be both grandiose and multinational:

> It was said that he had made a railway across Russia, that he provisioned
> the Southern Army in the American civil war, and he had at one time
> bought up all the iron in England. He could make or mar any company
> by buying or selling stock, and could make money dear or cheap as he
> pleased. All this was said of him in praise,—but it was also said that he
> was regarded in Paris as the most gigantic swindler that had ever lived;
> that he had made that City too hot to hold him[.]"[7]

Melmotte's is the profession of an outsider, of the cosmopolitan, international Jew.[8] But, the novel hastens to tell us, Melmotte's "Jewish" profession does not render him unattractive to society: "[I]t was known to all the world that a Royal Prince, a Cabinet Minister, and the very cream of duchesses were going to his wife's ball" (*TWWLN*, 31; vol. I, ch. iv). The effect of these and lesser folk flocking to Melmotte (exemplified most directly in the composition of his Railway's board, with its mix of nobility and Jewish operatives) is to state that we are all—most of us, given the way we live now—Jews when it comes to these kinds of moral choices. Mrs. Hurtle, though an American, appears to speak for society in general when she tells Paul Montague, "Such a man rises above honesty [. . .] as a great general rises above humanity when he sacrifices an army to conquer a nation. Such greatness is incompatible with small scruples. [. . . C]ommerce is not noble unless it rises to great heights. To live in plenty by sticking to your counter from nine in the morning to nine at night is not a fine life. But this man with a scratch of his pen can send out or call in millions of dollars" (*TWWLN*, 245–46; vol. II, ch. xxvi). Thus, Trollope the satirist is saying, in a society dominated by financial capitalism, older, "Christian" values are forgotten, and "Jewish" values are embraced, at least by proxy, through Melmotte.

The notion that "we are all potential Jews" targets those in society willing to abandon "English" values, but the satire here depends on the identification of "the way we live now" with the values of a stereotype—the financial Jew. This stereotypical use of Jewishness at first appears to be mitigated in the novel's portrait of Breghert. Although a financier, Breghert is a better man than Melmotte—painted as honest, a devoted father and, potentially, a loving husband. In his farewell letter to Georgiana, he says,

> I would not have allowed my losses to interfere with your settlement be-
> cause I had stated a certain income; and must to a certain extent have

compromised my children. But I should not have been altogether happy until I had replaced them in their former position, and must therefore have abstained from increased expenditure till I had done so. (*TWWLN,* 278–79; vol. II, ch. lxxix)

Breghert's even-handedness and thoughtfulness about money imposes another lash of "the whip of the satirist"[9] on the Christians in the novel, who more often than not view their children as sources, rather than recipients, of money. Here, Breghert shows his understanding of "economy" and the use-value of money in providing for his family, while Georgey immediately plans to exploit the exchange-value of the watch and chain he had sent her, "which somebody had told her had not cost less than a hundred and fifty guineas": "She could not wear them, as people would know whence they had come; but she might exchange them for jewels which she could wear" (*TWWLN,* 279; vol. II, ch. lxxix).

Breghert's honest humanity reinforces the ironic flocking of the novel's Christians to embrace "Jewish" values. But the function of this character is more complex than this. Despite his good nature, Breghert's stereotypical appearance as the financial Jew is emphasized for us—forced on us—in the narrator's description:

He was a fat, greasy man, good-looking in a certain degree, about fifty, with hair dyed black, and beard and moustache dyed a dark purple colour. The charm of his face consisted in a pair of very bright black eyes, which were, however, set too near together in his face for the general delight of Christians. He [. . .] had that look of command in his face which has become common to master-butchers, probably by long intercourse with sheep and oxen. But Mr. Breghert was considered to be a very good man of business [. . .] the leading member of a great financial firm. (*TWWLN,* 91; vol. II, ch. lx)

The narrator here flatly presents Breghert as physically unattractive, with a "Jewish" face, and carrying associations of "grease" and "sheep and oxen." Breghert, we learn, is to succeed Mr. Todd, the senior partner in Breghert & Todd ("the business had almost got beyond him"), whose name could be that of a gentile, and who is associated with "Lombard Street, the Exchange, and the Bank" (*TWWLN,* 91; vol. II, ch. lx). Thus we see a transition in Breghert's firm that foreshadows one in the larger society: we are entering a world, the novel says, where the unattractive Jew usurps the place of the holder of the older, traditional values ("the Bank"), and comes right into our homes and clubs. Lady Monogram describes this process and society's complicity in it:

There's the butcher round the corner in Bond Street, or the man who comes to do my hair. I don't at all think of asking them to my house. But if they were suddenly to turn out wonderful men, and go every-where, no doubt I should be glad to have them here. That's the way we live, and you are as well used to it as I am. (*TWWLN*, 90; vol. II, ch. lx)

Of course, this process implies that these "wonderful men" provide some-thing of value to the society that tolerates them, just as Melmotte is thought to. Marriage, however, is a more complicated question. Georgiana ticks off "ever so many instances [. . .] of 'decent people' who had married Jews or Jewesses" (*TWWLN*, 93; vol. II, ch. lx), and recognizes that "there was at present a general heaving-up of society on this matter"—another consequence of "the way we live now." Still, the Goldsheiner marriage is positioned as a golden exception, the marriage of Jewish and Christian aristocracies, with the conversion of young Goldsheiner to boot. Eventually, the marriage Georgina desires (not to "a Jew that had been, as to whom there might possibly have been a doubt [. . .] but to a Jew that was" (*TWWLN*, 92; vol. II, ch. lx) becomes "the vile sin that she had contemplated" (*TWWLN*, 275; vol. II, ch. lxxix).

In the end, Breghert serves a dual (racial and financial) function. First, his character makes the point that the exchange-value ethic which dominates society is not confined to the Jews, but is being embraced in modern society by all kinds of people. This point is problematized, however, since the ethic that is being embraced is presented as something "Jewish" to begin with. The problematization of the Jewishness of finance is deepened by Breghert's sec-ond function: he is the vigorous, "greasy" financial Jew who is in the process of moving from the role of usurper in our banks to that of usurper in our homes. Such an "upheaval" (as Georgey thinks of it) links the unstoppable pervasiveness of capitalism not with the autonomy of capital itself (as I tried to show Dickens doing in my chapter on *Little Dorrit*), but with the racial pervasiveness of the Jews. This ambiguity allows us to infer a double-edged meaning to Roger Carbury's denunciation of Melmotte as a "swindler":

> You can keep your house free from him, and so can I mine. But we set no example to the nation at large. They who do set example go to his feasts [. . .] And yet these leaders of fashion know [. . .] that he is what he is because he has been a swindler greater than all other swindlers. What follows as a natural consequence? Men reconcile themselves to swindling. (*TWWLN*, 44; vol. II, ch i)

Men must reconcile themselves to swindling—and often are the willing victims of it, as the novel's satire shows; but men, in this modern, capitalist society, must also reconcile themselves to the presence of—indeed intimacy with—those exemplars of capitalism, the Jews. This, the novel says, despite Trollope's delineation of humanity and decency in Breghert's character, is to be deplored.

Against this inevitable "upheaval," the twinned invasion of finance and Jewishness, *The Way We Live Now* offers an "economic" solution, articulated most clearly by Roger Carbury, who is the exemplar of the value-system threatened by the financial Jew. His announcement of his decision to share his estate with Hetta and Paul defines "economy":

> I would not dictate either to you or to him, but it is right that you should know that I hold my property as steward for those who are to come after me, and that the satisfaction of my stewardship will be infinitely increased if I find that those for whom I act share the interest which I shall take in the matter. It is the only payment which you and he make me for my trouble. (*TWWLN*, 472; vol. II, ch. c)

Such an attitude toward property and its uses seems to contrast sharply with Melmotte's actions in attempting to take back the money he has settled on Marie, and in pulling down the house at Pickering Park before it has even been paid for. At one level, then, Roger's philosophy, backed up by his actions, seems a nice counterbalance to the chrematistic invasiveness figured by Melmotte. But the solution works only on the surface, and is undercut in many different ways over the last quarter of the novel. To begin with, even though Melmotte is dead, his creation will live on. Fisker's boasts to Paul Montague indicate that there are many more would-be Melmottes waiting in the wings, and that the chrematistic values exemplified by Melmotte—though perhaps not of the destructive scope and strength of a Dickensian "pestilence"—are not easily eradicated:

> D'you think we're all going to smash [in San Francisco] because a fool like Melmotte [kills himself]? [. . .] These shares are at a'most nothing now in London. I'll buy every share in the market. [. . .] What [Melmotte]'s done'll just be the making of us [in San Francisco]. (*TWWLN*, 394; vol. II, ch. xcii)

Roger, of course, is no speculator and his "economy" is most of all a Nicklebian withdrawal from the world of commerce to that of the country. But Fisker's statement means that withdrawal from the "game" may not guarantee immunity: as chrematistic accumulation and financial capitalism grow, they will continue to bring riches to some and ruin to others. This year, it is Pickering Park that must be put up for sale to allow the Longstaffes to settle their financial obligations; next year, it might be Carbury Hall.

In addition, the invasive evils of capitalism are not confined to the financial world of the novel, but contaminate the most intimate human relationships—among Christians as well as Jews. Parents in the novel are routinely unable (or unwilling) to insulate their children from commodification, or to hold themselves aloof from the chrematistic desire to gain from the sale of these commodities. The tension between these forces and the ideal of economy is embodied in Lady Carbury. As an author, she doubles the industry and energy of Frances Trollope, whose novels supported her family during Anthony's adolescence.[10] But Lady Carbury's willingness to "sell" Hetta and her active encouragement of Felix's fortune-hunting undercut her economy by placing her in a long line of parents (Melmotte, Lord Nidderdale's father, Ruggles) willing to sacrifice children for financial gain. "How much better it would be to be childless," Lady Carbury exclaims when Hetta refuses to marry Roger: "[A]sk yourself whether you do not give as much pain [as the drunken Sir Felix], seeing what you could do for us if you would. But it never occurs to you to sacrifice even a fantasy for the advantage of others" (*TWWLN,* 15–14; vol. II, ch. lii). The debasement, essentially a monetization, of the family relationship here is different only in degree from the debasement expressed in Melmotte's bitterly ironic lament when Marie refuses to return the money he had settled on her: "Heavens and earth! That he should be robbed by his own child,—robbed openly, shamefully, with brazen audacity!" (*TWWLN,* 251; vol. II, ch. lxxvii).

Finally, even Roger's decision to "[conquer] his own heart"(*TWWLN,* 468; vol. II, ch. c) and allow Hetta and Paul to share in the estate fails to convince as a triumph of generosity over frustrated chrematistic desire (Roger's failure to possess Hetta). Roger's economy itself is conflicted: we are told that he believes in "the necessity of so living that the income might always be more than sufficient for the wants of the household" (473). And in the end his generosity does not come without strings; his decision to settle Carbury on Hetta's eldest boy depends "on [the] condition that such a boy should take the old name" (469)—that is, on the enactment in a symbolic sense of the chrematistic desire Roger claims to have given up. Thus the novel discredits its own solution in the end, disclosing the "Jewishness" Roger is making a stand against within his own character, and resonating with a strong cultural subtext postulating the "uncovertibility" of the Jews (and, by extension, of the "Jew" the novel sees in all of us).[11]

DANIEL DERONDA: "SPIRITUAL ECONOMY"

Daniel Deronda's identification of finance with "Jewishness" positions the Jew as "in" but not necessarily "of" the chrematistic ethic finance brings with it, while it positions most of the novel's Christians as, ironically, more chrematistic than the Jews. Thus, when Gwendolen goes to "Mr. Weiner" to pawn her necklace, his thoughts are merely business-like: "Mr. Weiner [had] nothing to remark except her proud grace of manner, and the superior size and quality of the three central turquoises."[12] Gwendolen's thoughts, however, are entirely focused on exchange-value: her "dominant regret was that after all she had only nine louis to add to the four in her purse: these Jew dealers were so unscrupulous in taking advantage of Christians unfortunate at play!" (*DD*, 19; bk. I, ch. 2).

This irony—that Christians are more "Jewish" than (some) Jews— suggests that the "Jewishness" being discussed is neither religious nor national, but moral: a "chrematistic" ethic traditionally associated with the Jews. In turn, this separation of Jews and chrematistics lays the foundation for the novel's project, which is the presentation of an "economic" solution to the ubiquitous and invasive evils of capitalistic life, an "economy" built firmly on the spiritual tradition of Judaism. In carrying out this project, *Daniel Deronda* attempts to legitimate the Jews, but also to legitimate authorship itself.[13]

Eliot, like Trollope and Dickens, represents the chrematistic through conflating gambling and finance; the games at Leubronn are equated rhetorically with the "wicked recklessness" of the speculation enacted by Grapnell & Co. which results in Mrs. Davilow's ruin. Part of humanity's vulnerability to the chrematistic ethic, we are told, is its propensity to make poor economic choices—as with the "respectable London Tradesman [. .] winning money in business and spending it showily"(*DD*, 8; bk. I, ch.1). But the evil here is more invasive, as well. Clearly, "ruin" in Mrs. Davilow's case is partly due to her ignorance. But it is also due to Grapnell & Co.'s malfeasance—"being also bent on amusing themselves, no matter how" (*DD*, 156; bk. I, ch. 15). The firm's actions, whether careless or fraudulent, penetrate even into county society where the machinations of finance are all but unknowable, and bring real, painful consequences: upon hearing the news of the family's ruin, Gwendolen equates her new position of "poverty and humiliating dependence" with "the chill sense that death had really come" (*DD*, 16; bk. I, ch. 2).

Even at the level of intimate relationships, a chrematistic ethic appears both widespread and invasively destructive in the world of the novel. Chrematistics as the accumulation of power and dominance is enacted in intent by Gwendolen (as Daniel notes, Gwendolen's marriage-venture is simply "another sort of gambling than roulette" [*DD*, 563; bk. VI, ch. 45]), and in actuality by Grandcourt.[14] The latter, described by Daniel as "that remnant of a human being" (*DD*, 404; bk. V, ch. 35), is a figure of the teleology of capital—the inevitable link between chrematistics and death. Grandcourt is presented as a monster, but he is also the type of an ethic practiced by many characters (the Alcharisi, Mr. and Mrs. Arrowpoint, and Mrs. Davilow, for example), and which has debased intimate and family relations by turning people into pieces in a game of power.

Eliot clearly offers various kinds of "economy" as solutions to the evils of capitalism. This "economy," in my view, operates on several levels. Most basically, it is a productive use of money for the building and preservation of home and family life. The Meyricks' "triple bond" ("family love, admiration for the finest work, the best action; and habitual industry" [*DD*, 197; bk. II, ch. 18]) typifies this kind of economy, as does Mirah when she tells Mordecai, "I work now. I shall get money to keep us" (*DD*, 582; bk. VI, ch. 47).

Such examples, however, are rare and, at least in Mirah's case, the ethic of "economy" has necessarily been supported by Daniel's relative affluence. But *Daniel Deronda's* economic solution runs deeper than the mere proper use of money; the book offers a "spiritual" economy as a more powerful opposing force to the chrematistic mindset described above. This kind of economy involves opposing capital with "spiritual capital" that can be used to improve the world. The existence of and value inherent in this "capital" becomes clear when Daniel offers to use his own (monetary) capital to publish Mordecai's writings. "That is not enough," Mordecai insists, "with something like a pale flame" in his face:

> You will take this inheritance which the base son refuses because of the tombs which the plough and the harrow may not pass over, nor the gold-seeker disturb; you will take the sacred inheritance of the Jew. (*DD*, 500; bk. V, ch. 40)

This meaning of this economy is deepened when Daniel is given his Grandfather's chest, which contains "manuscripts, family records, stretching far back" (*DD*, 748; bk. VIII, ch. 63)—the record of Daniel's ancestry and the confirmation of his spiritual Jewishness. But the chest also contains, as Eliot notes in her quotation from Milton, "a potency of life" (*DD*, 721; bk. VIII, ch. 60), and "that remainder of [Charisi] which he had prized and preserved for his offspring" (*DD*, 727; bk. VIII, ch. 61). In other words, the chest contains value that can be productive in the here and now (as Daniel senses when he feels himself "touching the electric chain of his own ancestry"); the chest represents a kind of "capital" accumulation that, potentially, produces life and improves humanity's lot. It stands in opposition to the novel's most potent emblem of chrematistic accumulation—the casket of "poisoned gems" which are the accumulated essence not of Grandcourt's "best young love," but of his "withered heart" (*DD*, 359; bk. IV, ch. 31).

At a more profound level, this "economy" is one of souls: when Mordecai dies his soul will not be lost, but will join Daniel's. In one sense, this union involves "an active replenishment [of Mordecai's] self, so Deronda might receive from Mordecai's mind the complete ideal shape of that personal duty and citizenship" which will become Daniel's career in statecraft. But "economy" here goes deeper than the exchange of ideology or knowledge—to a " sacramental solemnity," a more or less literal "marriage of our souls" (*DD*, 751; bk. VIII, ch. 63), and a way to "save the life within me from being stifled with this stifled breath" as Mordecai tells Daniel (*DD*, 497; bk. V, ch. 40). Thus Eliot describes a process which, as Catherine Gallagher notes, is the "moral economy for which both money-changing and art are exchanged in *Daniel Deronda*" (Gallagher, "George Eliot and *Daniel Deronda*," 58)—a pure form of accumulation and exchange which replaces the chrematistic forms to which it is opposed.

In the end, the outgrowth of this "economy" is to be tangible, productive changes in the real world. Mordecai introduces this notion in his talks with Daniel by deliberately contrasting spiritual and financial well being:

> I said, let my body dwell in poverty, and my hands be as the hands of the toiler; but let my soul be as a temple of remembrance [. . .] They said, "He feeds himself on visions," and I denied not; for visions are the creators and feeders of the world." (*DD*, 497; bk. V, ch. 40)

For Daniel, the most tangible productive outgrowth of this "economy" is to be "some ideal task, in which I might feel myself the heart and brain of a multitude—some social captainship which would come to me as a duty, and not be striven for as a personal prize" (DD, 750; bk. VIII, ch. 63). This task, standing here in opposition to chrematistic desire for a "personal prize," is the creation of a Jewish state:

> The ideal that I am possessed with is that of restoring a political existence to my people, making them a nation again, giving them a national centre such as the English have, though they too are scattered over the face of the globe." (*DD*, 803; bk. VIII, ch. 69)

That such a state would be "economic" rather than "chrematistic" is implied in both Mordecai's embrace of poverty and Daniel's repudiation of personal gain. As Gallagher points out, for Eliot a religious and national homeland for the Jews would certainly be a place opposed to the "Jewish-ness" of finance:

> In "The Modern Hep! Hep! Hep!," the last of the *Theophrastus Such* es-
> says, Eliot sums up the [effects of financial circulation] in the word
> "alienism." Alienism is a spiritual disease that, she tells us, is sometimes
> euphemistically called "cosmopolitanism." Jews are particularly prone
> to it because, having no homeland of their own, they are often forced to
> live in the medium of abstract universalism created by international fi-
> nance [. .] If Jews are to be virtuous, [Eliot] insists, they must have at
> least a spiritual nationality and at best a homeland. (Gallagher, "George
> Eliot and *Daniel Deronda*, 56)

Overarching all of this is the sense that *Daniel Deronda* is itself an act of "economy"—a productive use of signs to teach lessons of value and, as Gal-lagher says, a way for Eliot to use "her authorship" to "[purchase] her status as something other than a whore" (Gallagher, "George Eliot and *Daniel Deronda*, 60).[15] Hugo Witemeyer, in *George Eliot and the Visual Arts*, points out Eliot's belief, based in part on G. H. Lewes's critical writings on artistic "vision," in the instructive power of vivid picturing. Paraphrasing Lewes's article "Princi-ples of Success," Witemeyer describes Lewes's view of art's power to teach:

> The clear visions of the artist penetrate the layer of habit and "misty
> generality" which normally obscures our mental experience; thus the
> artist causes us to see things—often very familiar things—anew [. . .]
> By communicating his clear vision to an audience, the artist extends
> their perceptions and sympathies. For this reason, Eliot believed that
> vivid aesthetic picturing is a far more effective way of teaching than hor-
> tatory argument.[16]

Such a belief, as Witemeyer notes, prompts some of the contrasting pictorial representations in the novel:

> Throughout *Deronda*, George Eliot regularly visualizes Gwendolen and
> the other English characters in terms of the English portrait tradition,
> and especially of the "fancy" portraits that were fashionable among the
> upper classes in the seventeenth and eighteenth centuries. Conversely,
> Eliot visualizes Daniel and the other Jewish characters in terms of Italian
> Renaissance painting, especially that of Titian and the Venetian school.
> The contrasts between these two schools of painting reflect moral con-
> trasts between the two races and cultures represented. (95)

And thus positioned, the vivid imagery is a series of serious and very deliberate signs, designed both to valorize Judaism in itself, and teach moral lessons about social liberality and the anti-chrematistic value of Jewish spirituality, as Witemeyer implies:

> It is as though George Eliot were saying to her Protestant English audience: you have learned to appreciate the Italians despite their ethnic, religious, and cultural foreignness; you can learn to appreciate the Jews in the same way: both people are of Mediterranean origin, both have distinguished non-Protestant religious traditions, and the Italian Renaissance painting you admire realizes many motifs of Hebrew scriptures. Eliot's pictorialism, in other words, here becomes a sophisticated rhetorical device employed in the service of a liberal social vision. (98–99)

In the end, however, despite the novel's efforts to achieve its project of offering both a spiritual Jewishness and an economics of the spirit as counterpoints to "Jewish" finance, *Daniel Deronda*'s solutions fail to convince. This failure, in my view, involves both the attempt to define "Jewishness" as separate from finance, and the attempt to provide a credibly robust form of "economic" activity unimplicated in capitalism. In terms of Jewishness, Michael Ragussis points to the lack of a unified vision of the "Jew" as a problem in the novel. Eliot, he points out, really deals with two kinds of Jews, and clearly values one more than the other:

> [W]hile Mordecai represents the modern Jew inspired by the ancient Judaic vision, he does not prevent Deronda from keeping intact his prejudice against the modern shopkeeping Jew. [. .]Eliot has cut off Mordecai entirely from all wealth [. .] In so doing, [she] has unwittingly perpetuated an opposition that rests on certain well-known stereotypes about the Jews, for example, the opposition between "scholar and merchant" [. . .] that Disraeli undoes in inventing Sidonia. So, while Mordecai brings alive the ancient physiognomy and vision of the Hebrew prophets, Ezra Cohen is consistently measured against certain romantic notions of what Jewish identity should be— that is, against what the liberal, tolerant Christian requires—and is hardly ever allowed his own reality, his own integrity. [. .] The discovery that Mordecai and not the shopkeeping Ezra is Mirah's brother brings Deronda a personal relief that is ironically underscored by being represented as a kind of "deliverance." (Ragussis, 278–79)

One effect of this duality is that the novel is unable to shut financial capitalism out of Jewish life, except in the case of Mordecai, who is viewed by the Cohens and others as more or less unhinged (*DD*, 400; bk. IV, ch. 34). Although the Cohen family appears to Daniel in "a Venetian glow of colouring" (*DD*, 396; bk. IV, ch. 34), Ezra's appearance and manner suggest an inevitable Jewishness, a Breghertian combination of oiliness and financial acuteness: his "flourishing face" is "glistening on the way to fatness" (*DD*, 387; bk. IV, ch. 33); and his "glistening eyes seemed to get a little nearer together" when the talk turns to bargains and money.

Similarly, the novel expends significant energy on representing little Jacob as a beautiful, intelligent and realistically drawn child, yet portrays him constantly in terms of exchange. His "shwops" with Daniel are endearing at one level, but disturbing as well: "His small voice was hoarse in its glibness, as if it belonged to an aged commercial soul, fatigued with bargaining through many generations" (*DD*, 390; bk. IV, ch. 33). Jacob's duality also extends to his relationship with Mordecai, whose attempt to "print" himself on the young boy strikes the modern reader as a form of coercive commodification when compared with the reciprocal relationship Mordecai envisions with Daniel. In a sense, Jacob is the nexus where the two types of Jewishness come together; in him Eliot presents an engaging and lively character, and one in whom the "financial Jew" is clearly in the ascendant, despite Mordecai's passionate efforts. Ultimately, this persistent linkage of finance and Jewishness limits the scope of Eliot's critique of capitalism, just as it limits Trollope's. Unlike Dickens, whose sense of the systemic nature of capitalism and its evils seems to grow during his career, Eliot and Trollope fail convincingly to decouple Jewishness and chrematistics, and so offer the (British, and/or non-Jewish) reader the "out" of viewing financial capitalism as, at its root, somebody else's fault.

A second undercutting effect of the dualism in Eliot's presentation of Jewishness as a path to "economy" is suggested by the novel's pictorial method itself. On one hand, using Italian Renaissance motifs to valorize the "Jew" may help overcome Jewish foreignness and inculcate the value of a Jewish culture; but on the other hand it serves to sanitize the Jews, rendering them more palatable by making them look "Italian" and glossing over real aspects of Jewish life in the 1870s. Read in this way, the novel is not so much rejecting the links between Jews and commerce and the important Jewish role in British finance, as wishing it away and rendering it undiscussable. This problem becomes especially apparent at the close of the novel, where Daniel, supported by his own fortune and Sir Hugo's travelling outfit, must leave England to create a state based on the principles of spiritual economy I have been describing. Considering the novel narrowly, in terms of its handling of Jewishness and finance, such an ending is a form of capitulation—a statement that, in the fully capitalistic soil of England, and without an English fortune behind it, the "economic" solution is not hardy enough to survive.

*   *   *   *   *

It is tempting to look to literature as a counterweight to the increasing reach and power of financial capitalism during the nineteenth century, and to try to find ways in which novels (and works like the *Carol*) were able to offer remedies for the alienation inherent in capitalist society. Certainly, Dickens, Trollope and Eliot's works attempt to offer such a counterweight, as I have shown. However, our attempts to find relief from capitalism in the novels are doomed to failure, just as are the novels' attempts to provide it. The reader finds, in fact, that rather than providing a viewpoint from outside capitalism, the novels are implicated in it. For example, the novels' very preoccupation with financial capitalism leads them to use and re-use the techniques of capitalism (e.g., the "marketing" of Dickens's messages in *A Christmas Carol* and *Nicholas Nickleby*) even as they attempt to criticize it. In addition, the serial, in which all of the novels I have been considering appeared, epitomized the commodity text. Dickens's later novels were marketed via hundreds of thousands of bills and posters, and their sales tracked as precisely as were shares on the Stock Exchange; in them, the line between work of art and consumer product is utterly blurred. Finally, this confusion informs the role of the novelist, who must be both artist and capitalist in order to succeed in the literary market of the nineteenth century.

Nevertheless, each of the works I have examined tries to provide a counterweight to financial capitalism. Each, in its own way, examines the duality in a money society between chrematistic accumulation and "economic" uses of money. As we have seen, "economy" in this sense, derived from the Greek, refers to household management, and implies careful use (versus obsessive accumulation) of money to foster the growth and comfort of household and family. Dickens, Trollope and Eliot view chrematistic accumulation (typified by finance) in much the same way as Marx—accumulating money for its own sake is a sterile pursuit, and the teleology of capital, each author makes clear, is death.

Each author also attempts to use "economy" as the foundation of the counterweight or "solution" to the problems of living in a capitalist world. Many of these "economic" solutions are really "home economics"—that is, attempts to create insulated domestic enclaves in which the evils of capital-ism cannot penetrate. Such enclaves, typified by the Nicklebys' and Car-burys' walled gardens, are undercut by their own isolation from the real world, and function more as fervent wishes than as prescriptions for change. In addition, Dickens and Eliot examine various forms of "spiritual" econom-ics. One form of this involves commitment to a charitable ethic, in which money is used to enable others to manage their households (e.g., Scrooge founds the home economy of the Cratchit family). Another involves com-mitment to a spiritual ethic that eschews accumulation in favor of commit-ment to national and spiritual ideas—to the creation of a larger "home" in which true "economics" can be practiced (e.g., Daniel Deronda's commit-ment to building a Jewish state). Again, however, these attempts fail; they are undercut by their own implication in capitalism: Scrooge's charity requires the money he has accumulated through his financial operations.

These solutions fail in the end because they partake in the dilemma of the word "economics" itself; despite its original meaning, it has become in-escapably intertwined, for the nineteenth-century reader as well as for our-selves, with money, capital, flows of commodities, statistical rather than individual treatment of people—the essential components of capitalism, rather than the homely, domestic components of Aristotle's *oikonomiké*. This confusion, the warring concepts intertwined in the one word "economics" implies, in my view, that the projects of the works I have been considering, insofar as they were intended to present a counterweight to capitalism (Dick-ens's avowed project in the *Carol*, for example), were doomed to failure from the start. Georg Lukács describes capitalism as an "alien system" in which even our authors were "objects" rather than subjects.[17] Such a system implies a degree of "alienation" of the worker from his or her product, of the artist from his or her art; the relationship between artist and art, in the works I have been discussing, was mediated, through money, by capitalism itself, so pervasive and insidious in its effects that even artists of this caliber failed to transcend it. Each struggled to develop a counterweight or solution, but none was able to imagine a solution unimplicated in capitalism. In this sense, capitalism has become more than an economic system: like the water in a fishbowl, it has become the very medium in which artists and their works exist, an inescapable pre-condition of existence which, despite the best efforts of even the brilliant and well-intentioned, cannot be overcome.

Notes

NOTES TO THE INTRODUCTION

1. Mary Poovey, (ed.), "Introduction," *The Financial System in Nineteenth-Century Britain*, The Victorian Archives Series (Oxford: Oxford University Press, 2003), 4–5. (Additional references will appear in parentheses in the text.)
2. Poovey notes: "This mutually provocative interaction is [. . .] evident in the financial panics that punctuated the nineteenth century. These panics, which focused the country's attention on banks or discount houses, were often fuelled by newspaper accounts that a particular house was overextended. In reporting the angry crowds milling about Lombard Street, even a newspaper as staid as the *Times* could incite more worried investors to demand their money, and thus exacerbate the lenders' woes." (7).
3. In *The Economy of Literature* (Baltimore: Johns Hopkins University Press, 1978), Marc Shell provides a summary of Aristotle's use of "economics" and "chrematistics": "Aristotle suggests that the chrematist desires to earn an unnaturally infinite profit: 'Wealth-getting (*chrematistiké*) has no limit in respect of its end, and its end is riches and the acquisition of goods in the commercial sense. But the household branch (*oikonomiké*) of wealth-getting has a limit, inasmuch as the acquisition of money [as opposed to goods] is not the function of household management (*Politics* 1257b). Chrematistics, unlike economics, supports the unnatural illusion that "wealth consists of a quantity of money' (*Politics* 1257b) that can purchase and so seems to be homogeneous with anything in the market." (92)
4. Marx, Karl. *Capital*, Vol. I, tr. Ben Fowkes, (1867; London: Penguin Books, 1990) 229–30. (Additional references will appear in parentheses in the text.)
5. The injunctions from Deuteronomy are:
    XXIII: 19. Thou shalt not lend upon usury (*neshek*) to thy brother (*l'ahika*); usury of money, usury of victuals, usury of anything that is lent upon usury:
    XXIII: 20. Unto a stranger (*nokri*) thou mayest lend upon usury; but unto thy brother thou shalt not lend upon usury, that the Lord thy God may

bless thee in all that thou settest thine hand to in the land whither thou goest to possess it.
Quoted in Benjamin H. Nelson, *The Idea of Usury: From Tribal Brother-hood to Universal Otherhood* (Princeton: Princeton University Press, 1949), xv–xvii. Nelson suggests the importance of the idea of the stranger as an enemy with whom one is at war, quoting St. Ambrose: "From him exact usury whom it would not be a crime to kill" (4).

6. Marx describes the self-replicating growth of capital:
    The simple circulation of commodities—selling in order to buy—is a means to a final goal which lies outside circulation, namely the appropria-tion of use-value, the satisfaction of needs. As against this, the circulation of money as capital is an end in itself, for the valorization of value takes place only within this constantly renewed movement. The movement of capital is therefore limitless. (*Capital*, vol. I, 252–53)

7. Charles Dickens, *Our Mutual Friend*, 1865, ed. Adrian Poole (London: Penguin Books, 1997), 280; bk. II, ch. v. (Additional references will appear in parentheses in the text.)

8. Gallagher, Catherine. "The Bio-Economics of *Our Mutual Friend*," in *Frag-ments for a History of the Human Body, Part Three*, ed. Michel Feher with Romona Nadaff and Nadia Tazi (New York: Urzone, Inc., 1989), 364.

9. In "George Eliot and *Daniel Deronda:* The Prostitute and the Jewish Ques-tion," in *Sex, Politics, and Science in the Nineteenth-Century Novel*, ed., Ruth Bernard Yeazell, Selected Papers from the English Institute, 1983–84, new ser., no. 10 (Baltimore: Johns Hopkins University Press, 1986), Gallagher discusses the Victorian distinction between "writer" and "author":
    The activities of authoring, of procuring illegitimate income, and of alien-ating one's self through prostitution seem particularly closely associated with one another in the Victorian period. Thackeray identifies two reasons for this historical conjuncture: the development of cheap serial publica-tion (in which authors were often paid by the line) and the growth of a massive popular readership in the 1830s and 1840s. These conditions most directly affected what we now call popular literature, but the decreas-ing cost of publication, advances in education, and changes in copyright law made it impossible for any professional writer to claim to be inde-pendent of the marketplace. The author, moreover, does not go to market as a respectable producer with an alienable commodity, but with *himself or herself* as commodity. (43; Gallagher's emphasis)

NOTES TO CHAPTER ONE

1. Even appreciative critics have frequently been hard on *Nickleby's* structure. For example, in *Charles Dickens: His Tragedy and Triumph* (2 Vols., [New York: Simon and Schuster, 1952]), Edgar Johnson notes that the novel

"lacks the essential unity and coherence that blankets all of *Oliver* with its heavy evil. [. . .] In *Nickleby* [. . .] the diverse threads are loosely woven together , its varied scenes and characters related to each other in a sprawling picaresque improvisation in the eighteenth-century tradition of *Tom Jones* and *Roderick Random.*" Johnson adds, however, that "the triumphant achievement of the book is that [its] gratuitous interludes [Dotheboys Hall, the Mantalinis,' etc.] start into a life so far exceeding their structural importance as to represent, in fact, *Nicholas Nickleby's* most vivid claim upon our memories" (vol. I, 285). Others, like John Lucas in *The Melancholy Man: A Study of Dickens's Novels* (London: Methuen & Co. Ltd., 1970), view the novel as primarily apprentice work; Lucas says that the novel is at times an "incoherent muddle" which contains important themes articulated more fully in later novels (55). Still other critics, like Steven Marcus in *Dickens: from Pickwick to Dombey* (London: Chatto & Windus, 1965), have found unity in *Nickleby* at the thematic level: Marcus notes that the "aggressive force of intellect in the novel is directed against prudence—the conception that life should be lived close to the vest, that incessant work, cautious good sense, deliberate action and sobriety are the principal indications of virtue and the principal assurances of 'success'" (95). My own position in this chapter is closer to Marcus's than to Lucas's; I find *Nickleby* quite "unified" in the sense that it is deeply concerned with certain economic themes that it returns to again and again and looks at from multiple angles. However, I disagree with Marcus's contention that Ralph represents simply the "prudence" of the economic man; as I will argue, inherent in Ralph is the savagery and ultimate emptiness which Marx finds in capital, and Ralph embodies these elements of capitalism in the novel.
More recent critics have focused on looking for both themes and rhetorical structures useful in explaining what unity and coherence might be present amid *Nickleby's* complexity. Of these, I have found several helpful. For example, John Bowen, in "Performing Business, Training Ghosts: Transcoding *Nickleby*" (*ELH* Vol. 63, No. 1 [Spring, 1996], 153–75), argues that elements of the novel which may seem intrusive are actually linked to its major economic theme. He notes that "Dickens uses what have often been seen as residual survivals of older traditions—parable, fairy-story, moral typification—as abstraction in fiction in the service of a radical critique of abstraction in society, to analyse not old morals but new social and economic forces" (160). Tatiana Holway, in "The Game of Speculation: Economics and Representation" (*Dickens Quarterly* IX, No. 3 [Sept. 1992]: 103–114) also views *Nickleby* as a study of emerging economic forces; Holway focuses on "speculation" as economic activity and metaphor for the introduction of risk into society. Sylvia Manning also finds a kind of coherence in *Nickleby* which she sees as a "novel of the excluded subject and the desire for inclusion"; she argues in "*Nicholas Nickleby:* Parody on the

Plains of Syria" (*Dickens Studies Annual* 23 [1994]: 73–92) that the novel "is structured by the interaction of this theme and persistent use of parody. [. . . The] narrative peppers a plot that requires identification with the desire for inclusion, with parody that undermines it." (76–77). Similarly, Tore Rem argues in "Playing Around with Melodrama: The Crummles Episodes in *Nicholas Nickleby*" (*Dickens Studies Annual* 25 [1996]: 267–286), for a view of the novel that recognizes the need for "double vision." In her view, " the relationship between parody and melodrama constitutes a different sort of organizing principle from a plot- or character-centered one"(267). Rem notes that each of these "alternate portrayals of the same phenomena [. . .] gives life to the other and makes the overall picture more dynamic and complex" (280–81). Finally, Joseph Litvak, in *Caught in the Act: Theatricality in the Nineteenth-Century English Novel* (Berkeley: University of California Press, 1992), points out the existence side-by-side in the novel of "ludic" and "panoptic" theatricalities, and notes that the "ludic" Crummles world is strictly separated from Ralph's "panoptic" world (113–14). The lack of "dialectic" between these worlds, in my view, is in keeping with the novel's parodic structure as Rem describes it above; in addition, the lack of direct confrontation between the two theatricalities and the moral stances they represent signals the novel's ambivalence—its justifiably harsh criticism of and deep fascination with Ralph and his world—and its insistence on the reader's participation in the moral choices presented.

2. For example, John Lucas cites "the mismanagement of plot which produces the Cheerybles half-way through the book, and as a result of which Nicholas's fortune is guaranteed so early that interest in the rest of the novel has to be kept up by some fairly desperate manoeuvrres" (56); and Sylvia Manning refers to the denouement of the novel as "what the Cheeryble brothers finally engineer" (87).

3. Charles Dickens, *Nicholas Nickleby*, 1838–39, ed. Michael Slater (London: Penguin Books, 1978), 254; ch. 16. (Additional references will appear in parentheses in the text.)

4. Tatiana M. Holway, "The Game of Speculation: Economics and Representation," 103. (Additional references will appear in parentheses in the text.)

5. This preoccupation is reflected as soon as the novel begins; the first two chapters lay the groundwork by describing the system of financial capitalism as both corrupt and irrational.

6. The Pilgrim Edition of *The Letters of Charles Dickens*, Vol. One: 1820–1839, Eds. Madeline House and Graham Storey (Oxford: The Clarendon Press, 1965), 493–94. (Additional references will appear in parentheses in the text.)

7. In *Charles Dickens and his Publishers* (Oxford: Clarendon Press, 1978), Robert L. Patten notes that this transformation was well under way by the time Dickens wrote the letter I am discussing: "[T]he kind of economic

potency that *Pickwick* developed, and the relationship in that novel of process to end, necessitated the reworking of publisher-author arrangements. Was the copyright the right to the text, in whatever form it was published, or was it more narrowly restricted to copyright of the serial edition and editions bound from serial numbers? If stereotypes are made, how does one determine or limit the size of the edition for which copyright is sold? One solution to these problems is to make the author share in the work, and this is the solution which Chapman and Hall reached regarding *Pickwick*" (69–71).

8. C. R. B. Dunlop, "Debtors and Creditors in Dickens' Fiction." *Dickens Studies Annual* 19 (1990): 25–47; 34. (Additional references will appear in parentheses in the text.) Dunlop is citing John Vernon's *Money and Fiction: Literary Realism in the Nineteenth and Twentieth Centuries,* 69–71, 110.

9. Benjamin H. Nelson, *The Idea of Usury: From Tribal Brotherhood to Universal Otherhood,* 123–24. (Additional references will appear in parentheses in the text.) Quoting Bentham's *Defence of Usury,* Letter I, *Works,* vol. III, 3. (Bentham's emphasis.)

10. Manning says: "Chapter 49 is a braid of two stands; the recognition of mutual attraction between Kate and Frank, and the climax of Mrs. Nickleby's flirtation with the man in small-clothes. Which one is absurd?" (83).

11. The commercial/financial language continues throughout the scenes in which the Gentleman appears. For example, the Gentleman thinks that Mrs. Nickleby may be "daughter in law to the Lord Mayor and Court of Common Council" (624); he then asks her to "step down to the Royal Exchange and [. . .] take the cocked hat off the stoutest beadle's head" (625).

12. Malcolm Andrews, *Dickens and the Grown-up Child* (Iowa City: University of Iowa Press, 1994), 67–68

13. Versus directly converting the reader through the text itself—the project of *A Christmas Carol,* as I will argue in the next chapter.

14. Jeff Nunokawa, *The Afterlife of Property* (Princeton: Princeton University Press, 1994), 4. (Additional references will appear in parentheses in the text.)

15. See below, chapter three, pp. 89–91 for a more extended discussion of these "circulations" and their implications in the financial-capitalist world of *Little Dorritt.*

16. See note 3 in my introduction (p. 14 above) for Marc Shell's summary of Aristotle's use of "economics" and "chrematistics."

17. *Capital,* vol. I, 253–54; note 6; quoting Aristotle's *De Republica,* I, c. 8, 9.

18. *Capital,* vol. I, 267; the "('indicates an augmentation to the amount of money signified by "M."

19. Walter Bagehot, *Lombard Street,* 1873 (New York: John Wiley & Sons, 1999), 4–5.

20. Quoting St. Ambrose of Milan, *De Tobia,* xv: 51. Nelson goes on to show how the strict interpretation of Deuteronomy XXIII, 19–20 proved inconvenient

for the development of a modern commercial society, and how Calvin, Weber and others were influential in moderating the "war/brotherhood" dichotomy to include the middle ground of "competition." However, the starker split presented in Deuteronomy remained a part of the usury debate until the 1840s.

21. Both Ralph's Old-Testament and his entropic subtexts appear when we first see him in chapter two, as he stares into the ruined "garden" with its blasted fir tree—a scene of post-Edenic, pre-Christ unredeemed desolation (66).

22. See his prefaces to the 1839 and 1848 editions, *NN*, 46 and 51.

23. In his 1839 Preface, Dickens refers to the Grants as "the pride and honour" of the unnamed town in which they live (46).

24. Forster states that the meeting occurred but does not pinpoint a year (*The Life of Charles Dickens*, (2 vols. [London: Chapman & Hall, 1876]), vol. I: 158), Peter Ackroyd places the meeting in 1838 (*Dickens* [London: Sinclair-Stevenson Limited, 1990], 273). Ainsworth had grown up in Manchester and had access to the Grants, who often entertained artists, inventors and businesspeople. Ainsworth may have known the Grants through John Ainsworth, who wrote a "brief and quaint history of the family," according to T. H. Hayhurst's *An Appreciative Estimate of the Grant Brothers of Ramsbottom (The "Brothers Cheeryble.")*, (Bury: T. Crompton and Co., 1884), 30.

25. Rev. W. Hume Eliot, *The Story of the "Cheeryble" Grants* (Manchester: Sherrat and Hughes, 1906), 234–35. (Additional references will appear in parentheses in the text.)

26. The Grants' Presbyterianism figures largely in their story. The importance of religion to them and its link with their charitable activities is paralleled in contemporary accounts of other benevolent business-people, as in those examined by Howard L. Malchow in his study *Gentlemen Capitalists: The Social and Political World of the Victorian Businessman* (Stanford: Stanford University Press, 1992). For Robert Fowler, a banker and a Quaker, and William McArthur, a merchant and a Wesleyan, religion served both as a motivation for benevolence and a justification for successful commercial activities. (For example see Fowler's view of wealth as "stewardship" [171] and his need to rationalize his wealth through piety [211]). In Dickens's largely secular universe, the Cheerybles do not espouse any particular creed, but their dress (Charles wears a "good easy old-fashioned white neckcloth" and a "low-crowned broad-brimmed hat" when he encounters Nicholas [531; ch. 35]) and clannishness bear a Quaker subtext, and their familial piety provides a quasi-religious tone.

27. In *The Novelist and Mammon* (Oxford: Clarendon Press, 1986), Norman Russell describes a real and vibrant trade: "The Cheerybles [. . .] were importers and exporters in the German trade, and at the time the novel was written would have been mainly concerned with the import of fine wool from Saxony, and the export to Germany of finished textiles, cotton twist and yarn. Germany was England's best customer for worsted, used for light

fabrics, providing the Bradford manufacturers with profitable, if unexpansive, markets" (192). But none of the technical or financial details of the trade are reflected in the novel's description of the Cheerybles' firm.

28. Steven Marcus, *Dickens: from Pickwick to Dombey,* 112

29. T. H. Hayhurst, *An Appreciative Estimate of the Grant Brothers of Ramsbottom (The "Brothers Cheeryble."),* 53. (Additional references will appear in parentheses in the text.)

30. Dickens, Charles. *A Christmas Carol.* 1843, in *The Christmas Books,* Volume 1. Ed. Michael Slater, (London: Penguin Books), 1971, 78

31. Charles Dickens, *Dombey and Son,* 1848, ed. Raymond Williams (London: Penguin Books, 1992), 69.

32. Childers, Joseph W. "*Nicholas Nickleby*'s Problem of *Doux Commerce,*" *Dickens Studies Annual* 25 (1996), 49–65; 61 (Additional references will appear in parentheses in the text.)

33. Humphry House, *The Dickens World* 2nd ed. (London: Oxford University Press, 1942) 46, 47–49. (Additional references will appear in parentheses in the text.)

34. This control sometimes carries the subtext of real coercion. Childers notes: The control the Cheerybles exert over their world is not always articulated in terms of domestic virtues, and affections, and delicacy of feeling. For instance, when the brothers give Tim a gold snuff box stuffed with a large bank-note for his birthday, Charles warns the old clerk by "playfully" threatening his employee's cherished pet: "never say another word upon the subject or I'll kill the blackbird" (559; ch. 37). Charles, of course, would never do such a thing, but the threat carries a certain weight nevertheless. When one person tells another that she would never *think* of lying to him, rest assured that thought has just crossed her mind." (62; Childers's emphasis)

35. Hayhurst tells a different, less resonant version of this story in which the child, a toddler boy, falls into the Irwell while playing (23).

36. Alexander Welsh, *The City of Dickens* (Oxford: Clarendon Press, 1971), 124–26. Quoting *The City of God,* Bk. XV, ch. v.

37. Such protestations, like those about Krook, may also indicate that Dickens felt the Cheerybles' reality *needed* some kind of defense—reflecting, perhaps, Dickens's own ambiguity about the case he was making.

38. Edgar Johnson, *Charles Dickens: His Tragedy and Triumph,* 29.

39. "Spectacle depends on a distinction between vision and participation, a distance that produces desire in a spectator," Jaffe says, commenting on Scrooge's positioning as "a reader and interpreter of cultural signs" in *A Christmas Carol.* She adds that reading cultural signs in *A Christmas Carol* "includes an element of internalization—or, more precisely, what Louis Althusser calls interpellation [. . .] By this one-hundred-and-eighty-degree physical conversion, he becomes a *subject*" (Jaffe's emphasis). Thus

the spectator in such a situation, Jaffe notes, is invited to take an active role: "Visual representation inscribes the spectator as absence or lack, and these images, in their fullness, emphasize that lack. But the relation between spectator and image is reversed, as these commodities call out to the spectator to complete them" (Jaffe, "Spectacular Sympathy: Visuality and Ideology in Dickens's *A Christmas Carol*," *PMLA*, Vol. 109, no. 2, 259).

40. In the *City of Dickens*, Alexander Welsh rightly calls this sequence a "set piece" and links it to a tradition of urban satire that includes Gay and Johnson (4–6); however I am struck by the framing of the passage I have quoted, and believe that there Dickens is building on the set-piece to present a spectacle, like those Jaffe is describing, which breaks through the distance of satire and involves us as readers in its moral issues.

41. Thomas Richards, *The Commodity Culture of Victorian England*, (Stanford: Stanford University Press, 1990), 73.

42. Steven H. Star, Nancy J. Davis, Christopher H. Lovelock, and Benson P. Shapiro, *Problems in Marketing*, 5th ed. (New York: McGraw-Hill Book Company, 1977), 2.

43. Dorothy Van Ghent, "The Dickens World: A View from Todgers's," (1950), rpt. in *Dickens: A Collection of Critical Essays*, ed. Martin Price, Twentieth Century Views (Englewood Cliffs, NJ: Spectrum-Prentice-Hall, 1967), 30.

44. In "Playing Around with Melodrama: The Crummles Episodes in *Nicholas Nickleby*," Tore Rem notes: "The dark cloud that follows Ralph on his way to his death is . . . [an] example of the 'hypersignificant signs' of melodrama [. . .] Through the use of these melodramatic signs, a legible universe is displayed. A life that has order and meaning is communicated by showing this structured reality below the surface" (374; Rem is citing Peter Brooks, *The Melodramatic Imagination* (1985), 126). I would add that the kinds of devices Rem refers to produce the same effect as some of the "expressionist" techniques of movies like Fritz Lang's *Das Cabinet des Dr. Caligari* (1920) in which "oblique chimneys on pell-mell roofs, [. . .] windows in the form of arrows or kites and [. . .] treelike arabesques that were threats rather than trees [. . .] had the function of characterizing the phenomena on the screen as phenomena of the soul" (Siegfried Kracauer, *From Caligari to Hitler* [Princeton: Princeton University Press, 1947], 69 and 71).

45. Sylvia Manning, in "*Nicholas Nickleby*: Parody on the Plains of Syria," points out that the novel is shot through with parodies, primarily of other scenes in the novel. Manning's thesis is that *Nickleby* is a novel about the desire of the excluded subject for inclusion at a higher societal level. She notes that the "effect of the parody is to cast doubt upon every possibility of inclusion as it arises, upon the rationality of the desire for it and upon the ontological status of inclusion itself. The narrative peppers a plot that requires identification with the desire for inclusion, with parody that undermines it." (77). Manning points out that such parodies serve to surround the

moral standards the novel is avowing with ambiguity: "When Lillyvick and Snevellicci parody Kate and Hawk and Verisopht [ch. 30], what is parodied ultimately is the moral standard that defines the falsity of Hawk and his companions. Kate's purity is burlesqued here, and furthermore it is interrogated by Nicholas's flirtations, especially with Miss La Creevy. That purity is the basis of her marriage, so that it too, the "true" inclusion of the finale, is debunked. The comic impulse realized in parody threatens not just to relieve the serious but to relieve it of its credibility and of our emotional and unironic engagement" (85).

NOTES TO CHAPTER TWO

1. The Pilgrim Edition of *The Letters of Charles Dickens,* Vol. Three 1842–1843, eds. Madeline House and Graham Storey (Oxford: Clarendon Press, 1965, letter of 10 March 1843, 461. (Additional references will be cited in parentheses in the text.)

2. See note 3 in my introduction (p. 165 above) for Aristotle's definitions of "economics" and "chrematistics"; see pp. 26–27 of chapter one, above, for a more detailed consideration of Marx's uses of these terms.

3. Much critical discussion centers around the extent to which Scrooge's conversion is real, how radical the *Carol* is as an attack on capitalism, the middle class or both, and whether or not the *Carol* advocates some believably efficacious form of social change. T.A. Jackson sees the *Carol* as decisive move away from a feudal-paternalist ethic of benevolism—"the Cheeryble illusion"—to a notion that employers must be shamed and scared, through fear of revolution ("the terrors to come") into benevolence (Jackson, T.A. *Charles Dickens: The Progress of a Radical,* 294–5).
   Modern critics like Paul Davis focus more on the *Carol*'s relationship to Dickens's status as a successful middle-class achiever. Davis notes that the *Carol* was Dickens's attempt to deal with contradictory impulses. On the one hand, "[h]e wanted to reassure the readers whom *Chuzzlewit* had alienated that he still embodied their belief in entrepreneurial achievement and success. He was still 'the inimitable Boz,' the literary magician who alone could have created and produced the *Carol*. The book itself represented these bourgeois values. Its hand-tinted illustrations and the gold leaf on the binding attested to the success and authority of its creator. [. . .] At the same time Dickens also wanted to speak for the urban poor and reach a working-class audience like the one he addressed in Manchester" (*The Lives and Times of Ebenezer Scrooge* [New Haven: Yale University Press, 1990], 11).
   Caroline McCracken-Flesher continues to explore the *Carol* as an expression of middle-class values, summarizing critical debate about the problem of Scrooge's conversion being embedded in the money ethic of capitalistic society, and noting the value of carefully modulated individual benevolence

("Scrooge's redemptive gesture recognizes the necessity only for repletion, not for surfeit"—charity mixed with middle-class prudence) as a solution to the problems the *Carol* poses:

Although Don Richard Cox [*PMLA* 90 (1975), 22–23] has intriguingly argued that "the 'conversion' [. . .] Scrooge experiences is not a holy revelation but an economic [one]," and that "Scrooge simply exchanges one set of economic values for another [coming to] the rather secular conversion that it is not money that brings happiness in life, but rather what money can buy" [. . .], Eliot Gilbert [*PMLA* 91 (1976) 22] has tellingly asked in return: "What [. . .] is to be said of a critic who appears to believe that, because the decision to buy a turkey and the decision not to buy a turkey both involve financial considerations, there is therefore no important difference in the end between having a turkey and not having a turkey?" Pushing the point home, Gilbert continues, "Surely only someone with the most austerely abstract notions of spirituality could be as careless as this about the distinction between eating and starving." Obviously, Scrooge shifts from getting to spending money, but he does so to participate in a carefully modulated exercise of unostentatious giving, and of giving according to need. ("The Incorporation of *A Christmas Carol:* A Tale of Seasonal Screening," *Dickens Studies Annual* 24 [1996] , 97–98)

J. Hillis Miller views the *Carol* as an attempt to reform capitalism through believing in and acting on individual benevolence:

Dickens seems to believe and to want his readers to believe that the camel may go through the needle's eye after all, a rich man may enter the kingdom of heaven, if he is generous enough and loving enough: 'He became as good a friend, as good as Master, and as good a man, as the good old city knew, or any other good old city, town, or borough, in the good old world.' ("The Genres of *A Christmas Carol*," *The Dickensian* [1993], 204).

James M. Brown (*Dickens: Novelist in the Marketplace* [(Totowa, NJ: Barnes and Noble Books),1982] does not discuss the *Carol,* but describes a "loosely integrated" middle-class entrepreneurial value set (a model for "good capitalism" stressing individual benevolism, much like what Scrooge embraces in the end) which he places in opposition to the exchange-value ethic of a commercial society (42). Audrey Jaffe (discussed in the text) feels that the values the redeemed Scrooge is converted to are those of middle-class consumerism.

4. Audrey Jaffe, "Spectacular Sympathy: Visuality and Ideology in Dickens's *A Christmas Carol,*" 254. (Additional references will appear in parentheses in the text.)

5. Charles Dickens, *A Christmas Carol,* 89–90. (Additional references will be cited in parentheses in the text.)

6. Leonore Davidoff and Catherine Hall, *Family Fortunes: Men and Women of the English Middle Class, 1780–1850* (London: Hutchinson, 1987), 234–35.

(Davidoff and Hall's emphasis.) (Additional references will be cited in parentheses in the text.) Davidoff and Hall's quotes from Taylor's *Self Cultivation Recommended* (1817) are from 17 and 41.

7. Erich Auerbach, "Figura," 1944, in *Scenes from the Drama of European Literature,* tr. Ralph Mannheim (New York: Meridian Books, 1959), 11–76; 72. (Additional references will be cited in parentheses in the text.)

8. Robert Tracy, "'A Whimsical Kind of Masque': The Christmas Books and Victorian Spectacle," *Dickens Studies Annual* 27 (1998): 114–15. (Additional references will be cited in parentheses in the text.)

9. Malcolm Andrews, *Dickens and the Grown-up Child,* 69. (Additional references will be cited in parentheses in the text.)

10. The quotation from Ruskin is from the Preface to the Second Edition of *Modern Painters* (1844); Popular Edition, 1906, I, xxxi-xxxii.

11. See Forster's comments on Dickens's boyhood reading as described in the "Autobiographical Fragment" (*Life,* I, 9–10). Harry Stone points out, "Dickens was convinced that the literature he read as a child had been crucial to his imagination. He was equally certain that the literature he read as a youth kept him from perishing. The literature of childhood was the source of all of his 'early imaginations'; the literature of youth 'kept alive my fancy, and my hope of something beyond that place and time.'" (From *Dickens and the Invisible World* [Bloomington: University of Indiana Press, 1979], 3; Stone quotes Dickens's "Dullborough Town," *Uncommercial Traveller* [1860], Oxford Illustrated Dickens [Oxford: Oxford University Press, 1989], 126; and the "Autobiographical Fragment" [Forster, *Life,* I, 9].)

12. Here we see another trope—that of the "thoughtful" and sickly child whose sensibility seems far beyond his years; again, this trope occurs widely in Dickens's work, often presenting the child as a superior alternative to the adults around him or her—a child of acute sympathy, like Little Nell, or one, like Paul Dombey, who represents non-commercial values. This trope is closely associated with the child Dickens himself, and is linked with the pathos of neglected gifts. Forster refers to the child Dickens as sickly or ill several times in the *Life*—often juxtaposing sickness with thoughtfulness or imagination; for example:

    I have the picture of him[at William Giles' school] very strongly in my mind as a sensitive, thoughtful, feeble-bodied little boy, with an amount of experience as well as fancy unusual in such a child. (*Life,* vol. I, 12)

13. "A Christmas Tree," *Household Words* (21 December 1850), rpt. in *Charles Dickens: Selected Journalism, 1850–1870,* ed. David Pascoe (London: Penguin Books, 1997) 10. (Additional references will be cited in parentheses in the text.)

14. The full passage is quoted in chapter three, pp. 88–89, below. The danger Marx perceives derives from money's ability to allow social power itself to become private property—a commodity: "[M]oney is itself a commodity, an

external object capable of becoming the private property of any individual. Thus the social power" ["the social incarnation of all human labour"] "becomes the private power of private persons." (*Capital*, vol. I, 229–30).

15. Quoted in Davidoff and Hall, 234.

16. My thinking on this point was influenced by the following passage from Paul Davis's *The Life and Times of Ebenezer Scrooge:* "Robert Patten ['Dickens Time and Again,' *Dickens Studies Annual* 2 (1972): 170] has described the dynamic of the Carol as one in which the narrator's voice is for the reader comparable to the voices of the spirits to Scrooge: 'In insisting on the analogy between the narrator's voice and the Caritas Ghosts, Dickens provides one way of taking their eruption into the fictional world: our senses respond to his voice as Scrooge does to the ghosts, and we respond to the stories he tells as Scrooge does to the times which the Ghosts present. The *Carol* becomes the analogue to Scrooge's experience'" (Davis, 64–65).

17. "The Absent Jew in Dickens: Narrators in *Oliver Twist, Our Mutual Friend,* and *A Christmas Carol,*" *Dickens Studies Annual* 24 (1996): 50: "In *A Christmas Carol,* Scrooge is never referred to as Jewish. Yet [. . .] the overall scenario of a conversion at Christmas time suggests that Scrooge's Jewishness might haunt this text. [. . .] Scrooge's Jewishness might explain not only why he never went home, but also why he tells the Ghost of Christmas Present that he has *never* celebrated Christmas." (Grossman's emphasis; additional references will be cited in parentheses in the text.)

18. Scrooge is presented as a money-lending businessman, hardly distinguishable from the following portrait of a real petty-financier described by financial Journalist David Morier Evans in 1845:

> Of the third-rate class of bill brokers, Mr. Thomas Rogers is a fair specimen. This [. . .] is what the bill agents and needy ones term "a fifty and sixty percenter"; and he must have good names at the back of a bill, as endorsees, before he writes out a cheque on his bankers. It is doubtful, however, whether this gentleman, with all his caution, and relish for law to enforce his rights, has made his business pay of late. Among the fraternity he is regarded as a shrewd man, and as one who is awake to all the manoevres of his calling. These people visit the second-class coffee-houses and taverns; and one or two of the Hebrew persuasion, who do a great deal of business, visit Garraway's and the Auction Mart. When bills are discounted, or loans advanced at these houses, the borrower may expect to be paymaster for refreshment; and under such circumstances the lenders are always in excellent condition for feeding.

To 1843 readers of the *Carol,* Scrooge would appear to be a representative not of individual eccentricity (as *Our Mutual Friend*'s Dancer or Elwes would), but of a large class, as Evans points out:

Of second and third-class bill brokers, or discounters, a great number exist both in the City and the outskirts, the repeal of the usury laws having increased the desire of many to enter into this description of business, for the sake of making the most of surplus capital. These discounters number—attorneys, tradespeople, and petty shopkeepers, who, at the risk of getting twenty, thirty, or fifty per cent. for their money, jeopardize what they already possess. (D. M. Evans, *The City; or, the Physiology of London Business; with Sketches on 'Change, and at the Coffee Houses* [London: Bialy Brothers, 1845], 21)

19. *Politics* 1258b; quoted in Marc Shell, "The Golden Fleece and the Voice of the Shuttle: Economy in Literary Theory," 94. (Additional references will be cited in parentheses in the text.)

20. Thomas Carlyle, *Past and Present* (1843) *The Works of Thomas Carlyle, X,* (London: Chapman & Hall, 1901), 59.

21. "If a man asks Mr [Nathan] Rothschild, what is his opinion of the Funds, he answers that they must be better & at the very same time he acts contrary to himself & sells to knock them down. It is a deplorable circumstance that in so great a Country as this, Your Lordship and Colleagues should be the Sport [&] the caprice of a Jew party, it is truly lamentable." (Anonymous letter to Lord Liverpool in 1818, when he was considering a plan to reduce government dependence on the City, quoted in David Kynaston, *The City of London: Vol. One: A World of its Own 1815–1890.* London: Pimlico-Random House, 1994.) Nathan Rothschild's son Lionel was made a peer in 1885. Evans, in *The City,* reports that Isaac Lyon Goldsmid was a baronet by 1845 (72).

22. Ragussis, Michael. *Figures of Conversion: The "Jewish Question" and English National Identity* (Durham: Duke University Press, 1995). Woodcuts published in 1764 by Henry Roberts (52) and in 1836 by C. J. Grant (53). (Additional references will be cited in parentheses in the text.)

23. "As use-values, commodities are, above all, of different qualities, but as exchange-values they are merely different quantities, and consequently do not contain an atom of use-value," (*Capital,* vol. I, 269).

24. Collins, Philip, "The Reception and Status of the *Carol,*" *The Dickensian* (1993), 175.

25. Patten, Robert L. *Dickens and his Publishers,* 10

26. "Pray do not suppose," he wrote in 1852, "that I ever write merely to amuse, or without an object. [. . .]. Without [an "object" or thematic purpose], my pursuit—and the steadiness, patience, seclusion, regularity, hard work and self-concentration, it demands—would be utterly worthless to me." (From a letter to Mrs. Cropper, 20 December 1852; quoted in Paul Schlicke, *Oxford Reader's Companion to Dickens* [Oxford: Oxford University Press, 1999], 411–12).

27. "*George Eliot and Daniel Deronda,*" 40. (Additional references will be cited in parentheses in the text.)

NOTES TO CHAPTER THREE

1. Many of these critical works start from a Marxist point of view. For example, Grahame Smith in *Dickens, Money and Society* (Berkeley and Los Angeles: University of California Press, 1968) discusses the importance and use of exchange-value as a consequence of money worship and alienation in Dickens's presentation of Victorian society. In *Charles Dickens: The Progress of a Radical* (1937; New York: Haskell House Publishers), T.A. Jackson places Dickens's radicalism in the context of his time, but fails to make his case that Dickens portrayed the working class (as opposed to the middle class) "from the inside" (298), or that Dickens came to see revolution "as the only road to hope" (173). Other critics approach financial issues in Dickens's novels from the starting point of the Victorian opposition between Mammon and "the human spirit of man," as Norman Russell notes in *The Novelist and Mammon* (Oxford: Clarendon Press, 1986). From Russell's perspective Mammon-worship was a "moral, rather than political" problem (8); he places Dickens's obvious contempt for Mammon worship in a philosophical context, contrasting Dickens's disdain for the "wrong-headed applications" of utilitarianism and laissez-faire standpoints used to support Mammon-worship (13–14), with "good business," meaning generative activities, rooted in early 19th century middle-class values, which produce more than "cash-nexus" relationships between people. Russell also takes up the theme of the novelist's relation to Mammon, which he paints as equivocal: money misused was Mammon-worship, but used wisely meant security, support for family values and economic growth for the nation. James M. Brown, in *Dickens: the Novelist in the Marketplace* (Totowa, NJ: Barnes and Noble Books, 1982), discusses Dickens's position as an artist with "a self-conscious stand in the literary market of the day," and contrasts this position with the "business ethos" Dickens is against: "an attitude to business which elevates it into the primary or sole concern of life, so that the imaginative spiritual and religious life lapses into an extension of the economic, to be regarded the same qualitative terms" (26). Other, more recent critics, who approach the issue of Dickens and financial capitalism through structuralism, linguistics and other tools (e.g., Tatiana Holway, Jeff Nunokawa, Audrey Jaffe), are discussed in the text.

2. Quoted in *Capital*, vol. I, 923.

3. For example, building on Edmund Wilson's "Dickens: The Two Scrooges" (1941), Alexander Welsh (*Dickens: From Copyright to Copperfield* [Cambridge, MA: Harvard University Press, 1987]) links Dickens's early trauma with Erikson's concept of the "moratorium" to explain Dickens's novelistic development after his trip to America in 1841. Welsh uses the Warren's episode to help explain Dickens's "need to justify a rise in the world, so desired by the sons of the nineteenth century" (158); Welsh examines how the attitude toward money changes in novels after *Martin Chuzzelwit*, with

selfishness giving way, in *Dombey and Son,* to concern for "being and identity" (80), but says little about the psychological impact, in the novels, of living under a system of financial capitalism. Similarly, Harry Stone, in *The Night Side of Dickens* (Columbus: Ohio State University Press, 1994), discusses psychological preoccupations (cannibalism, passion, compulsion, etc.) in the novels and links these preoccupations interestingly to business and money. For instance Stone argues that Carker's managerial ethic is "nothing more or less than blatant cannibalism" (201), and points out that "the sin of valuing money more than human beings" drives the action in *Great Expectations.* Despite these insights, however, Stone never steps back to examine the impact of the system of financial capitalism on life in the novels in any structured way. Cultural approaches like that of Thomas Richards and structural and linguistic viewpoints like that of Audrey Jaffe (both referenced in the text) have been more helpful to me in examining the "nervous" world of the novels than psychoanalytical or psychological criticism per se. In addition, for the general idea of the "nervous" world of Dickens's novels, and the link between this nervousness and metonymic writing, I am indebted to Dorothy Van Ghent's 1950 essay, "The Dickens's World: The View from Todgers's."

4. *Dictionary of National Biography,* VI, 923.

5. Evans is cited often in financial histories like David Kynaston's *The City of London Vol. One: A World of its Own 1815–1890;* Kynaston refers to Evans's "pioneering, authoritative and eminently readable survey *The City* [. . .] published in 1845" (140). Books by Evans include *The Commercial Crisis 1847–1848* (1848) and *Speculative Notes, or Notes on Speculation* (1864).

6. David Morier Evans, *The Commercial Crisis: 1847–1848* (London: Letts, Son, and Steer, 1848) 82–83. (Additional references will appear in parentheses in the text.)

7. Quoted in Evans, *Commercial Crisis,* 23–4.

8. Quoted in Evans, *Commercial Crisis,* 41.

9. David Morier Evans, *Speculative Notes, or Notes on Speculation* (London: Groombridge and Sons, 1864) 36. (Additional references will appear in parentheses in the text.)

10. David Morier Evans, *The City,* 2: " The bankers of the present day are neither the Jews nor the goldsmiths, who, by extortion, once crippled the resources of our country, and considered themselves the privileged phlebotomizers of royalty [.]" However, there was ample precedent for Perez and other non-English speculators to operate in London, as experts in foreign securities; Evans perhaps describes the events that brought Perez to grief in *The City:* "It is impossible to give a description of the failures that occurred during the celebrated "*Spanish Panic*" in May 1835. A decline of 20 to 30 per cent. in the Peninsular securities within a week or ten days, ruined a considerable number " (46; Evans's emphasis).

11. Walter E. Houghton, *The Victorian Frame of Mind* (New Haven: Yale University Press, 1954); Newman, *Parochial and Lay Sermons*, 8, No. 11, 159, is quoted on 183; the second quotation is from 190.

12. Tom Lutz, *American Nervousness, 1903* (Ithaca: Cornell University Press, 1991), 2, xii.

13. Brian Rosenberg, *Little Dorrit's Shadows* (Columbia, MO: University of Misssouri Press, 1996) 47 and 56; Rosenberg quotes Horton's *Interpreting Interpreting: Interpreting Dickens's Dombey* (Baltimore: Johns Hopkins University Press, 1979), 12–13.

14. Charles Dickens, *Little Dorrit* (1857), eds. Stephen Wall and Helen Small, (London: Penguin Books, 1998), 109–10; bk. I, ch. ix. (Additional references will appear in parentheses in the text.)

15. Reference to *Robinson Crusoe* quoted in Penguin Edition of *Little Dorrit*, note 13, 857.

16. Marx goes on from this point to talk about "economic" uses of money versus "chrematistic" accumulation, typified by the capitalist's drive to amass more and more money for its own sake. (See *Capital*, I, 253–54 and note 6, and 257; see note 3 of my Introduction [on p. 165 above] for definitions of these terms.) The present argument is primarily focused on the amorality of capital—one consequence of chrematistic accumulation. I discuss the usefulness of the chrematistic/economic dichotomy as a fundamental theme in Dickens's critique of capitalism in chapters one and two above.

17. *Trades' Unions and Strikes: their Philosophy and Intention* (London, 1860), 35–36; quoted in *Capital*, vol. I, 925–6.

18. Tatiana Holway, "Imaginary Capital: The Shape of the Victorian Economy and the Shaping of Dickens's Career," *Dickens Studies Annual* 27, (1998): 34. (Additional references will appear in parentheses in the text.)

19. Jean Baudrillard. *Selected Writings*, 10; quoted in Thomas Richards, *The Commodity Culture of Victorian* England, 267. Richards notes the "production and consumption of [. . .] commodities as complementary parts of a *commodity culture* in which the dominant system of representation is what [Debord] calls 'spectacle.'" (Guy Debord, *Society of the Spectacle*, 1; quoted in Richards, 268; Richards's emphasis). (Additional references to Richards's book will appear in parentheses in the text.)

20. Charles Dickens, "Railway Dreaming" (1856) in *Charles Dickens: Selected Journalism 1850–1870*, 174.

21. Charles Dickens, "Some Recollections of Mortality" (1863), in *Charles Dickens: Selected Journalism 1850–1870*, 103. (Additional references will appear in parentheses in the text.)

22. Barbara Weiss, "Secret Pockets and Secret Breasts: *Little Dorrit* and the Commercial Scandals of the Fifties," *Dickens Studies Annual* 10 (1982): 70.

23. David Morier Evans, *Facts, Failures & Frauds: Revelations Financial, Mercantile, Criminal* (1859; New York: Augustus M. Kelley Publishers, 1968) 228. (Additional references will appear in parentheses in the text.)

24. Weiss notes that Dickens was a regular reader of *The Times*, which covered the Sadlier affair extensively (Weiss, 73). In addition, Edgar Johnson cites the following passage from one of Dickens's letters to Forster: "Mr. Merdle's complaint, which you will find in the end to be fraud and forgery, came into my mind as the last drop in the silver cream-jug on Hampstead Heath." (Letter of 4/56 to Forster; cited in *Charles Dickens: His Tragedy and Triumph*, II, 888.)

25. For example, in the sketch of Perez, the City operator discussed earlier, Evans's companion casually refers to "suicide, expatriation—all the fearful consequences of this kind of life!" (*Speculative Notes*, 54). In the same book Evans presents in great detail the activities and death-scene of a financial swindler who committed suicide to avoid imprisonment (262). And Trollope's Melmotte, to avoid "the indignities and penalties to which the law might have subjected him," "deliver[s] himself" through "a dose of prussic acid." From *The Way We Live Now*, (1875), ed. John Sutherland, The World's Classics (Oxford: Oxford University Press, 1982), 319; vol. II, ch. LXXXIII.

26. The idea of metonymy as an "opportunistic" trope based on contiguity rather than logic comes from works by Roman Jacobson ("The metaphoric and metonymic poles") and Paul de Man (*Allegories of Reading*); I discuss metonymy and Dickens's use of it to mirror and critique the "opportunistic" nature of financial capitalism in more detail below, in chapter four.

27. I will argue in chapter four that in the world of *Our Mutual Friend* the metonymic process I have just described ranges beyond the sphere of finance, that it is, in the novel, depicted as structural—foundational to and endemic in the capitalist society England has become by the 1860s. Such a sense of widespread chaos underneath the surface is certainly suggested in *Little Dorrit*, but here, in my view, the critique is limited, treating finance as an entity that can still be separated from the society in which it operates.

28. Daniel P. Scoggin, "Speculative Plagues and the Ghosts of *Little Dorrit*," *Dickens Studies Annual* 29 (2000): 234–36.

29. "Marriage" in general, in *Little Dorrit* as in *Middlemarch* or *Anna Karenina*, does not imply such a happy ending. What we as readers seek is an ending where the generative and the human triumph and where a marriage can believably be described as "inseparable and blessed," as opposed to "diseased" marriages like Fanny's, Pet's, or Mr. Dorrit's intended union with Mrs. General.

30. *The City of London Vol. I*, 33. (Additional references will appear in parentheses in the text.)

31. Limited liability reform for stock companies, begun in the 1820s for certain banking companies, was designed to prevent small shareholders from becoming liable for far more than their original investments; this reform comes too late for Mr. Dorrit, but for Dickens's readers the existence of the reform would have emphasized the unfairness of Mr. Dorrit's imprisonment.

32. D. A. Miller, *The Novel and the Police* (Berkeley: University of California Press, 1988), 88–89.

33. William J. Palmer, *Dickens and New Historicism* (New York: St. Martin's Press, 1997), 24–29.

34. James M. Brown, *Dickens: the Novelist in the Marketplace*, 96–97.

35. Dickens himself was deeply concerned with capital accumulation. For example, during the writing of *Little Dorrit* Dickens was busy with negotiations for purchasing Gad's Hill Place, which he termed "a dream of my childhood." During these negotiations, the issue of capital accumulation weighed on his mind, as noted by Fred Kaplan in *Dickens: A Biography* (New York: William Morrow and Co., Inc., 1988): "At moments, the negotiations seemed 'to be a sort of Chancery suit which will never be settled.' He did not want to overpay, as a matter both of principle and of patrimony. He felt that he needed to keep in mind that his savings were small, that he had a large family for which to provide, and that his earnings depended on is maintaining his reputation, popularity, and health" (347–48; quotations from letters to Wills, 2/9/1855 and 3/2/1856).

36. From Bagehot's *Estimations in Criticism*, vol. II, 193; quoted in House, 47.

NOTES TO CHAPTER FOUR

1. "The metaphoric and metonymic poles," in David Lodge, ed., *Modern Criticism and Theory: A Reader* (London: Longman, 1988), 57–58. (Additional references will appear in parentheses in the text.)

2. De Man points out:

   The demystifying power of semiology, within the context of French historical and thematic criticism, has been considerable. It demonstrated that the perception of the literary dimensions of language is largely obscured if one submits to the authority of reference. It also revealed how tenaciously this authority continues to assert itself in a variety of disguises, ranging from the crudest ideology to the most refined forms of aesthetic and ethical judgement. It especially explodes the myth of semantic correspondence between sign and referent, the wishful hope of having it both ways, of being, to paraphrase Marx in the German Ideology, a formalist critic in the morning and a communal moralist in the afternoon, of serving both the technique of form and the substance of meaning.

   From *Allegories of Reading: Figural Language in Rousseau, Nietzsche, Rilke, and Proust* (New Haven: Yale University Press, 1979), 5–6. (Additional references will appear in parentheses in the text.) The passage de Man goes on to analyze appears in *Swann's Way* (Paris: Pleiade, 1954), 82ff.

3. The metonymic nature of London's commercial and urban environment is clear in this 1853 description of Holborn:

> Holborn is a business street. It has a business character; there is no mistaking it. Shop and plate-glass windows side by side on each hand; costermongers and itinerant vendors all along the pavement; the houses covered with signboards and inscriptions; busy crowds on either side; omnibuses rushing to and fro in the centre of the road, and all around that indescribable bewildering noise of human voices, carriage-wheels, horses' hoofs, which pervades the leading streets of crowded cities.

From Max Schlesinger, *Saunterings in and About London*, English edn. by Otto Wenckstern (London: Nathaniel Cooke, 1853), 12–13. Quoted in Lynda Nead, *Victorian Babylon: People, Streets and Images in Nineteenth-Century London* (New Haven: Yale University Press, 2000), 50–51

4. Roland Barthes, "The Death of the Author," in *Image—Music—Text*, Tr. Stephen Heath (New York: Hill and Wang, 1977), 145. (Additional references will appear in parentheses in the text.)

5. Marx's discussion of commodity fetishism is quoted at length above in chapter two, p. 61.

6. "Speculation and Virtue in *Our Mutual Friend*," in *Making a Social Body: British Cultural Formation, 1830–1864* (Chicago: University of Chicago Press, 1995), 158. Quoting Sir John Clapham, *An Economic History Of Modern Britain: Free Trade and Steel, 1850–1886* (Cambridge: Cambridge University Press, 1932), 371. Poovey's article is one of several sources which consider the articles of M. L. Meason (see below) in relation to *Our Mutual Friend*. Others are Michael Cotsell's "The Book of Insolvent Fates: Financial Speculation in *Our Mutual Friend*," cited below, and Wilfred P. Dvorak's "Dickens's Ambivalence as a Social Critic in the 1860s: Attitudes to Money in *All the Year Round* and *The Uncommercial Traveller*," also cited below.

7. Dvorak provides a sketch of Meason's career:

> Percy Fitzgerald calls Meason a soldier, a world traveller, and an exceedingly good and popular writer whom Dickens held in great affection [*Memories of Charles Dickens*, pp. 313–14]. Meason contributed to *Household Words* occasionally, in 1855–56 and 1859, mostly on military subjects. Evidently he fancied himself something of an expert of financial matters in the 1860s—a view with which Dickens must have concurred. Meason's books—on finance and speculation, mainly reprinting his periodical essays—include *The Bubbles of Finance* (1865), *The Profits of Panics* (1866), *Turf Frauds and Turf Practices* (1868), *Three Months After Date and Other Tales* (1875), and *Sir William's Speculations: Or, The Seamy Side of Finance* (1866).

From "Dickens's Ambivalence as a Social Critic in the 1860s: Attitudes to Money in *All the Year Round* and *The Uncommercial Traveller*," *The Dickensian* (1984), 102–03.

8. M. L. Meason, "Starting the Rio Grande Railway," *All the Year Round*, XIV (1865), 342, 368.

9. M. L. Meason, "Amateur Finance," Part II, *All the Year Round*, XIV (1865), 329, 87. (Meason's emphasis.) (Additional references will appear in parentheses in the text.)

10. M. L. Meason, "How the Bank was Wound Up," in *The Bubbles of Finance: Joint-Stock Companies, Promoting of Companies, Modern Commerce, Money Lending, and Life Insuring. By a City Man*. (London: Samson, Low, Son, and Marston, 1865), 87–88.

11. In another article, Meason implicates biology in capital accumulation via the metaphor of infanticide. The narrator in "The Bank of Patagonia (Limited)" describes initial problems the young bank is facing, noting that these were not unusual or insuperable problems for a fledgling company:

But slight as were its difficulties, they were quite sufficient to make me long for greater profits, when a tempter, in the shape of a solicitor, put into my head that I might make much more money out of the concern that I had done hitherto, by filing a petition [the narrator retained some shares after the flotation] for the winding-up of the bank, and dividing the costs that were incurred with the lawyer, who prompted me thus to kill, as it were, my own offspring. (*The Bubbles of Finance*, 232–33)

Mary Poovey's comments on this article underline the link between capitalist structures and the biology of the family:

According to this metaphor, infanticide has been rendered painless—and, more to the point, lucrative—by the limited liability acts, which not only limited the investor's fiscal liability, but also absolves investors' families, as well as the corporation's (noninvesting) directors, from all fiscal responsibility. ("Speculation and Virtue in *Our Mutual Friend*," 163)

12. In "The Book of Insolvent Fates: Financial Speculation in *Our Mutual Friend*," *Dickens Studies Annual* 13 (1984), Michael Cotsell notes:

Since 1825 there had been a financial crisis about every ten years, and Victorians had come to believe that there was a horrible inevitability in this pattern. [. . .] The fall of Overend, Gurney proved them right. It is tempting to speculate that Dickens knew something about the desperate state of affairs in this great house [. . .] The *Household Words* article on the 1857 crisis, "The City of Unlimited Paper" [by John Hollingshead], had complained that the Bank of England's good gold had gone to the support of such "paper" houses. A few years after that crisis, tension had developed between the Bank and the discount houses over the Bank's cautious policy, and in 1860 Overend, Gurney tried to "intimidate" the Bank by making a massive overnight withdrawal. This might well have seemed like bad paper trying to destabilize gold. (139–40)

13. In "The Bio-Economics of *Our Mutual Friend*," Catherine Gallagher summarizes the debate about the value of human waste:

> One popular belief held that each nation had a God-given capital of fertilizing elements including human waste and decomposing human bodies. A way had to be found, sanitary reformers argued, to return this capital to the food-producing earth, for if it were not returned, it would, first, not bear sufficient interest as food to keep the population alive, and second, become itself the seed of death rather than life. For although there was considerable disagreement over how large concentrations of decomposing matter caused disease, everyone agreed that they did. Hence dead and decomposing human matter was organized into the sanitarian's bio-economy as both potential illth and wealth. (359)

And Christopher Hamlin's discussion of the advocates of sewage recycling reveals the pervasiveness of metonymy as a figure for describing the waste-money relationship, and positions recycling human waste as a revenue opportunity for the state:

> [Health of Towns Commissioner Lyon] Playfair [. . .] was most rhapsodic: a pound of urine was a pound of wheat; the excretions of each adult male yielded an acre of turnips. The impediment to sanitary improvement had always been cost, and the only solution, higher rates. But sewage promised a "supply of money [. . .] for carrying out [. . .] all the necessary works for promoting the health and comfort of the people altogether independent of rates," noted Smith [of Deanston, another Commissioner]. There would even be a surplus for "architectural and other improvements." The nation was losing about two million pounds per year, Playfair told Peel.

From *Public Health and Social Justice in the Age of Chadwick: Britain, 1800*–1854, Cambridge History of Medicine [Cambridge: Cambridge University Press, 1998], 238.

14. *Unto This Last;* "Ad Valorem" (1862), in *Ruskin's Works: Sesame and Lilies and Unto this Last* (New York: John W. Lovell Company, 1884), 82–83.

15. F. Somner Merryweather, *Lives and Anecdotes of Misers; or the Passion of Avarice Displayed* (London: Simkin, Marshall, and Co., 1850), 111. (Additional references will appear in parentheses in the text.)

16. In "Homophobia, Misogyny, and Capital: The Example of *Our Mutual Friend*," in *Between Men: English Literature and Male Homosocial Desire* (New York: Columbia University Press, 1983), Eve Kosofsky Sedgwick notes that the novel's links between biology and economics include all the "unmentionable" bodily functions :

> *Our Mutual Friend* is the only English novel that everyone *says* is about excrement in order that they may *forget* that it is about anality. For the

Freudian insights, elided in the critics' moralistic yoking of filth and lucre, are erotic ones. They are insights into the pleasures, desires, bonds, and forms of eros that have to do with the anus. And it is precisely the repression of these pleasures and desires that, in Freud, turns feces into filth and filth into gold. A novel about the whole issue of anal eroticism, and not merely a sanitized invective against money or "filthy lucre" or what some critics have come to call "the dust-money equation," would have to concern itself with other elements in the chain Freud describes: love between man and man, for instance; the sphincter, its control, and the relation of these to sadism; the relations among bodily images, material accumulation, and economic status. It would also offer some intimations, at least, of adult genital desire, and repression, in relation to the anus. Furthermore a novel that treated these issues would necessarily cast them in the mold of a particular, historical vision of society, class, power, money, and gender. (164; Sedgwick's emphases. Additional references will appear in parentheses in the text.)

Sedgwick's comment helps describe the coercive component of Eugene's conversion, as I argue below; but, in this context, it also reinforces the idea that the novel is deeply concerned with processes and mechanisms of transformation within the human body, and that this concern helps the novel drive home the point that "capitalistic" forces are at work within our own bodies.

17. A mid-century London guidebook illustrates the extent of the sewage problem, which was not significantly improved until the early 1860s:

> The ordinary daily amount of London sewerage discharged into the River Thames on the north side has been calculated at 7,045,120 cubic feet, and on the south side 2,457,600 cubic feet, making a total of 9,502,720 cubic feet, or a quantity equivalent to a surface of more than thirty-six acres in extent and six feet in depth.

From the 1845 "Report of the Average Discharge of Sewage through the principal outlets printed by order of the Court of Sewers for Westminster and Middlesex, Oct. 3rd, 1845."

> Cited in Peter Cunningham, *Handbook for London, Past and Present*, 2 vols. (London: John Murray, 1849), vol. I: xxxiii-xxxiv.

18. *Charles Dickens: The World of His Novels* (Cambridge, MA: Harvard University Press, 1958), 281. (Additional references will appear in parentheses in the text.)

19. "The Bio-Economics of *Our Mutual Friend*," 364. (Additional references will appear in parentheses in the text.)

20. In this sketch the narrator calls Monmouth Street "the burial place of the fashions":

> We love to walk among these extensive groves of the illustrious dead, and to indulge in the speculations to which they give rise; now fitting a deceased coat, then a dead pair of trousers [. . .] We have gone on speculating in this

way, until whole rows of coats have started from their pegs, and buttoned up, of their own accord, round the waists of imaginary wearers.

From *Sketches by Boz* (1839), ed. Dennis Walder (London: Penguin Books, 1995), 98.

The mechanisms of spectacle and "speculation" here parallel those used in the description of Venus's shop window, but the difference in the objects on view ("dry stick" versus "trousers") and the difference in narrative tones ("We love to walk among these extensive groves" versus a "muddle of objects [. . .] among which nothing is resolvable into anything distinct") support the change in focus for which I argue.

21. Jeff Nunokawa's analysis of the nineteenth-century novel's attitudes to the home as a refuge from the conmmodified marketplace supports this view:

The nineteenth-century novel never ceases remarking the reach of market forces into the parlors, bedrooms, and closets of a domestic realm that thus never ceases to fail in its mission to shelter its inhabitants from the clash of these armies.

Nunokawa goes on to add that the question of whose property a woman is arises when commodification is allowed to "invade" the Victorian home:

Trouble arises when women are cast as such property in the Victorian novel less because the proprietor's grasp goes too far when it reaches her than because that grasp is always loosened when the shadow of the commodity falls upon the object that it holds (*The Afterlife of Property,* 4, 7).

22. Joseph Litvak uses the term "panoptic" to describe a world view that combines an obsessive, accumulative drive with paranoid observation of others who may threaten or further the accumulation—a formulation very close to the kind of role Boffin enacts deliberately, and Rokesmith perhaps involuntarily, in *Our Mutual Friend.* In his analysis of *Nicholas Nickleby,* Litvak notes:

[Ralph's] ruthlessly excited critique of worldliness [. . .] voices the specifically male, and male-violent, theatrical ethos that occupies much of the novel. For the dog-eat-dog world view that Ralph implies here gets enacted most recurrently and spectacularly in his relationship with his nephew. Borrowing from recent Foucault-inspired readings of Dickens, we could call the theatricality inherent in that relationship "panoptic" or "paranoid." (*Caught in the Act,* 113–14)

23. *The Invisible Woman: The Story of Nelly Ternan and Charles Dickens* (1990; rpt. London: Penguin Books, 1991), 168–70.

24. Adrian Poole links this passage with "several New Testament phrases [. . .] most notably the following: 'Know ye not, that so many of us as were baptized into Jesus Christ were baptized into his death? Therefore we are buried with him by baptism into death: that like as Christ was raised up from the dead by the glory of the Father, even so we also should walk in newness of life' (Romans 6.3–4)" (*OMF,* note 2, 814). This plunge into Christ's death echoes Eugene's metonymic plunge into the river and coma, and his rebirth.

25. In 1847, Forster notes, Dickens's "accounts for the first half-year of *Dombey* were so much in excess of what had been expected from the new publishing arrangements, that from this date all embarrassments connected with money were brought to a close. His future profits varied of course with his varying sales, but there was always enough, and savings were now to begin" (*Life* vol. II, 15).

26. The Pilgrim Edition of *The Letters of Charles Dickens*, Vol. Ten: 1862–1864, ed. Graham Storey. (Oxford: Clarendon Press, 1998), 287.

27. Of the various "authors" in the novel, Jenny Wren most closely enacts the role of the artist who must sell his or her work to live—an important component of Dickens's own career-long dilemma as an artist; her crucial role in the resolution of the Eugene-Lizzie plot (her ability to decipher Eugene's inarticulate signs) may reflect Dickens's fundamental faith in his own art, perhaps, and his refusal to accept the limitations "the market" seemed to force upon the artist.

    Venus figures the artist truly tempted to use his art in the service of accumulation, and illustrates that refusing to succumb to this temptation has both a cost and a reward. One thinks here of Forster's comment on the novel: "The book thus begun and continued under adverse influences, though with fancy in it, descriptive power, and characters well designed, will never rank with his higher efforts" (*Life*, vol II: 367). A troubled Dickens, producing in this novel (as in *Little Dorrit*) something reflective of his times and critical of his society, pays a price for his honesty—or at least for his refusal to recreate past successes, to produce the commodities that would sell best.

    Finally, the image of the child John Harmon "sitting with his little book on these stairs" (*OMF*, 185; bk. I, ch. xv) links Harmon/Rokesmith with Dickens and both with the imagination of childhood at risk—one of the "costs" of capitalism most fully developed in earlier worlds like *Nicholas Nickleby* and *A Christmas Carol*. The application of this trope (the neglected child, reading) to Harmon/Rokesmith puts him at the center of the Dickens universe, and casts his efforts to deal with the effects of capitalism as an attempt to rescue childhood, and, in so doing, to retrieve Dickens's own childhood as well.

28. Rosemarie Bodenheimer, in "Dickens and the Identical Man: *Our Mutual Friend* Doubled," *Dickens Studies Annual* 31 (2002), notes: "John Harmon has to create himself through a tale that asserts a continuity of self despite his experience of gaps in memory, consciousness and time. [. . .] Harmon's story is told as a struggle to incorporate trauma while not being sucked back into its circular disorientation" (171). On Bella, Lisa Surridge comments that, "while it appears to be John Harmon who violates the sanctity of the home with his secret past, assumed name, and suspicion of murder, the real angst surrounds Bella. She must unlearn her wilfulness [. . .] and 'mature' into 'adult' submission" ("'John Rokesmith's Secret': Sensation. Detection

and the Policing of the Feminine in *Our Mutual Friend,*" *Dickens Studies Annual* 26 [1997], 274).

29. Forster (*Life,* vol. II, 365–367) notes that Dickens was anxious about his ability to keep up the necessary production for a twenty-number serial as early as March 1864. "A start with three full numbers done, though more than enough to satisfy the hardest self-conditions formerly, did not satisfy him now. . . . [On 29 March he writes,] 'I have grown hard to satisfy, and write very slowly.'" Later, "[i]n April and May [1865, Dickens] suffered severely; and after trying the sea went abroad for more complete change. 'Work and worry, without exercise, would soon make an end of me. If I were not going away now, I should break down. No one knows as I know to-day how near to it I have been.'" Finally, after Staplehurst, "the immediate result was that another lost number was added to the losses of the preceding months, and 'alas!' he wrote at the opening of July, 'for the two numbers you write of! There is only one in existence. I have just begun the other.'"

30. To Thomas Mitton, 13 June 1865. The Pilgrim Edition of *The Letters of Charles Dickens,* Volume Eleven, 1865–1867, ed. Graham Storey (Oxford: Clarendon Press, 1999), 56–57. (Additional references will appear in parentheses in the text.)

31. For example, see letter to Catherine Dickens, 11 June 1865 (Pilgrim *Letters,* Vol. Eleven: 52); letters to T. J. Arnold, Thomas Headland, Charles Lever and W. C. Macready, all of 12 June 1865 (52–53); and letters in Georgina's hand to J. B. Buckstone and John De Gex of 13 June 1865 (54–55): to De Gex Dickens writes, "I am too much shaken to write many notes. Not by the beating and dragging of the carriage in which I was [. . .] but by the work afterwards to get out the dying and the dead. Which was terrible."

32. Just before his death Bradley sits "[r]igid before the fire, as if it were a charmed flame that was turning him old, [. . .] with the dark lines deepening in his face, its stare becoming more and more haggard, its surface turning whiter and whiter as if it were being overspread with ashes, and the very texture and colour of his hair degenerating" (*OMF,* 779; bk. IV, ch. xv.).

33. In the same way, Dickens's problems with his left side signal the "metonymy" that can be brought on in the body by stroke and other vascular problems—impairments and alienations from his own body ("there was no I") beginning to inscribe themselves on Dickens's body just as he was inscribing similar metonymic transformations on the world of *Our Mutual Friend.* For example, see the "one sided" amble of Mr. Boffin and the divided, doubled parlor of the Boffins, both in bk. I, ch. v.

34. In 1865, when asked to contribute toward a national memorial for Shakespeare, Dickens refused, commenting that a poet's "last monument is in his works" (Peter Ackroyd, *Dickens,* 947).

NOTES TO THE CONCLUSION

1. The description of Albert Grant is from W. T. C. King, *History of the London Money Market* (London: George Routledge & Sons, Ltd., 1936), 232–33. A *Bankers' Magazine* article from August 1865 announced the conversion of Overend, Gurney to the joint-stock form and the identified the new board of directors:

   The directors include Mr. Henry Edmund Gurney, Mr. John Henry Gurney, Mr. Robert Birkbeck, all members of the old house; and the other gentlemen are Mr. H. F. Barclay, Mr. Thomas A. Gibb, Mr. Harry G. Gordon, chairman of the Oriental Bank Corporation, and Mr. W. Rennie, of Messrs. Cavan, Lubbock, and Co."

   From "Overend, Gurney and Co., Limited," *The Bankers' Magazine* CCLVII (August, 1865), 1018–19.

2. "Stockbroking and the Stock Exchange," *Fraser's Magazine* n.s. 14 [July 1876]; in Mary Poovey (ed.), *The Financial System in Nineteenth-Century Britain*, 166–67. (Additional references will appear in parentheses in the text.) Poovey notes that this article was "typical" in its "anxieties about the role Jewish financiers play in the stock market" (124).

3. Niall Ferguson, *The House of Rothschild: Money's Prophets*, 1798–1848 (1998; rpt. Harmondsworth: Penguin Books, 1999), 133. (Additional references will appear in parentheses in the text.) Anti-Semitic reaction to Jewish success in the sphere of high finance had a long history as well: Ferguson quotes City insider Henry Thornton's account of Nathan Rothschild's role in relieving the Bank of England during the Panic of 1825:

   "[T]he Jew King of the City Rothschild. [. . .] by dint of a little persuasion and exhortation [. . .] was induced to bring out his gold, first charging 2 and one-half per cent commission, then saying he did it out of public spirit." (136)

4. "The National Debt and the Stock Exchange," *Blackwood's Edinburgh Magazine* 66 (December 1849), by W. E. Aytoun; in Mary Poovey (ed.), *The Financial System in Nineteenth-Century Britain*, 127–28. (Additional references will appear in parentheses in the text.)

5. Ferguson provides no citation for the quotation from Shaftesbury.

6. The dissonance I have been suggesting can be seen in outline by comparing two citations from Niall Ferguson's *Empire: The Rise and Demise of The British World Order and the Lessons for Global Power* (2002; rpt. New York: Basic Books, 2002) which contrast masculine heroism with "Jewish" financial cosmopolitanism. The first is from Ruskin's inaugural lecture as Slade Professor at Oxford, 1870:

   There is indeed a course of beneficent glory open to us, such as never was yet offered to any poor group of mortal souls. But it must be—it is with us, now, 'Reign or Die' [. . .] And this is what [England] must either do, or perish: she must found colonies as far and as fast as she is able, formed of her most energetic and worthiest men;—seizing every piece of fruitful waste ground she can set her foot on. (222)

The second citation is from Ferguson's analysis of the economic benefits of imperial expansion:

Most of the huge flows of money from Britain's vast stock of overseas investments flowed to a tiny elite of, at most, a few hundred thousand people. At the apex of this elite was indeed the Rothschild Bank, whose combined capital in London, Paris and Vienna amounted to a staggering £41 million, making it by far the biggest financial institution in the world. The greater part of the firm's assets was invested [in the latter part of the nineteenth century] in government bonds, a high proportion of which were in colonial economies like Egypt and South Africa. Nor is there any question that the extension of British power into those economies generated a wealth of new business for Rothschilds. (*Empire*, 282)

7. *The Way We Live Now*, 31; vol. I, ch. iv. (Additional references will appear in parentheses in the text.)

8. In her essay "George Eliot and *Daniel Deronda:* The Prostitute and the Jewish Question," Catherine Gallagher quotes George Eliot on the idea of "cosmopolitanism" that Melmotte's kind of Jewishness represents:

Although Eliot argues [in "The Modern Hep! Hep! Hep!"] that the Jews have not yet been made "viciously cosmopolitan by holding the world's money-bag," and hence resolving "all national interests" into "the algebra of loans," she fears that such cosmopolitanism would result from any relaxation of their separatism. (56)

(Additional to references to Gallagher's essay will appear in parentheses in the text.)

9. *An Autobiography* (1883; Harmondsworth: Penguin Books, 1996), 225.

10. In *An Autobiography*, Trollope pays tribute to his mother's industry and economy:

[After *The Domestic Manners of the Americans* (1832), b]ook followed book immediately,—first two novels and then a work on Belgium and Western Germany. She refurnished the house which I have called Orley Farm, and surrounded us again with moderate comforts. Of the mixture of joviality and industry which formed her character it is almost impossible to speak with exaggeration. The industry was a thing apart;—kept to herself. It was not necessary that any one who lived with her should see it. She was at her table at four in the morning and had finished her work before the world had begun to be aroused. (21)

11. This subtext ("the Jew never changes") is expressed in two related tropes: first, that of the Jew unshakable in his or her Judaism and unwilling to convert; and second, that of the false or fraudulent conversion. In 1844, Disraeli's Sidonia articulates the first of these tropes—describing the Jews'

unchanging nature in terms of a racial purity that explains their ability to survive oppression:

The fact is you cannot destroy a pure race of the Caucasian organisation. It is a physiological fact; a simple law of nature which has baffled Egyptian and Assyrian kings, Roman Emperors, and Christian inquisitors. No penal laws, no physical tortures, can effect that a superior race should be absorbed in an inferior, or be destroyed by it. The mixed persecuting races disappear; the pure persecuted race remains. (*Coningsby* [1844, rpt. Everyman's Library, London: J. M. Dent & Sons Limited, 1933], 207–08)

The second trope—the false or fraudulent conversion of Jews (for money, advantage, etc.)—is captured, interestingly, in a mid-century book in which a Jewish writer attacked conversionist societies for spending their money on persons to whom religion is nothing but a matter of pounds, shillings, and pence—who are Jews to-day, call themselves Christians to-morrow, in the prospect of certain advantages, and, for a few shillings more, would turn Mohammedans the day after!" (Ragussis, *Figures of Conversion,* 52–53)

Ragussis is quoting from M. J. Lissack, *Jewish Perseverance, or The Jew, at Home and Abroad: An Autobiography,* 2nd ed. [London: Hamilton, Adams, 1851], 191. Clearly Lissack does not regard these "persons" as examples of "Jewish perseverance," but his attack on the conversionist societies for their gullibility only serves to foreground the issue of the unconvertibility of "real" Jews.

Fledgeby, in *Our Mutual Friend,* illustrates the unquestioning acceptance of the subtext of the unchanging Jew in the 1860s; he is able to use Riah's appearance to his financial advantage as long as it expresses Jewishness: "he felt that to relinquish an inch of [Riah's] baldness, an inch of his grey hair, an inch of his coat-skirt, an inch of his hat-brim, an inch of his walking-staff, would be to relinquish hundreds of pounds" (*OMF,* 275; bk. II, ch. v).

12. *Daniel Deronda* (1876), ed. Terence Cave (London: Penguin Books, 1995), 19; bk. I, ch. 2. (Additional references will appear in parentheses in the text.)

13. Catherine Gallagher notes the connections between authorship and whoredom, and links these with Jewishness and usury:

At times, Aristotle speaks of poetic making as a method of natural reproduction; at other times, he speaks of the written word as an arbitrary and conventional sign multiplying unnaturally in the mere process of exchange. The former idea of language promotes the metaphor of literary paternity; the latter the metaphor of literary usury and, ultimately, literary prostitution. ("George Eliot and *Daniel Deronda,*" 40)

Gallagher bases her discussion on Marc Shell's *The Economy of Literature,* 91–102.

14. Rather than mastering Grandcourt as she plans, Gwendolen becomes his possession:

'He delights in making the dogs and horses quail; that is half his pleasure in calling them his,' she said to herself as she opened the jewel-case with a shivering sensation. 'It will come to be so with me; and I shall quail. What else is there for me?' (*DD*, 427; bk. V, ch. 35)

15. Gallagher locates this tension at the intersection of Eliot's personal and authorial lives:

Eliot's great anxiety about how much she would make from her book seems entirely determined by the illicitness of her relationship to George Henry Lewes. Eliot alone of all Victorian authors felt as a constant reality the interchangeability, the equivalence of difference, between prostitution and authorship. ("George Eliot and *Daniel Deronda*," 59)

16. Hugo Witemeyer, *George Eliot and the Visual Arts* (New Haven and London: Yale University Press, 1979), 36–37. (Additional references will appear in parentheses in the text.) Witemeyer is paraphrasing G.H. Lewes, "The Principles of Success in Literature," *Fortnightly Review*, I (1865), 188.

17. Lukács, Georg. *History and Class Consciousness* (1922); rpt. trans. Rodney Livingstone (Cambridge, MA: The MIT Press, 1971), 90, 134–35.

Works Cited

WORKS BY DICKENS

Dickens, Charles. *A Christmas Carol.* 1843. In *The Christmas Books,* Volume 1. Ed. Michael Slater. London: Penguin Books, 1971.

——. *Charles Dickens' Uncollected Writings from Household Words: 1850–1859.* Ed. Harry Stone. Bloomington: Indiana University Press, 1968.

——. *Dombey and Son.* 1848. London: Penguin Books, 1992.

——. *Little Dorrit.* 1857. Eds. Stephen Wall and Helen Small. London: Penguin Books, 1998.

——. *Nicholas Nickleby.* 1839. Ed. Michael Slater. London: Penguin Books, 1978.

——. *Our Mutual Friend.* 1865. Ed. Adrian Poole. London: Penguin Books, 1997.

——. The Pilgrim Edition of *The Letters of Charles Dickens.* Vol. One: 1820–1839. Eds. Madeline House and Graham Storey. Oxford: The Clarendon Press, 1965.

——. The Pilgrim Edition of *The Letters of Charles Dickens,* Vol. Three 1842–1843. Eds. Madeline House and Graham Storey. Oxford: Clarendon Press, 1965.

——. The Pilgrim Edition of *The Letters of Charles Dickens,* Vol. Ten: 1862–1864. Ed. Graham Storey. Oxford: Clarendon Press, 1998.

——. The Pilgrim Edition of *The Letters of Charles Dickens,* Vol. Eleven: 1865–1867. Ed. Graham Storey. Oxford: Clarendon Press, 1999.

——. *Selected Journalism: 1850—1870.* Ed. David Pascoe. London: Penguin Books, 1997.

——. *Sketches by Boz.* 1839. Ed. Dennis Walder. London: Penguin Books, 1995.

OTHER PRIMARY SOURCES

Carlyle, Thomas. *Past and Present.* 1843. *The Works of Thomas Carlyle, X.* London: Chapman & Hall, 1901.

Cunningham, Peter. *Handbook for London, Past and Present.* 2 vols. London: John Murray, 1849.

Disraeli, Benjamin. *Coningsby.* 1844. Everyman's Library. London: J. M. Dent & Sons Limited, 1933.

Eliot, George. *Daniel Deronda.* 1876. Ed. Terence Cave. London: Penguin Books, 1995.

Elliot, Rev. W. Hume. *The Story of the "Cheeryble" Grants, from the Spey to the Irwell.* Manchester: Sherrat and Hughes, 1906.

Hayhurst, T. H. *An Appreciative Estimate of the Grant Brothers of Ramsbottom (The "Brothers Cheeryble.")* Bury: T. Crompton and Co., 1884.

Marx, Karl. *Capital: A Critique of Political Economy,* Vol. I. 1867. Tr. Ben Fowkes. London: Penguin Books, 1990.

Meason, M. L. "Amateur Finance," Parts I, II, and III. *All the Year Round,* XIV (1865), 329, 56–60; 330, 87–91; 331, 110–115.

———. *The Bubbles of Finance: Joint-Stock Companies, Promoting of Companies, Modern Commerce, Money Lending, and Life Insuring. By a City Man.* London: Samson, Low, Son, and Marston, 1865.

———. "Starting the Rio Grande Railway." *All the Year Round,* XIV (1865), 342, 368–372.

Merryweather, F. Somner. *Lives and Anecdotes of Misers; or the Passion of Avarice Displayed.* London: Simkin, Marshall, and Co., 1850.

Ruskin, John. *Unto This Last* (1862). In *Ruskin's Works: Sesame and Lilies and Unto this Last.* New York: John W. Lovell Company, 1884.

Trollope, Anthony. *An Autobiography.* 1883. Ed. David Skilton. Harmondsworth: Penguin Books, 1996.

———. *The Way We Live Now.* 1875. Ed. John Sutherland. The World's Classics. Oxford: Oxford University Press, 1982.

BIOGRAPHY, LITERARY CRITICISM AND HISTORY

Ackroyd, Peter. *Dickens.* London: Sinclair-Stevenson Limited, 1990.

Andrews, Malcolm. *Dickens and the Grown-Up Child.* Iowa City: University of Iowa Press, 1994.

Auerbach, Erich. "Figura." (1944). Tr. Ralph Mannheim. *Scenes from the Drama of European Literature.* New York: Meridian Books, 1959, 11–76.

Barthes, Roland. "The Death of the Author." In *Image—Music—Text.* Tr. Stephen Heath. New York: Hill and Wang, 1977, 142–48.

Bodenheimer, Rosemarie. "Dickens and the Identical Man: *Our Mutual Friend* Doubled." *Dickens Studies Annual* 31 (2002), 159–74.

Bowen, John. "Performing Business, Training Ghosts: Transcoding *Nickleby.*" *ELH* Vol. 63, No. 1 (Spring, 1996), 153–75.

Brown, J.M. *Dickens: Novelist in the Marketplace.* Totowa, NJ: Barnes and Noble Books, 1982.

Childers, Joseph W. "*Nicholas Nickleby*'s Problem of *Doux Commerce.*" *Dickens Studies Annual* 25 (1996), 49–65.

Collins, Philip. "The Reception and Status of the *Carol.*" *The Dickensian* (1993), 170-76.

Cotsell, Michael. "The Book of Insolvent Fates: Financial Speculation in *Our Mutual Friend.*" *Dickens Studies Annual* 13 (1984), 125–142.

Davidoff, Leonore and Hall, Catherine. *Family Fortunes: Men and Women of the English Middle Class, 1780–1850.* London: Hutchinson, 1987.

Davis, Paul. *The Lives and Times of Ebenezer Scrooge.* New Haven: Yale University Press, 1990.

de Man, Paul. *Allegories of Reading: Figural Language in Rousseau, Nietzsche, Rilke, and Proust.* New Haven: Yale University Press, 1979.

Dunlop, C. R. B. "Debtors and Creditors in Dickens' Fiction." *Dickens Studies Annual* 19 (1990): 25–47.

Dvorak, Wilfred P. "Dickens's Ambivalence as a Social Critic in the 1860s: Attitudes to Money in *All the Year Round* and *The Uncommercial Traveller.*" *The Dickensian* (1984), 89–104.

Ferguson, Niall. *Empire: The Rise and Demise of The British World Order and the Lessons for Global Power.* New York: Basic Books, 2002.

Forster, John. *The Life of Charles Dickens.* 2 vols. London: Chapman & Hall, 1876.

Gallagher, Catherine. "The Bio-Economics of *Our Mutual Friend.*" *Fragments for a History of the Human Body, Part Three.* Ed. Michel Feher with Romona Nadaff and Nadia Tazi. New York: Urzone, Inc., 1989, 345–365.

——. "George Eliot and *Daniel Deronda:* The Prostitute and the Jewish Question." *Sex, Politics, and Science in the Nineteenth-Century Novel.* Ed., Ruth Bernard Yeazell. Selected Papers from the English Institute, 1983–84, new ser., no. 10. (Baltimore: Johns Hopkins University Press, 1986), 39–62.

Grossman, Jonathan H. "The Absent Jew in Dickens: Narrators in *Oliver Twist, Our Mutual Friend,* and *A Christmas Carol.*" *Dickens Studies Annual* 24 (1996): 37-55.

Hamlin, Christopher. *Public Health and Social Justice in the Age of Chadwick: Britain, 1800–1854.* Cambridge History of Medicine. Cambridge: Cambridge University Press, 1998.

Holway, Tatiana M. "The Game of Speculation: Economics and Representation." *Dickens Quarterly* IX, No. 3 (Sept. 1992): 103–114.

——. "Imaginary Capital: The Shape of the Victorian Economy and the Shaping of Dickens's Career." *Dickens Studies Annual* 27, 1998; pp 23–43.

Houghton, Walter E. *The Victorian Frame of Mind.* New Haven: Yale University Press, 1957.

House, Humphry. *The Dickens World.* 2nd ed. London: Oxford University Press, 1942.

Jackson, T.A. *Charles Dickens: The Progress of a Radical.* 1937. New York: Haskell House Publishers, 1973.

Jakobson, Roman. "The metaphoric and metonymic poles." In David Lodge, ed., *Modern Criticism and Theory: A Reader.* London: Longman, 1988, 57–61.

Jaffe, Audrey. "Spectacular Sympathy: Visuality and Ideology in Dickens's *A Christmas Carol.*" *PMLA,* Vol. 109, no. 2, 254–265.

Johnson, Edgar. *Charles Dickens: His Tragedy and Triumph.* 2 Vols. New York: Simon and Schuster, 1952.

Kaplan, Fred. *Dickens: A Biography.* New York: William Morrow and Co., Inc., 1988.

Kracauer, Sigfried. *From Caligari to Hitler: A Psychological History of the German Film.* Princeton: Princeton University Press, 1947.

Litvak, Joseph. *Caught in the Act: Theatricality in the Nineteenth-Century English Novel.* Berkeley: University of California Press, 1992.

Lucas, John. *The Melancholy Man: A Study of Dickens's Novels.* London: Methuen & Co. Ltd., 1970.

Lukács, Georg. *History and Class Consciousness.* 1922. Tr. Rodney Livingstone. Cambridge, MA: The MIT Press, 1971.

Lutz, Tom. *American Nervousness, 1903.* Ithaca: Cornell University Press, 1991.

Manning, Sylvia. "*Nicholas Nickleby:* Parody on the Plains of Syria." *Dickens Studies Annual* 23 (1994): 73–92.

Marcus, Stephen. *Dickens: From Pickwick to Dombey.* London: Chatto & Windus, 1965.

McCracken-Flesher, Caroline. "The Incorporation of *A Christmas Carol:* A Tale of Seasonal Screening." *Dickens Studies Annual* 24 (1996): 93–118.

Miller, D.A. *The Novel and the Police.* Berkeley: University of California Press, 1988.

Miller, J. Hillis. *Charles Dickens: The World of His Novels.* Cambridge, MA: Harvard University Press, 1958.

———. "The Genres of *A Christmas Carol.*" *The Dickensian* (1993), 193–206.

Nead, Lynda. *Victorian Babylon: People, Streets and Images in Nineteenth-Century London.* New Haven: Yale University Press, 2000.

Nunokawa, Jeff. *The Afterlife of Property.* Princeton: Princeton University Press, 1994.

Palmer, William J. *Dickens and New Historicism.* New York: St. Martin's Press, 1997.

Patten, Robert L. *Charles Dickens and His Publishers.* Oxford: Clarendon Press, 1978.

Poovey, Mary. *Making a Social Body: British Cultural Formation, 1830–1864.* Chicago: University of Chicago Press, 1995.

Ragussis, Michael. *Figures of Conversion: "The Jewish Question" and English National Identity.* Durham: Duke University Press, 1995.

Rem, Tore. "Playing Around with Melodrama: The Crummles Episodes in *Nicholas Nickleby.*" *Dickens Studies Annual* 25 (1996): 267–286.

Richards, Thomas. *The Commodity Culture of Victorian England.* Stanford: Stanford University Press, 1990.

Rosenberg, Brian. *Little Dorrit's Shadows: Character and Contradiction in Dickens.* Columbia, MO: University of Misssouri Press, 1996.

Russell, Norman. *The Novelist and Mammon: Literary Responses to the World of Commerce in the Nineteenth Century.* Oxford: Clarendon Press, 1986.

Schlicke, Paul. *Oxford Reader's Companion to Dickens*. Oxford: Oxford University Press, 1999.

Scoggin, Daniel P. "Speculative Plagues and the Ghosts of *Little Dorrit*," *Dickens Studies Annual* 29: 2000, 233–66.

Shell, Marc. "The Golden Fleece and the Voice of the Shuttle: Economy in Literary Theory." In *The Economy of Literature*. Baltimore: Johns Hopkins University Press, 1978, 89–112.

Sedgwick, Eve Kosofsky. "Homophobia, Misogyny, and Capital: The Example of *Our Mutual Friend*." In *Between Men: English Literature and Male Homosocial Desire*. New York: Columbia University Press, 1983; 161–179.

Smith, Grahame. *Dickens, Money, and Society*. Berkeley and Los Angeles: University of California Press, 1968.

Stone, Harry. *Dickens and the Invisible World*. Bloomington: University of Indiana Press, 1979.

——. *The Night Side of Dickens: Cannibalism, Passion, Necessity*. Columbus: Ohio State University Press, 1994.

Surridge, Lisa. "'John Rokesmith's Secret': Sensation, Detection and the Policing of the Feminine in *Our Mutual Friend*," *Dickens Studies Annual* 26 (1997), 265–284.

Tomalin, Claire. *The Invisible Woman: The Story of Nelly Ternan and Charles Dickens*. 1990. Rpt. London: Penguin Books, 1991.

Tracy, Robert. "'A Whimsical Kind of Masque': The Christmas Books and Victorian Spectacle." *Dickens Studies Annual* 27 (1998): 113–130.

Van Ghent, Dorothy. "The Dickens World: A View from Todgers's" 1950. *Dickens: A Collection of Critical Essays*. Price, Martin, ed. Twentieth Century Views. Englewood Cliffs, NJ: Spectrum-Prentice-Hall, 1967.

Weiss, Barbara. "Secret Pockets and Secret Breasts: *Little Dorrit* and the Commercial Scandals of the Fifties." *Dickens Studies Annual* 10 (1982): 67–76.

Welsh, Alexander. *The City of Dickens*. Oxford: Clarendon Press, 1971.

——. *From Copyright to Copperfield: The Identity of Dickens*. Cambridge, MA: Harvard University Press, 1987.

Witemeyer, Hugo. *George Eliot and the Visual Arts*. New Haven and London: Yale University Press, 1979.

BUSINESS, FINANCE AND FINANCIAL HISTORY

Bagehot, Walter. *Lombard Street: A Description of the Money Market*. 1873. New York: John Wiley & Sons, 1999.

Evans, David Morier. *The City; or, the Physiology of London Business; with Sketches on 'Change, and at the Coffee Houses*. London: Bialy Brothers, 1845.

——. *The Commercial Crisis, 1847–8*. London: Letts, Son, and Steer, 1848.

——. *Facts, Failures & Frauds: Revelations Financial, Mercantile, Criminal*. 1859. New York: Augustus M. Kelley Publishers, 1968.

——. *Speculative Notes and Notes on Speculation, Ideal and Real.* London: Groombridge and Sons, 1864.

Ferguson, Niall. *The House of Rothschild: Money's Prophets 1798–1848.* 1998. Harmondsworth: Penguin Books, 1999.

King, W. T. C. *History of the London Money Market.* London: George Routledge & Sons, Ltd., 1936.

Kynaston, David. *The City of London: Vol. One: A World of its Own 1815–1890.* London: Pimlico-Random House, 1994.

Malchow, H. L. *Gentlemen Capitalists: The Social and Political World of the Victorian Businessman.* Stanford: Stanford University Press, 1992.

Nelson, Benjamin H. *The Idea of Usury: From Tribal Brotherhood to Universal Otherhood.* Princeton: Princeton University Press, 1949.

"Overend, Gurney and Co., Limited." *The Bankers' Magazine* CCLVII (August, 1865): 905–09.

Poovey, Mary (Ed.). *The Financial System in Nineteenth-Century Britain.* The Victorian Archives Series. Oxford: Oxford University Press, 2003.

Star, Steven H., Davis, Nancy J., Lovelock, Christopher H., and Shapiro, Benson P. *Problems in Marketing.* 5th ed. New York: McGraw-Hill Book Company, 1977.

Index